TI

Intellectual Property Law Series

EC INFORMATION TECHNOLOGY LAW

By
Robbie Downing
MA (Oxon), Lic Spec en Droit Européen (Brussels)
Solicitor (England & Wales)
King's College, London, UK

JOHN WILEY & SONS
Chichester • New York • Brisbane • Toronto • Singapore

Published in the United Kingdom by
Chancery Law Publishing Ltd
Baffins Lane
Chichester PO19 1UD

Published in North America by
John Wiley & Sons Inc
7222 Commerce Center Drive
Colorado Springs, CO 80919
USA

Typeset by Vision Typesetting,
Manchester

Printed in Great Britain by
Bookcraft (Bath) Ltd

ISBN 0471 95049 1

A copy of the CIP entry for this book
is available from the British Library

First published in March 1995

©

Robbie Downing
1995

To Mum and Dad

"The information society is on its way. A 'digital revolution' is triggering structural changes comparable to last century's industrial revolution with the corresponding high economic stakes. The process cannot be stopped and will lead eventually to a knowledge-based economy."

European Commission, *Europe's Way to the Information Society. An Action Plan*, 19 July 1994

Contents

CONTENTS

Preface

The information technology industry has always been characterised by rapid growth and change. European Community law on IT is no different. After a slow start, there is an increasing range of EC legislation dealing with specific issues raised by information technology. These issues are critical to the industry. One of the most important is the extent to which law and regulation should provide incentives for innovation and exploitation of the results given the impact on competition. This is one of a number of common themes of EC IT law which this book seeks to explore.

But what is actually meant by the IT industry? At the core of the sector's activity is the manipulation of information in digital form and, as "digitisation" spreads, so does the scope of the industry itself. The traditional definition of the sector as one which revolves around computers is therefore no longer adequate; arguably it now needs to encompass telecommunications as well. For this reason, this book also deals with EC regulation of the telecoms sector which has clear parallels with Community law governing computer hardware, software and services.

The rapid pace at which IT law develops will quickly date any publication on the subject. For instance, this book does not include discussion of the European Court of Justice's judgment in the *Magill* cases which will have important consequences for the interface between intellectual property and competition law. The ECJ had originally been expected to decide the cases by the end of summer 1994 but no date for judgment had been fixed by the time of writing. The cases are difficult but, whatever the ECJ's eventual decision, its absence from this book should not invalidate the discussion in this book of common themes of EC IT law.

It is worth pointing out right at the start that the subject of EC IT law is important not just for those who advise within the IT industry. Many of the questions involved in the application of EC law in this field raise issues which will be familiar to those outside the industry. So the book endeavours to explain the law in a way which is accessible to those who may put off the area by the lack of a technical background. For this reason, Chapter 2 starts with a brief explanation of those technical characteristics of the industry which are important for the application of EC law.

I am very grateful to those colleagues and friends and a brother who have read and commented on drafts of various chapters of the book. I would particularly like to thank Jonathon Stoodley (DGIII, European Commission), Joanna Goyder (Baker & McKenzie, Brussels), Lionel Bentley, Maleiha Malik and Aileen McColgan (King's College), Guy Jones (New England Consulting) and Andrew Downing (Telsis Limited). The book is immeasurably better as as result of their help. All remaining errors are entirely my own.

My thanks also to Lynda Martin Alegi (Baker & McKenzie, London) for arranging permission to use the table of national implementing measures for the Software Directive and to David Wilson at Chancery for his help and encouragement.

I have sought to state the law on the basis of materials available to me on 1 October 1994.

Robbie Downing
King's College, London
October 1994

Tables

CASES

CONVENTIONS AND AGREEMENTS

EC REGULATIONS

NATIONAL LEGISLATION

Glossary of Abbreviations

API	Application Programming Interface
CD-ROM	Compact Disk - Read Only Memory
CFI	Court of First Instance
CISC	Complex Instruction Set Computing
CL&P	Computer Law and Practice
CMLR	Common Market Law Reports
CMLRev	Common Market Law Review
COREPER	Committee of Permanent Representatives
CPC	Community Patent Convention
CPU	Central Processing Unit
DoJ	Department of Justice
EBLR	European Business Law Review
EC	European Community or Communities
ECJ	European Court of Justice
ECLR	European Competition Law Review
ECR	European Court Reports
ECSC	European Coal and Steel Community
ECU	European Currency Unit
EIPR	European Intellectual Property Review
ELR	European Law Review
EPC	European Patent Convention
ETSI	European Telecommunications Standards Institute
EU	European Union
Euratom	European Atomic Energy Community
FM	Facilities Management
FSR	Fleet Street Reports
FTC	Federal Trade Commission
GATT	General Agreement on Tariffs and Trade
GUI	Graphical User Interface
ICCLR	International Company and Commercial Law Review
IIC	International Review of Industrial Property and Copyright Law
IJL&IT	International Journal of Law and Information Technology
IP	Intellectual Property
IPR	Intellectual Property Right
ISDN	Integrated Services Digital Network
IT	Information Technology
JBL	Journal of Business Law
LAN	Local Area Network
MEP	Member of European Parliament

MQR	Measure of Equivalent Effect to a Quantitative Restriction
MS-DOS	Microsoft Disk Operating System
NDA	Non-Disclosure Agreement
NRA	National Regulatory Authority
NTP	Network Termination Point
NZBLC	New Zealand Business Law Cases
OECD	Organisation for Economic Cooperation and Development
OEM	Original Equipment Manufacturer
OJ	Official Journal
ONP	Open Network Provision
PC	Personal Computer
PNO	Public Network Operator
PSTN	Public Switched Telephone Network
R&D	Research and Development
RAM	Random Access Memory
RISC	Reduced Instruction Set Computing
ROM	Read Only Memory
RSI	Repetitive Strain Injury
SEA	Single European Act
SSO	Software and Services Organisation
TA	Telecoms Administration
TCLR	Trade and Competition Law Reports (NZ)
TEN	Trans-European Network
TEU	Treaty on European Union
TO	Telecoms Organisation
TPM	Third Party Maintainer
TRIPs	Agreement on Trade-Related Aspects of Intellectual Property Rights
UCC	Universal Copyright Convention
UK	United Kingdom
UNESCO	United Nations Educational, Scientific and Cultural Organisation
US	United States of America
VAR	Value Added Reseller
VDU	Visual Display Unit
WAN	Wide Area Network
WIPO	World Intellectual Property Organisation
YEL	Yearbook of European Law

Part 1

Commentary

Chapter 1
Introduction

The information technology industry is a key industry for the European   **1.1**
Community. In its paper on *An Industrial Competitiveness Policy*,[1] the European
Commission estimates that the value of the data processing and telecoms
market to the Community in 1995 will be 290 billion ECU (about US$ 350
billion). As well as the importance that comes from the sheer size of the
industry, the Commission also points out that: "the conditions of access to
information, to the networks carrying it and to the services facilitating use of
the data are playing an increasing role in industrial competitiveness."

Competitiveness is at least partly determined by the effectiveness with   **1.2**
which European industry is able to develop and exploit new technology. Laws
and regulation are critical in this context because they provide incentives for
the development of new technology. However, the incentive provided by laws
and regulation takes the form of exclusive rights over technology. Society loses
if this exclusivity goes so far as to stifle competition excessively. One of the key
issues underlying much of IT law is how to strike the balance between, on the
one hand, the incentive provided by exclusivity and, on the other, control of
that exclusivity. For example, if the law grants Lotus exclusive rights over its
well-known spreadsheet software, Lotus 1-2-3, should those rights extend to
the way in which the spreadsheet interacts with the user? If competitors cannot
use the Lotus 1-2-3 user interface, their spreadsheet programs may be less
attractive to customers because of the need to retrain staff to use alternative
products. This is one of many examples in the IT industry which show that
exclusive rights granted by intellectual property legislation must be sensitive to
the potential impact on competition.

Law and regulation also play a role in controlling potential abuses of the   **1.3**
technology. For instance, information technology has enabled vast stocks of
personal data to be assembled. Inevitably, there are calls for regulation of the
uses to which this data can be put. Another example is the growing concern
over injury which can result from excessive use of workstations. Do we need
specific rules to reduce the risk of personal injury?

The first problem which a book on information technology law has to   **1.4**
address is its scope. Most laws will affect the IT industry in the same way that
they affect many others. However, in some cases, the issues raised by the IT
industry are qualitatively different and worthy of separate study. The main
focus of this book is on EC legislation which is specifically directed at the new
technologies. Until recently there has been little specific regulation of the IT

---

[1] COM(94)319 of 14 September 1994.

industry at either a national or Community level. After initial intervention by national laws, the Community has recently entered the scene with a variety of legislation devoted entirely to issues raised by IT. The most obvious example is the 1991 Software Directive[2] which requires Member States to ensure that computer programs are protected by national copyright law. Another example is the Semiconductor Chip Directive[3] which requires Member States to give protection under national intellectual property law to semiconductor chip topographies. Further legislation is in the pipeline.

1.5 This book also aims to describe general EC rules which raise particular issues for the IT industry. The most important of these is EC competition law which matters for two main reasons. Firstly, its application raises a number of key issues for the IT industry; secondly, it acts as the principal foundation of the balance which IT legislation has to strike between exclusive rights and the benefits of sustaining competition.

1.6 This still leaves the question of what is meant by the words "information technology". This is not a term which is often used in legal circles but, since this is a book on the law, it seems appropriate to look briefly at how information technology has been defined in EC law.

1.7 In a 1986 Council Decision,[4] information technology was taken to mean:

> "the systems, equipment, components and software required to ensure the retrieval, processing and storage of information in all centres of human activity (home, office, factories, etc.), the application of which generally requires the use of electronics or similar technology" Art 1(13).

1.8 So the focus of the IT industry is on technology to process information. This includes the manufacture of the equipment (hardware), as well as the instructions or code (software) which causes the hardware to function. The inclusion of the words "all centres of human activity" highlights the degree to which we are all affected by IT. It will have escaped very few people's notice, for example, that the home market is now a major focus for sales of computers. As the IT commentator, Professor Nick Negroponte, has observed: "Twenty five million American homes now have PCs and they're not using them just to play Nintendo."[5]

Which is not to suggest that adults are the only target of marketing to the home. WordPerfect recently announced that it will use Disney characters to advertise its software to children.[6]

1.9 When computers were first made available to commercial users in the 1960s, the hardware was cumbersome and expensive while the software was primitive and often included in the total price. As a result, the computer would typically

---

[2] Council Dir 91/250 on the legal protection of computer programs (OJ 1991 L122/42). See Appendix A4.
[3] Council Dir 87/54 on the legal protection of topographies of semiconductor products (OJ 1987 L24/36). See Appendix A2.
[4] Council Dec 87/95 (OJ 1987 L36/31).
[5] *Computer Weekly* 5 May 1994, 47
[6] *Computer Weekly* 14 April 1994, 2.

be used centrally to process large amounts of data such as wage slips or invoices. Since then, three developments have transformed the industry. The first of these has resulted from advances in technology that have enabled the same processing power of the original large machines to be made available in machines which are a fraction of the size. One of the major recent influences in the hardware market has been the move from mainframes to client-server systems where powerful desktop machines are connected to a network through a server. Inevitably, mainframe suppliers such as IBM have been hit hard by these moves. In 1992, the company lost US$ 5 billion—the largest US corporate loss ever recorded up until that time. IBM is planning still further reductions in a workforce of 235,000 which at one time numbered 400,000.[7]

1.10 The second, related development has been the advance in software technology which has enabled hardware to be employed for a vastly increased range of functions. This in turn led to the birth and rapid growth of an industry devoted exclusively to software development and marketing—one that is now as important as the hardware industry, if not more so. Witness the activities of the antitrust authorities. In the 1970s, IBM was investigated by a US Department of Justice concerned about IBM's dominance of the computer industry. At about the same time, the European Commission also embarked on a massive investigation of IBM's practices culminating in a settlement in 1984. In contrast, in 1993, it was the turn of Microsoft, the leading producer of PC software, to attract the attention of the antitrust authorities in both the US and Europe. Echoing the result of earlier investigations into IBM, Microsoft settled the cases in July 1994 by giving undertakings to both the US Department of Justice and the Commission.[8] The IBM and Microsoft settlements will crop up frequently in the discussion of competition law and the IT industry.

1.11 The third major development has been the globalisation of world markets. This is reflected in recent application of competition law; for example, negotiations to settle the Microsoft investigation were conducted jointly by the US Department of Justice and the European Commission. The international nature of many IT markets also influences intellectual property protection of new technologies. The signing in April 1994 of the GATT Uruguay Round Agreement on Trade-Related Aspects of Intellectual Property Rights (TRIPs) will have a significant impact on intellectual property law within the IT industry.

1.12 In parallel with these developments, the growing sophistication of telecoms technology has enormously increased the number and variety of tasks to which hardware and software can be put. The computer industry is based on the manipulation of data in digital form and the buzz word in today's IT industry is "convergence"—that is, the spread of digitisation to other industries. Given the increasing digitisation of the telecoms industry as well as its importance to the computer industry, this book includes coverage of telecoms. Similarly, we

---

[7] *Computer Weekly* 4 August 1994, 8.
[8] *Computer Weekly* 21 July 1994, 1. See Appendix A10.

can expect other industries to join the IT industry and, as the media industry becomes increasingly digitised, it will be more difficult to argue that that industry should be left out of a book on IT law.

1.13   The purpose of this book is to identify common themes in EC IT law; it is not to provide an exhaustive description of all the many areas of law which affect the IT industry. Even the briefest of such treatments would be impossible in a single volume of remotely manageable proportions. For this reason, the book does not deal with issues such as anti-dumping law, even though it can be immensely important to the IT industry.[9]

1.14   As the book's title makes clear, only European Community law is covered in the following chapters. And since a great deal of national law remains intact throughout the Community, only a partial picture can be provided of the position in each Member State. The transfer of EC law to a national level is often effected in widely differing ways by the Member States. Some differences are permitted by Community law; others are not.

1.15   The specific issues of EC IT law can only be fully appreciated with a basic understanding of Community law. Chapter 2, therefore, includes an introduction to Community law and concludes with a selection of reading for those who need more detailed analysis of how these laws are usually applied. For those who are not computer literate, the next chapter begins with a brief description of the technology to which the law applies.

---

[9] There are numerous examples of decisions imposing anti-dumping duties on products in the IT industry: for example, Council Reg 2860/93 imposing a definitive anti-dumping duty on imports of certain types of electronic microcircuits known as Eproms (OJ 1993 L262/1).

Chapter 2
The Basics

1. The technology

An understanding of the technology is a prerequisite to analysis of the law   **2.1**
which applies to that technology. This chapter starts with a brief explanation
of those characteristics of the technology which figure in the application of EC
law.

The entire IT industry is built on the electronic manipulation of data   **2.2**
recorded in a digital format. A group of 1s and 0s is used to represent numbers
as well as words. In the computer, the 1s and 0s are reproduced by the "on"
and "off" state. In computer jargon, each 1 or 0 is known as a bit (from binary
digit) and a group of 8 bits is called a byte. One byte can represent 256 binary
values (00000000 to 11111111 (which equals 255)). These values can be used
to signify the numbers 0-9, the letters A-Z as well as other characters through
the use of a coding scheme such as ASCII (American Standard Code for
Information Interchange).

The earliest computers relied on valves (or vacuum tubes) to produce the on   **2.3**
and off states. That function is now performed by solid state transistors based
on semiconductor material and incorporated into integrated circuits housed
on chips. The processing power of today's computer is made possible, firstly, by
the incredible number of transistors and other components which can be put
on a chip and, secondly, the speed at which the chips operate. For example, it
has been reported that a processor in Digital Equipment's Alpha AXP range
can process more than one billion instructions per second. The chip has 9.3
million transistors and runs at 300 MHz (300 million cycles per second).[1]

The modern computer is made up of several distinct elements. A processor   **2.4**
manipulates digital information which may be fetched from an immediate
memory source (Random Access Memory or RAM) or a longer term storage
device such as a magnetic internal disk drive or a floppy disk (or diskette).
Input to the processor may come from another source such as a keyboard.
Once the processor has manipulated the input data, the results will be stored or
sent to a visual display unit (VDU), printer or other form of output. The
processor, memory, keyboard, VDU and printer are all examples of computer
hardware.

In the earliest computers of the 1940s, the way in which the components   **2.5**
were interconnected determined how the computer functioned. Changing this
configuration to perform another function involved time-consuming, manual

---

[1] *Computer Weekly* 15 September 1994, 12.

alteration to the wiring. In contrast, the speed and flexibility of the modern computer derives from its ability to respond to instructions recorded in digital form. These digital instructions are called software. It is not always straightforward to distinguish between software and hardware. Sometimes, instructions are permanently recorded on Read Only Memory or ROM. Reflecting this more permanent nature, the instructions are known as "firmware". Moreover, a particular configuration may be "hardwired" into a chip to improve processing speed such as Application Specific Integrated Circuits (ASICs).

2.6 The most basic instructions used to make a chip function will be recorded on that chip. They are known as microcode. The microcode instruction set has traditionally tended to encompass a wide range of functions—so-called Complex Instruction Set Computing or CISC. More recently, chips have been designed with a much reduced number of instructions to improve speed—so-called Reduced Instruction Set Computing or RISC. The result of the joint venture between IBM, Motorola and Apple is a RISC-based personal computer, the PowerPC.

2.7 At its most basic level, hardware responds to digital, machine-readable instructions. However, these instructions may be represented in higher level computing languages understandable by (at least some) humans. There are a wide range of languages such as BASIC, FORTRAN and C. The human readable software is called source code. It is turned into machine readable (object) code, through the process of "compilation". Nowadays, so-called fourth generation languages (4GL) are used automatically to generate source code to perform functions specified by the programmer.

2.8 As the technology led to greater flexibility, so different industry sectors came to be established according to the way in which the technology was applied. This process of change continues relentlessly to redefine the industry. To begin with, computers were large, inflexible and expensive to run and were only suitable for high volume processing of simple transactions. This made them ideal for universities, governments and large corporations. The main costs involved in these "mainframes" were the hardware itself and running costs. The software would often be licensed free with the hardware or would be written by the user for a specific task. In the 1970s, hardware became cheaper and more flexible and software became more sophisticated and expensive to develop. This led to the creation of an independent market for software. At the same time, smaller and cheaper hardware—mini-computers—began to be available to a wider market.

2.9 In the 1970s, hardware technology developed to the point where it became possible to incorporate a processor within a single chip. These microprocessors were the building blocks for a new product, the microcomputer or PC, and a new industry. At first quite basic, the chips on which they are based are now so powerful that microcomputers can take on and beat world champion chess players. In 1994, a computer based on Intel's Pentium chip knocked Gary Kasparov out of a chess championship.[2]

---

[2] *Computer Weekly* 8 September 1994, 4.

Increases in the power of smaller computers during the 1980s and   **2.10**
improvements in software and hardware enabled networks to be developed
which could replace the centralised mainframe. It became both cheaper and
much more flexible for many firms to buy a number of PCs connected to a
network via a small computer or PC called a server. This move toward
distributed computing or client/server technology in the late 1980s and early
1990s was one of the main reasons for a rapid decline in mainframe prices. Now
that mainframe prices are much lower, doubts have emerged as to whether the
hidden cost of managing individual use of computing power in fact outweighs
the cost of a central mainframe.

The growing use of networks also highlights one of the main characteristics   **2.11**
of the IT industry today. As hardware and software become more sophisticated, so it becomes more difficult to ensure that they all work together. To be
compatible, hardware and software must be designed so that they understand
the same set of instructions. The point at which the hardware and software
interconnect is called the interface. Perhaps the most important issue in IT law
today is the question of control over interfaces. If a firm has control over the
design of an interface and the product in which it is incorporated is successful,
there is a danger that that control will extend to other products which need to
work with the successful product.

This issue has become very significant in the software industry. As the   **2.12**
software market developed, it became cheaper and easier for the hardware to
be controlled by an operating system whilst the specific uses which a user
wanted, such as a database or spreadsheet, could be fulfilled by separate,
applications software. In order to work as intended, the interface between the
operating system and the applications program must be written according to
the same rules or specification. Control over that interface specification could
give control over the sale of both products because any entrant into the market
would be reliant on information which would have to be obtained from
another supplier. Later we will look at how the law can give rise to this type of
control (see para **4.29** *et seq*).

Two comments are worth making at this stage. Firstly, control over an   **2.13**
interface will probably only be of general concern if one of the products is
successful. However, once the product is successful that success can snowball as
more products are sold to fit in with the relevant interface. The greater the
success, the more market power that is conferred by control over the interface.
Secondly, such control will not necessarily give rise to a barrier to entry to the
market, not least because the designer of the interface may need to make the
specification widely available to ensure that third parties can make products
which work with the first product.

The success of Microsoft's MS-DOS and Windows software provides an   **2.14**
excellent example of both these features. Part of the reason for the incredible
success of those products has been that Microsoft made the Application
Programming Interface (API) widely available in order to ensure that third
parties would market software products which run in the Windows environment. This is no doubt one reason why it has been reported that Apple may

now license its operating system, System 7;[3] something which until now it has refused to do. It is worth noting that Microsoft still has control over the Windows API and this has led to calls, for example, by the industry body, Public Windows Interface (PWI), that such an important interface should be opened to industry influence.[4]

2.15   In addition to technical interfaces—the interface between hardware and software, another important interface exists between applications software and the person using it—the "user interface". As in the case of technical interfaces, access to this interface can also be the key to the market place. Once a user interface has become well-established, it may be difficult for other suppliers to gain a foothold in the market without access to the popular interface because customers would have to retrain staff to use an alternative user interface.

2.16   Not all technical interfaces are under the control of a single supplier ("proprietary interfaces"). In some cases, the relevant interface specifications are freely available ("open systems") so that both hardware and software can be produced by third parties to fit into the open "architecture". The most well-known example of an open operating system is UNIX. It was originally written in the early 1970s by programmers working for Bell Telephone Labs, part of AT&T, the US telephone corporation, and was aimed to be a simple, hardware independent, multiuser operating system. AT&T did not market the operating system itself but made the source code widely available which allowed UNIX to become the basis for a popular open system standard, particularly on mid-range systems. However, many of the operating systems derived from UNIX which were put on the market were not compatible. This led to moves to set up industry consortia such as the Open Software Foundation (OSF) to lay down UNIX standards. The downside of sharing this role amongst many is naturally that standards become more difficult to agree and to change to keep up with developments in technology.

2.17   So proprietary systems continue to thrive precisely because they may be the best systems available. Customers recognise that the best standards may be those owned and controlled by a single firm and being locked into that system may be a price worth paying for the most technologically advanced system. The UNIX system may be better placed now that UNIX System Laboratories has been acquired by Novell and the X/Open Group has been given a greater role in ensuring UNIX standardisation.

2.18   Standards are not just relevant to interfaces and, in fact, play a central role in the IT industry. We have seen that *de facto* standards can exist as a result of the commercial success of a product to which other products must connect. Other standards may be mandatory because they have been laid down by government, for example, with a view to protecting health and safety. These standards may well differ from one country to another. One of the Community's most important objectives is to create a single market. This may

---

[3] *Computer Weekly* 1 September 1994, 19.
[4] *Computer Weekly* 10 March 1994, 20.

require standards to be agreed at a Community level. Like industry agreement over standards, this can be a difficult and time-consuming process.

Electronic processing of digital information is the basic foundation of the IT industry. The spread of "digitisation" is extending the scope of that industry. Telecommunications is the best example. Two factors suggest that a description of the IT industry should cover telecoms as well. Firstly, we have seen that the growth in the IT industry nowadays has come from reliance on networks. These may be small or Local Area Networks (LANs). But there is growing use of the telecoms network to create larger networks, Wide Area Networks (WANs). Secondly, the network infrastructure in most developed countries is progressively converting from traditional copper wire connections which are more suitable for non-digital (or analogue) transmissions to optical fibre which rely on light for fast transmission of digital signals. **2.19**

The telecoms network is still mainly used for voice traffic. However, digital non-voice traffic is becoming more important. This traffic may rely on a modem to change digital signals into analogue signals for transmission across the network and to translate them back on receipt. Digital exchanges and increasing reliance on optical fibres has allowed the creation of large scale digital networks such as the Integrated Services Digital Network (ISDN) which can carry voice, data and even video. The final result of telecoms digitisation will be the "information superhighways" envisaged by US Vice President Al Gore. **2.20**

Another reason for treating telecoms as part of the IT industry is that the issues raised by regulation of the telecoms industry have clear parallels in the rest of the IT industry. Opening up the telecoms networks to competition can give power to those who have control over the network. The methods of dealing with that control are different to those used in the hardware and software sectors but at least one of the most basic issues is the same—the need to mould regulation and apply laws in order to avoid or control market power. **2.21**

The spread of digitisation to other industries—or, as some would call it, "convergence"—means that the IT industry of the future may encompass other industries as well, in particular, the media industry. When multimedia is fully adopted in commerce and in the home, it will not be possible to exclude the media industry from a description of the IT industry. As yet, it is appropriate to limit the IT industry to hardware, software (and services) and telecoms. **2.22**

A number of themes recur in the discussion of EC IT law. Firstly, the technology changes at a rapid pace. Traditionally, the law has been able more or less to keep up with the process of change by occasional, belated adjustment. The pace of change in the IT industry creates real dangers that law and regulation will be left behind by the technology. Secondly, the interconnection and interoperability of the products and services which make up the IT industry increase the possibility that market power will arise from control over interface and other standards. Again, there is a challenge for the law to deal with these issues in a sensitive and speedy way. Finally, the extension of digital networks is, to use a hackneyed phrase, making the world smaller. This can **2.23** only increase competition between firms from many different countries and increase the need for international accord over the issues which are now being addressed by the European Community. Before addressing the issues and themes in detail, we turn to the EC law background to EC IT law.

2. **What is EC law?**

(i) **Institutional structure**

2.24   We begin with a brief guide to the Community institutional structure. The Community's structure is complex and the way it functions often obscure and confusing. Changes introduced by the Maastricht Treaty on European Union (TEU) which came into force in November 1993 have added to the complexity and increased confusion, not least over terminology.

2.25   Until the TEU, EC law was the abbreviation for law of the European Communities. It was used to describe law derived from any one of the three European Communities. The first Community, the European Coal and Steel Community (ECSC), was set up in 1952 by six countries: France, Germany, Italy and the Benelux countries. In 1957, those same six countries set up two further Communities: the European Economic Community (EEC) and the European Atomic Energy Community (Euratom). A further six Member States have since joined the Communities: the UK, Ireland and Denmark (1973), Greece (1980), Spain and Portugal (1986). Austria, Sweden, Finland and Norway are scheduled to join in January 1995. Perhaps a little inaccurately, the three Communities are often referred to collectively as "the Community".

2.26   As a result of the 1965 Merger Treaty, the institutions established to run each of these three Communities were transformed into institutions common to all of three Communities. Since that date, the Community institutions discussed below have existed:

(a) Council

2.27   This body is made up of representatives of the Member States. It holds the most power in the Community and adopts almost all legislation. In fact, there is not one Council but many; one for each sector. For example, the Industry Ministers from each Member State attend the Internal Market Council and Ministers responsible for the telecoms portfolio attend the Telecommunications Council. There is a "chief" Council, the European Council, whose members are the Heads of State or Government of the Member States but this meets much less frequently than the other Councils, usually only twice a year. It does not adopt legislation; rather it lays down broad policies for the Community.

2.28   The work of the Council is directed by the Presidency which each Member State takes in turn for a six-month period. The detailed work of the Council is carried out by working parties. Most decisions are taken by the Committee of

Permanent Representatives (like many Community institutions, known by its French acronym, COREPER) which is made up of the ambassadors of the Member States to the Community (COREPER II) or their deputies (COREPER I). Agreement at this level is generally just rubber-stamped at the meeting of the Council itself. It is only if there is disagreement within COREPER II that discussion is required at ministerial level.

(b) Commission

This is the Community's executive body. In charge of a staff numbering some **2.29** 17,000 officials, there are 17 Commissioners who are appointed by the Member States collectively. Two are nominated by each of the larger Member States and one each by the other Member States. In January 1995, President Delors will complete a ten-year period of tenure as President of the Commission and will be replaced by Jacques Santer, Luxembourg's current Prime Minister, who has been appointed for an initial term of five years.

The Commission's main functions are to make proposals for legislation to **2.30** the Council and to ensure that EC law is respected. It has the power to adopt decisions, for example, in applying the competition rules. It also has the power under Article 169 to bring Member States before the European Court of Justice for failure to comply with their obligations under Community law.

(c) European Parliament

The original title for this institution was the Assembly but it has always called **2.31** itself the European Parliament and this title was confirmed by Treaty in 1987. Since 1979, it has been directly elected by universal suffrage. It has 567 members (increased from 518 by the TEU for the elections in June 1994). Its powers (or lack of them) are explained in the section in this chapter on the procedure for the adoption of legislation (see para **2.41** *et seq*).

(d) European Court of Justice (ECJ)

The ECJ ensures that the institutions respect the law through challenges to **2.32** their acts brought by other institutions, Member States, businesses or even individuals under Articles 173 and 175. The ECJ also ensures the uniform application of EC law throughout the Community through cases referred to it by the national courts of the Member States under Article 177 and through actions brought against the Member States under Articles 169 and 170. The TEU has conferred on the ECJ the power to fine Member States which fail to comply with ECJ rulings (Art 171).

In 1989, a first tier court, the Court of First Instance (CFI) was established. **2.33** Its jurisdiction, after the most recent extension in 1994 (OJ 1994 L66/29), encompasses all actions brought by natural or legal persons. It was set up as a court designed to deal with cases involving significant issues of fact with which the ECJ was not well-equipped to deal. For example, it has jurisdiction over all appeals brought by individuals and companies against decisions of the Commission applying EC competition rules. There is an appeal from the CFI to the ECJ on points of law. Case numbers for the CFI begin with "T" (from the French "Tribunal"). Cases before the ECJ begin with "C". The ECJ and CFI will be referred to collectively as the ECJ.

2.34   The entry into force of the Treaty on European Union has brought about some important changes to the Community's structure. Firstly, the TEU substantially alters the Treaty on the European Economic Community and renames it the European Community Treaty (or EC Treaty). Secondly, the TEU provides for cooperation between the 12 Member States in the fields of justice and home affairs and foreign and security policy. These additional areas do not fall within the competence of the existing Communities and, for the most part, only involve political cooperation between the Member States. It is for this reason that the post-Maastricht system is sometimes represented as a series of pillars supporting the European Union:

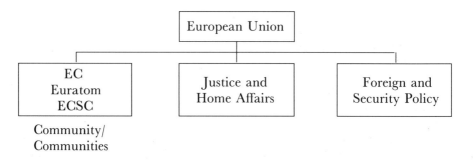

2.35   In the areas falling outside the Community's competence, the Community institutions play a much reduced role. It is basically only the Council which is borrowed as an institution for decisions on justice and home affairs and foreign and security policy. Recognising this wider role, the Council has renamed itself the Council of the European Union (EU Council). The other institutions retain their old names. EEC law is now EC law but it is still frequently referred to as Community law. This book is exclusively concerned with EC law.

(ii) Sources of Law

2.36   There are two principal sources of EC law: the Treaty itself and legislation adopted on the basis of the Treaty.

2.37   The aims of the Treaty, as expanded by the TEU, are laid down in Article 2:

> "The Community shall have as its task, by establishing a common market and an economic and monetary union and by implementing the common policies or activities referred to in Articles 3 and 3a, to promote throughout the Community a harmonious and balanced development of economic activities, sustainable and non-inflationary growth respecting the environment, a high degree of convergence of economic performance, a high level of employment and of social protection, the raising of the standard of living and quality of life, and economic and social cohesion and solidarity among Member States."

These aims are probably wider than many people think. They are **2.38** supplemented by a list of specific policies in Articles 3 and 3a. These include the creation of the internal market, the development of trans-European networks and a contribution to the "flowering of the cultures of the Member States" (Art 3(p)).

The Treaty could not achieve its aims solely by the application of the rules **2.39** contained in the Treaty. The EC Treaty grants powers to adopt specific measures such as the Commission's power to adopt decisions implementing EC competition rules. The Treaty also confers a wide range of powers to adopt subsidiary legislation. There are two basic forms of legislation: directive and regulation. The difference between the two lies in their effect on national law (see para **2.47** *et seq*). The TEU introduced an express requirement that the Community act:

> "only if and in so far as the objectives of the proposed action cannot be sufficiently achieved by the Member States and can therefore, by reason of the scale or effects of the proposed action, be better achieved by the Community" (Art 3 EC).

It remains to be seen how this "principle of subsidiarity" will be applied in EC law but, for example, the Commission was influenced by the principle in amending its draft Data Protection Directive (see para **7.5** *et seq*).

The ECJ has played a pivotal role in the impact of the EC Treaty in national **2.40** law by giving automatic effect to many of its provisions without the need for specific incorporation into national law. In addition, it is a source of law itself since it has relied on certain general principles in interpreting EC law, for example, fundamental human rights drawn from the European Convention on Human Rights (*Nold* v *Commission* Case 4/73 [1974] ECR 491; [1974] 2 CMLR 338).

(iii) **Procedure for adoption of legislation**

It is vital to understand the way in which the institutions are involved in the **2.41** adoption of legislation. There seems to be a good deal of confusion over their respective roles. The situation has not been improved by still further procedures for the adoption of legislation introduced by the TEU. We have now reached the point where academics argue over whether there are 20 or only 19 different procedures for the adoption of Community legislation.

The system is best described from an historical viewpoint. When the **2.42** Communities were first set up, the Parliament had an extremely limited role to play. In most cases, the Commission would make a proposal and the Council would then adopt it, assuming sufficient Member States could agree so as to satisfy the voting requirement laid down in the Treaty provision on which the legislation was based. In general, the Parliament's role was limited to giving an opinion which the Council was free to ignore.[5]

---

[5] Since 1975, the Parliament has played a greater role in the adoption of the Community budget.

2.43   When the Parliament became democratically elected in 1979, naturally there were calls for increased power. A limited step in this direction was taken in 1987 by the Single European Act (SEA) which amended the (then) EEC Treaty. The SEA introduced the "cooperation procedure" for some legislation.[6] The procedure is only available where the Treaty provision on which the legislation is based permits the legislation to be adopted by qualified majority.[7] Unlike simple majority, in the case of qualified majority, each Member State is allotted a certain number of votes depending on its importance; for example, the larger Member States such as the UK have ten votes whilst the smallest Member State, Luxembourg, only has two votes. Legislation is approved if a specified total number of votes (54 out of a total of 76), are cast in favour. The allocation of votes is such that one of the larger Member States cannot block a proposal unless it has the support of at least two other Member States. In fact, this voting system dates back to the original Treaties but had rarely been resorted to as a result of the compromise of a political crisis in 1966 prompted by France's General De Gaulle. The concern caused by the system came to the fore again in 1994 in discussions on new voting rules for the enlarged Community.

2.44   Under the cooperation procedure, the Council, on the basis of a Commission proposal and after consulting the Parliament, adopts a "common position" by qualified majority. Unlike the traditional, simple procedure, this common position is merely a statement of intent rather than final legislation. The common position is then transmitted to the Parliament for a second reading. If the Parliament approves the common position or fails to act, the common position is adopted by the Council by qualified majority. If, however, the Parliament rejects the common position, the Council can only adopt it by unanimous agreement. Alternatively, if the Parliament proposes amendments, the common position is returned to the Commission for it to consider the proposed amendments. The proposal, as amended by the Commission, is then sent to the Council for a second reading. The Council acts by qualified majority unless it wishes to amend the proposal in which case it must act unanimously.

2.45   There is no doubt that the cooperation procedure has increased the Parliament's influence. It can make it more difficult for the Council to adopt legislation by rejecting the common position or by proposing amendments (provided the Commission incorporates the amendments in the revised proposal). The Software Directive followed the cooperation procedure and the Parliament had a clear influence over the final text—it was the the Parliament which proposed a decompilation right, a vital part of the Directive. Nevertheless, it is difficult to argue that the Parliament has any real power under the cooperation procedure. Indeed, the decompilation right in the final text of the Directive is rather different to the Parliament's proposal. Moreover, one disadvantage of the procedure is its complexity. Even if the Parliament plays a greater role, democratic legitimacy is scarcely improved by the

---

[6] The procedure is now set out in Art 189c EC.
[7] Described in Art 148 EC.

difficulty which any voter would have in following the procedure with a view to assessing how their MEP or his or her party had performed.

The TEU introduced more procedures, in particular, the so-called **2.46** "co-decision procedure".[8] This procedure follows the basic structure of the cooperation procedure with some important changes. Firstly, the Parliament is not dependent on the Commission endorsing its amendments (although the Council has to act unanimously if the Commission expresses a negative opinion). Secondly, if the Parliament does propose amendments or reject the common position, the Council can call for a Conciliation Committee— made up of representatives of the Council, the Parliament and the Commission—to seek to agree a text which can command the support of a qualified majority of the Council and a majority of MEPs. Finally, whatever happens, the new procedure gives the Parliament a veto. If the Parliament rejects the common position or does not approve the text agreed by the Conciliation Committee, the Council cannot adopt the proposal whatever the support for it amongst the Member States. Clearly, this is an important difference to the cooperation procedure but not only is this a negative power but there is also little doubt that this power has been achieved at the expense of any clarity in the procedure. The first to gain will no doubt be Brussels lobbyists faced with even more arcane procedures to advise on and follow.

(iv) **Effect of EC law on national law**

The ECJ has played an important role in the impact of EC law on national **2.47** law. In 1964, it held that some provisions of the Treaty must be applied directly by national courts. For example, a national court must enforce EC competition law when it applies. There is still some doubt whether this would require a national court to award damages but it seems likely that this will be the case. The ECJ has also held that regulations apply automatically in national law without the need for implementation.

A more difficult question was whether directives could be directly effective. **2.48** The ECJ has held that a national court must interpret national law where possible in accordance with Community law.[9] In addition, it is now well-established that a directive will be directly effective provided it is sufficiently clear, precise and unconditional but it can only be invoked against the State and not against individuals or firms. The ECJ recently made it clear that directives cannot establish obligations on individuals in the absence of implementation by the Member State.[10] However, the ECJ has held in *Francovich* v *Italy* (Cases C-6 & 9/90 [1991] ECR I-3357; [1993] 2 CMLR 66) that, in certain circumstances, even if a directive is not directly effective, individuals can sue the Member State for failure to implement the directive. It

---

[8] Set out in Art 189b EC.

[9] *Marleasing* v *La Comercial Internacional de Alimentación* Case C-106/89 [1990] ECR I-4135; [1992] 1 CMLR 305.

[10] *Paola Faccini Dori* v *Recreb* Case C-91/92 Judgment of 14 July 1994. Not yet reported.

is still not clear what those circumstances are. It may be that such an action will not be available for a genuine mistake in interpretation.[11]

3. Free movement rules

2.49 One of the fundamental objectives of the EC Treaty is the creation of an internal market characterised by the free movement of goods, persons, services and capital (Arts 3(c) and 7a EC). For the purposes of this book, the most important of these Treaty obligations is the removal of barriers to trade in goods and services.

(i) Articles 30 and 36: free movement of goods

2.50 With a brevity which belies its significant contribution to the creation of the internal market, Article 30 states simply that "quantitative restrictions on imports and all measures having equivalent effect shall, without prejudice to the following provisions, be prohibited between Member States."

2.51 In keeping with the 1957 Treaty of Rome timetable, quantitative restrictions, such as quotas, were eliminated. However, this highlighted the extent to which trade within the Community was affected by measures having an equivalent effect to quantitative restrictions (MQRs). For example, if Germany laid down stringent mandatory safety standards for VDUs but standards in France were less demanding, VDUs manufactured to French standards could not be sold in Germany. In other words, divergent national technical rules can lead to the protection of a national market from competition from imports from other Member States. It is clear from this example that national rules can lead to this result even if they do not discriminate against imports and apply in exactly the same way to imports as they do to domestic production.

2.52 In *Procureur du Roi* v *Dassonville* (Case 8/74 [1974] ECR 837; [1974] 2 CMLR 436), the ECJ defined MQRs to include "all trading rules enacted by Member States which are capable of hindering, directly or indirectly, actually or potentially, intra-Community trade" (para 5).

2.53 This definition gives enormous scope to the application of Article 30 and would clearly catch the German rule in the above example.[12] There are three important qualifications to the application of Article 30. Firstly, in the famous *Cassis de Dijon* case (*Rewe-Zentral* v *Bundesmonopolverwaltung fur Branntwein* Case 120/78 [1979] ECR 649; [1979] 3 CMLR 494), the ECJ held that the barriers to trade caused by a national rule would not be caught by Article 30 provided that the rule applied in the same way to both domestic production and imports and that the rule was necessary to fulfil certain "mandatory requirements".

---

[11] See, *e.g.*, discussion by Steiner (1993) ELR 3.
[12] See also Commission Directive 70/50 (OJ 1970 L13/29) in which the Commission gave guidance on the scope of the definition of MQRs.

These included the protection of public health and the defence of the consumer. The stringent German VDU safety standards in the hypothetical example could escape the control of Article 30 on this basis because they apply in the same way to imports and domestic production. The German government would have to show that the standards were the least restrictive way of achieving one of the mandatory requirements, such as the protection of public health. The list of mandatory requirements given by the ECJ in the *Cassis de Dijon* case is not exhaustive and the ECJ has subsequently added to the list, for example, protection of the environment (*Commission* v *Denmark* Case 302/86 [1988] ECR 4607; [1989] 1 CMLR 619).

Secondly, in recent cases, the ECJ has circumscribed the scope of trading **2.54** rules laid down in the *Dassonville* case. The problem which faced the ECJ was that the wide definition laid down in that case caught national rules which did not stop the import of products from other Member States but could affect the overall level of imports. Even if these rules did not protect national production, Member States would have to justify the rules on the basis of one of the mandatory requirements. In a number of cases, for example, the ECJ was faced with the question whether Article 30 caught national rules which limited shopping on Sunday. Initially, it held that such restrictions were trading rules within the *Dassonville* definition but could be justified on the basis of a mandatory requirement (*Torfaen* v *B & Q* Case C-145/88 [1989] ECR 3851; [1991] 1 CMLR 383). More recently, the ECJ seems to have recognised that there is no point in subjecting such rules to the *Cassis de Dijon* test. In *Keck & Mithouard*,[13] the ECJ was asked whether Article 30 covered a French law which prohibited sale below cost. In a departure from its existing jurisprudence, the ECJ held that national rules controlling "certain selling arrangements" were not caught by Article 30 at all provided that:

> "those provisions applied to all affected traders operating within the national territory and provided that they affect in the same manner in law and in fact the marketing of domestic products and of those from other Member States" (para 16).

It remains to be seen precisely which selling arrangements are outside Article 30[14] but the ECJ has now confirmed that the prohibition does not cover Sunday trading rules.[15]

Finally, for national rules which are caught by Article 30 and do not satisfy **2.55** the test laid down in the *Cassis de Dijon* case, Article 36 provides a number of ways by which Member States can justify such rules. It exempts from Article 30

> "prohibitions or restrictions on imports...justified on grounds of public morality, public policy or public security; the protection of health and life of humans,

---

[13] Cases C-267 & 268/91. Judgment of 24 November 1993. Not yet reported.
[14] See Chalmers, *Repackaging the Internal Market—The Ramifications of the Keck Judgment* (1994) ELR 385.
[15] *Punto Casa* v *Sindaco del Commune di Capena* Cases C-69&258/93. Judgment of 2 June 1994. Not yet reported.

animals or plants; the protection of treasures possessing artistic, historic or archaeological value; or the protection of industrial and commercial property."

2.56   So if a trading rule which can affect trade between Member States either applies in a different way to imports or domestic production or is not justified on the basis of a mandatory requirement, then the Member State will have to justify the rule on the basis of one of the items listed in Article 36. As in the case of reliance on mandatory requirements, the Member State must also show that the national rule goes no further than is necessary to achieve the aim specified in Article 36. Moreover, Article 36 adds an important proviso that "such prohibitions or restrictions shall not, however, constitute a means of arbitrary discrimination or a disguised restriction on trade between Member States."

2.57   This brief discussion shows that the ECJ's caselaw seeks to strike a balance between, on the one hand, those national rules creating barriers to trade which can be justified by the Member State and so escape control and, on the other, those which are struck down because they cannot be justified. In the case of national rules which are justified, the resulting barrier to trade can only be eliminated by legislation at a Community level. In the VDU example, if the French and German standards for VDUs followed standards laid down at a Community level, French VDUs could be sold in Germany without any need for reliance on Article 30. While Article 30 effects a limited negative integration, full integration of the Community's national markets can only be achieved by collective positive integration.[16]

2.58   Positive integration can take different forms. For example, EC legislation may require Member States to change their rules. Alternatively, the legislation may be less interventionist and merely require Member States to recognise that rules laid down by other Member States are "equivalent" because they achieve the same aim albeit by different rules, so-called mutual recognition of equivalence. The power to adopt Community legislation is discussed later in this chapter (see para **2.73** *et seq*).

(ii) Article 30 and intellectual property

2.59   Intellectual property rights (IPRs), such as patents, copyright and trade marks, are granted by the national laws of each Member State and in respect of their own territory. One question which came before the ECJ was whether it was possible for owners of these national IPRs to rely on those rights to exclude products lawfully sold in other Member States. For example, if a VDU producer had patents for the same technology in both France and Germany, could that producer rely on the German patent to prevent the import of VDUs which incorporated the technology and which had been sold by that producer in France under the equivalent (or parallel) patent? Or could Article 30 be employed to control the use of IPRs where the effect of the IPR was to create a

---

[16] *Cf.* Van Empel, *EEC and Intellectual Property* (1991) Bar European Group News 1.

barrier to trade between Member States? There were arguments that the Treaty could not undermine national IPRs in this way. Article 222 states that "This Treaty shall in no way prejudice the rules in Member States governing the system of property ownership."

Even if Article 222 could be narrowly defined, one of the justifications listed in Article 36 is the "protection of industrial and commercial property". Now that the ECJ has recognised that this covers copyright, it is more common to use the term "intellectual property".

In *Deutsche Gramophon* v *Metro* (Case 78/70 [1971] ECR 487; [1971] CMLR **2.60** 631), the ECJ was faced with the question whether Article 30 applied where an owner of an IPR in one Member State attempted to stop the import of products sold under the parallel right in another Member State. Deutsche Gramophon owned rights similar to copyright in sound recordings which it had manufactured in Germany and sold under parallel rights in France through its French subsidiary. The ECJ held that Deutsche Gramophon could not rely on its German rights to stop the resale of those recordings in Germany. Under German law, if the recordings had been marketed in Germany, Deutsche Gramophon would not have been entitled to control resale—its rights would have been "exhausted". The ECJ held that EC law required the same effect to follow from sale in another Member State provided that the sale was effected by Deutsche Gramophon or with its consent.

The ECJ rejected the argument that Article 30 could not apply because of **2.61** Article 222 or, indeed, the exception provided by Article 36. The ECJ said:

> "Amongst the prohibitions or restrictions on the free movement of goods which it concedes Article 36 refers to industrial and commercial property. On the assumption that those provisions may be relevant to a right related to copyright, it is nevertheless clear from that article that, although the Treaty does not affect the existence of rights recognised by the legislation of a Member State with regard to industrial and commercial property, the exercise of such rights may nevertheless fall within the prohibitions laid down by the Treaty. Although it permits prohibitions or restrictions, which are justified for the purpose of protecting industrial and commercial property, Article 36 only admits derogations from that freedom to the extent that they are justified for the purpose of safeguarding rights which constitute the specific subject-matter of such property." (Case 78/70 [1971] ECR 487; [1971] CMLR 631 para 11).

Thus, the ECJ recognised that a balance had to be struck in the application of **2.62** Article 30 to intellectual property rights. Article 30 can control the use of parallel rights to divide up the Community into separate markets but there must be a limit to its application otherwise national IPRs could be harmonised down to the lowest common denominator.

The ECJ relied on two concepts to resolve this conflict. Firstly, it said that **2.63** there is a distinction between the existence of a right and its exercise—Article 30 could not prejudice the existence of an IPR but it could control its exercise. This distinction can be criticised on a number of grounds. Firstly, it is almost impossible to apply since it is difficult to see how a right exists if it cannot be exercised.[17] Secondly, it is argued that the distinction is misleading because Article 30 does not catch the behaviour of the owner of the right at all but rather it controls the national law which grants the right.[18] In other words, it is the existence of one aspect of the IPR which is attacked by Article 30. If Article 30 does apply, the IPR can never be relied upon in those circumstances. The existence/exercise theory draws attention away from this important point. However, we will see later that the theory is suited to describing the way in which the competition rules apply to IPRs.

2.64   In the *Deutsche Gramophon* case, the ECJ also refers to the concept of the specific subject-matter of an IPR. The concept is also difficult to apply but it does reflect the fact that there must be some limit to the intervention of the ECJ in the national determination of the scope of IPRs. This can be demonstrated by the ECJ's decision in *Warner Brothers* v *Christiansen* (Case 158/86 [1988] ECR 2605; [1990] 3 CMLR 684). Mr. Christiansen, who owned a video rental shop in Denmark, visited London where he bought a video cassette of the James Bond film "Never Say Never Again". He advertised the video for rental in Denmark. In Denmark, the owner of copyright of a prerecorded film can control rental even after sale. No such right existed in the UK. It was argued that Warner's rights had been exhausted on sale in the UK so that the additional Danish right to control rental could not be relied upon to prevent Mr Christiansen from renting out the video. The ECJ noted that the Danish rule did not discriminate between national products and imports and that the application of Article 30 would undermine the Danish system. The ECJ upheld the rental right.

2.65   There are a number of justifications for the ECJ's approach in the *Warner* case. It could be argued quite simply that rental rights are not exhausted on first sale in Denmark so it is inconsistent for the right to be exhausted by sale in another Member State. Indeed, the Danish rule did not have the effect of stopping the import of the video; it only required the payment of a royalty for rental. This result is fully in line with the ECJ's approach to royalties for performance (as opposed to reproduction) of copyright works.[19] It can also be argued that the ECJ was recognising in the *Warner* case the limit to the power of negative integration and the vital part played by positive integration. The ECJ might have been influenced by the fact that the Commission had embarked on a programme for harmonisation of copyright which included a proposal for a Directive on rental rights.[20] The case indicates a clear reluctance on the part of the ECJ to control national intellectual property rights where what is really required is harmonisation.

---

[17] See, *e.g.*, Guy & Leigh, *The EEC and Intellectual Property* (Sweet & Maxwell, 1981). The distinction still has its supporters. See, *e.g.*, Friden (1989) CMLRev 193.

[18] See, *e.g.*, Marenco & Banks, *Intellectual Property and the Community Rules on Free Movement: Discrimination Unearthed* (1990) ELR 224, 236.

[19] See, *e.g.*, *Basset* v *SACEM* Case 402/85 [1987] ECR 1747; [1987] 3 CMLR 173.

[20] See Green Paper on Copyright and the Challenge of Technology COM(88)172, para 4.11.2 followed by a proposal by the Commission (OJ 1991 L53/35), culminating in Council Dir 92/100 (OJ 1992 L346/61).

The *Warner* case may be important in determining how Article 30 applies to **2.66** the distribution of software since it recognises that even though the value of the video cassette depended on the recording of the James Bond film, the cassette could be treated as a good (rather than a service) for the purposes of the free movement rules. Rules on the free movement of services do exist but we will see that they do not necessarily apply in the same way as the rules on free movement of goods (see para **2.68** *et seq*).

In applying EC free movement rules to IPRs, care has to be taken to **2.67** distinguish the various types of IPRs. We have seen that copyright raises specific issues because the rights which go to make up copyright have different characteristics. It is also worth noting that some issues remain to be resolved. Consent is clearly essential to the doctrine of exhaustion (*Pharmon* v *Hoechst* Case 19/84 [1985] ECR 2281; [1985] 3 CMLR 775) but there is still uncertainty over how this is applied to assignments. The ECJ recently gave some guidance on this question in a case involving a trade mark assignment.[21]

(iii) Article 59: free movement of services

The EC Treaty also requires the removal of barriers to trade in services. Article **2.68** 59 requires the abolition of restrictions on freedom to provide services within the Community "in respect of nationals who are established in a State of the Community other than that of the person for whom the services are established." There are further rules on freedom to establish in another Member State (Arts 52–58).

The application of the principle of free movement to services is not always as **2.69** straightforward as the application of the principle to goods. One reason for this is that there is often nothing tangible which crosses a national frontier. Furthermore, there is no express equivalent to Article 36 to qualify the application of Article 59. However, the ECJ now seems to be developing its jurisprudence along the same lines as its case law on Article 30 so as to catch non-discriminatory rules which cannot be justified on the basis of certain mandatory requirements.[22]

As in the case of Article 30, IPRs may be obstacles to the free movement of **2.70** services. This is best illustrated by a case which may well be an important analogy for the application of both free movement and competition rules to transactions in the information technology field.

In *Coditel* v *Ciné Vog* (Case 62/79 [1980] ECR 881; [1981] 2 CMLR 362), a **2.71** French film producer, Films les Boétie, had granted a Belgian Company, Ciné Vog, the exclusive right to show in public in Belgium the film "Le Boucher". For an initial period, Ciné Vog was only permitted to show the film in cinemas and not on television. During that initial period, the film was shown on German television with the permission of Films les Boétie. A Belgian cable

---

[21] *IHT Internationale Heiztechnik* v *Ideal-Standard* Case C-9/93. Judgment of 22 June 1994. Not yet reported.
[22] See the Commission's interpretative communication concerning the free movement of services across frontiers (OJ 1993 C334/3).

television company, Coditel, picked up the signal and transmitted the film to subscribers to its cable network. A Belgian Court awarded Ciné Vog damages against Coditel for breach of copyright. The case was subsequently referred to the ECJ for a decision as to whether it was consistent with the free movement rules for Ciné Vog to be able to stop the transmission of the film by Coditel. The ECJ upheld Ciné Vog's rights. Although there is no express protection for intellectual property from the application of Article 59 as there is from Article 30 in Article 36, the ECJ applied similar principles. It held that films were different from other copyright works because the copyright holder was entitled to a royalty for each showing of the film. In other words, the right to control the performance of the film was not exhausted when it was first shown. Moreover, the Treaty did not prevent the copyright holder from imposing limits on where the film was shown and those limits could be based on Member State territories, particularly given that national broadcasting monopolies are based on those territories.[23]

(iv) **Relying on the free movement rules**

2.72   Articles 30 and 59 are directly effective so individuals are entitled to rely on them before a national court without the need for the Member State to have enacted specific legislation. It follows that a national court must not apply national legislation which is incompatible with Article 30 or Article 59. In case of doubt, the national court can seek guidance on the interpretation of those Articles by means of a preliminary reference to the ECJ under Article 177. Finally, individuals are probably entitled to damages from a Member State which breaches Article 30 although the position is not clear in all Member States.[24]

4. **Harmonisation legislation**

2.73   One of the predominant themes in the discussion of the principles of free movement was that there is a limit to the integration which can be achieved solely by negative means. Thus, many divergent national rules which create a barrier to trade can be justified on the basis of the protection of health. Although the ECJ has strictly applied the exceptions listed in Article 36, there is clearly a need for agreement at a Community level on legislation to achieve positive harmonisation. There are a number of powers granted by the Treaty to this effect.

---

[23] There was a second case on these facts involving the competition rules: *Coditel* v *Ciné Vog* Case 262/81 [1982] ECR 3381; [1983] 1 CMLR 49. See para 2.110.

[24] In the UK, for example, any right to damages has been severely curtailed by the Court of Appeal in *Bourgoin* v *MAFF* [1986] 1 CMLR 267.

(i) **Article 100: common market**

The original 1957 Treaty of Rome gave power to the Council to adopt   **2.74**
directives to harmonise national rules which directly affected "the establishment or functioning of the common market." A number of significant steps
were taken on the basis of this power towards the creation of a common
market. However, there was a growing realisation in the 1980s that insufficient
progress was being made towards the creation of a common market. One of the
reasons for the lack of progress was the requirement in Article 100 for
unanimous agreement among Member States. This was difficult to achieve
when there were only six Member States. It was becoming almost impossible
to achieve once that number had reached 12 with the addition of Spain and
Portugal in 1986. It looks as though the number could reach 16 with the
addition of Austria, Finland, Sweden and Norway scheduled for the beginning
of 1995. A further problem with the traditional approach to the creation of the
common market resulted from the attitude which was generally taken towards
creating a level playing field. In many cases, the Commission's proposals
would endeavour to create "Euro-products", every detail of which would be
laid down at a Community level. Not only did this make consensus difficult to
achieve but also led to problems in keeping pace with technological advances.

In 1986, the Commission produced a White Paper which confirmed the   **2.75**
need for the completion of the single market.[25] In a novel move, the White
Paper listed about 300 specific measures which were considered necessary for
completion of the single market and set down an eight-year timetable ending
on 31 December 1992—the famous 1992 deadline. This Internal Market
Programme has been described by its architect as "marking the turning point
in the fortunes of the Community."[26]

One key element of the White Paper was the recognition of the need for a   **2.76**
new approach to standardisation.[27] Instead of seeking complete uniformity, a
new approach was advocated. This would involve establishing basic general
criteria—"essential requirements"—which a product would have to meet in
order to circulate freely within the Community. The relevant European
standards bodies would then be given a mandate to draw up a standard which
would be sufficient evidence of meeting the basic general criteria. However,
the standard would not usually be compulsory. It would be open to a
manufacturer to prove compliance with the general criteria by other means.
The White Paper included some proposals in the IT field such as for a directive
on the legal protection of computer programs. It also called for the urgent
adoption of the Semiconductor Chip Directive which was subsequently
adopted on the basis of Article 100.[28]

We have seen that one brake to harmonisation came from the conditions for   **2.77**
reliance on Article 100, in particular, the requirement for unanimous

---

[25] White Paper on Completing the Internal Market COM(85)310 of 14 June 1985.
[26] Lord Cockfield, *The European Union: Creating the Single Market* (Wiley Chancery, 1994)
[27] Confirmed by Council Resolution of 7 May 1985 on the new approach to technical harmonisation
and standardisation (OJ 1985 C136/1).
[28] Council Dir 87/54 on the legal protection of topographies of semiconductor products (OJ 1987
L24/36). See Appendix A2 and para 3.4 *et seq.*

agreement amongst the Member States. In a parallel development to the White Paper, in 1986, the Member States agreed to a number of important changes to the Treaty of Rome at least partly to facilitate progress towards the single market. One vital change introduced as a result of this agreement (which became the 1987 Single European Act) was the introduction of a new power for the Council to legislate: Article 100a.

(ii) Article 100a: internal market

2.78 By way of derogation from Article 100, Article 100a gives the Council the power to adopt legislation to complete the internal market. Unlike Article 100, the Council can act by qualified majority. There are a number of qualifications to this new power. Firstly, it is only available "save where otherwise provided" in the Treaty. In other words, if a specific power is granted elsewhere in the Treaty, the Council has to rely on the more specific power.[29] Secondly, the involvement of the European Parliament is enhanced. Originally, measures adopted under Article 100a had to follow the cooperation procedure. Since the TEU came into force, those measures must follow the more complex co-decision procedure (see para **2.46**). Thirdly, the power under Article 100a is not available for legislation affecting fiscal provisions, the free movement of persons or the rights and interests of employed persons (Art 100a (2)). Fourthly, the Commission's proposals on health, safety, environmental and consumer protection must take as a base a high level of protection (Art 100a (3)). Finally, Article 100a(4) gives Member States the power to apply national rules justified on the basis of the exceptions listed in Article 36 or in order to protect the environment and the working environment. This power is in turn subject to limitations and, despite original fears that it would undermine the creation of the internal market, it has rarely been used.

2.79 A number of the important pieces of legislation in the information technology field have been adopted on the basis of Article 100a, in particular, the Software Directive which followed the cooperation procedure. The Article has been relied on for number of important pieces of legislation in the telecoms field, for example, the Council's Framework Directive on Open Network Provision.[30]

2.80 One aspect of the 1992 programme which has suffered delay is the removal of all border controls. An attempt to speed up the process, the Schengen Agreement, has been approved by nine Member States (all except the UK, Ireland and Denmark). IT enthusiasts will be interested to hear that one of the principal delays to implementing the agreement is the difficulty in finalising the necessary supporting IT system. There is also concern over data protection in the light of reports that up to six million items of personal data may need to be assembled.[31]

---

[29] Although the ECJ seems to take a rather flexible approach: see *Commission* v *Council (Titanium Dioxide Waste)* Case C-300/89 [1991] ECR I-2867; [1993] 3 CMLR 359.

[30] Council Dir 90/387 on the establishment of the internal market for telecommunications services through the implementation of open network provision (OJ 1990 L192/1).

[31] *Computer Weekly* 24 March 1994, 38.

(iii) **Other powers**

The Treaty also contains certain specific powers which have been extended by   **2.81**
the Single European Act and the TEU. Some legislation is adopted on the
basis of several powers. In the event that there is a conflicting procedure, the
ECJ insists that the most appropriate legal basis is chosen (*Commission* v *Council
(Titanium Dioxide Waste)* Case C-300/89 [1991] ECR I-2867; [1993] 3 CMLR
359). Specific powers have been relied on for the adoption of legislation in the
IT field. For example, the VDU Work Directive (see para **3.27** *et seq*) was
based on Article 118a (social policy) and the proposal for a Database Directive
(see para **5.3** *et seq*) is based on Article 57(2) (establishment), Article 66
(services) as well as Article 100a.

Where there is no specific power, Article 235 of the Treaty confers a general   **2.82**
power to adopt legislation necessary to achieve the objectives of the
Community. For example, the Council Decision on developing Integrated
Services Digital Network (ISDN) as a Trans-European Network (TEN) was
based on Article 235.

(iv) **Harmonisation and IPRs**

We have seen that Articles 30 and 59 effect a limited negative integration and   **2.83**
leave some barriers to trade. This is equally true in the case of intellectual
property rights (IPRs). Since IPRs play a key role in the IT industry, the
removal of the barriers to trade is important for the industry. In addition,
harmonisation at a Community level has been seen to be necessary in order to
resolve uncertainty about the protection of new technologies such as
semiconductor chips and computer programs. For these reasons, discussion of
legislation to harmonise IPRs forms a major part of this book.

5. **Competition rules**

(i) **Importance**

The system of competition law set up by the Treaty of Rome is as fundamental   **2.84**
to the Community as the creation of an internal market based on free
movement and harmonisation.[32] The starting point for understanding why a
law is required to protect competition is the underlying economic theory.[33]
This theory relies on market models to demonstrate that society's resources are
most efficiently used where there is perfect competition rather than monopoly.
Both models depend on the basic principle that the higher the market price the
more producers will supply but the less customers will demand. The market

---

[32] See Art 3 EC.
[33] For a basic introduction to the economics of competition law, see Fishwick, *Making Sense of
Competition Policy* (Kogan Page, 1993). See also Lipsey, *An Introduction to Positive Economics* (OUP,
1989, 7th ed).

price will tend towards the price which clears the market, that is, where supply equals demand.

2.85   Perfect competition exists in a market when certain conditions are fulfilled. In particular there must be enough producers and customers of a product such that no individual producer or customer can influence the market price and that price is the only factor which customers take into account in deciding where and how much to buy. In addition, there must be no barriers to entry to or exit from the market and everyone must be fully informed about market conditions. The model shows that the marginal cost of each profit-maximising producer will equal price, that is, each rational producer will keep on producing until the marginal cost has risen to the point where the last product adds no more to cost than to revenue. If the average cost of the output represented by this marginal cost exceeds the most efficient level, other more efficient producers will enter the market until there is enough additional supply for the market price to fall. The equilibrium market price will gravitate towards the level at which producers earn no more than the most efficient cost of production plus sufficient profit to keep them in the market. The benefits of perfect competition are that society's resources are directed toward the lowest cost production of what consumers want (reflected in their willingness to buy).

2.86   The model of perfect competition can be compared to the monopoly model where there is a single producer of a product. This producer can influence the price by varying output. The model shows that the monopoly producer can increase profits by reducing output so as to force the price above marginal cost and above the competitive level. Profits are increased because demand falls by proportionately less than the price rises; in technical jargon, the demand is inelastic at the competitive price level. In conditions of perfect competition, demand is elastic—if a producer increases its price above the competitive level, purchasers will buy from others and demand for its products will fall to zero.

2.87   Comparing our two models, we see that society's resources will not be as efficiently allocated and employed in the case of monopoly as under conditions of perfect competition. This basic theory underlies most competition laws including EC competition law. Thus, on the one hand, Article 86 controls the behaviour of firms which have a strong position on the market (in the words of Article 86, a dominant position). On the other hand, Article 85 is aimed at agreements between independent firms which eliminate competition.

2.88   But do these models really help us to apply competition law in practice? The first point is that the models do not reflect real life. The conditions required for perfect competition are so artificial that the model will never exist in real life. For example, in many markets, purchase decisions are based on factors other than price so producers will do their utmost to distinguish their products from competing products, for example, by advertising. Does this make advertising a bad thing? Some could be argued to be wasteful but it is worth bearing in mind that, not only does advertising allow firms to confirm reputations, say for quality, but it also pays for commercial television. It is not easy to see how the simple theoretical models help to determine the application of competition law to this type of "imperfect" competition.

Another condition of perfect competition is that producers cannot reduce   **2.89**
marginal cost by producing more; yet these "economies of scale" are a
common feature of markets in the real world. Blind adherence to the benefits of
the model of perfect competition will do away with any efficiencies from size.
In addition, the combination of the resources of more than one firm may be
required, for example, to develop a better product. Indeed, modern society
could not function without the pooling of resources to produce the complex
products which we take for granted. In other words, ensuring efficiency by
aiming for perfect competition may be at the expense of other (perhaps
greater) efficiencies and benefits.

Some markets can only sustain a few efficient producers. Where (for this   **2.90**
reason or others) there are only a few players—so-called "oligopoly"—the
operation of the market may be utterly different from the models of either
monopoly or perfect competition. In particular, even in the absence of
agreement, firms may be wary of altering their price because of predicted
reactions from others. Thus, because a price reduction could be followed
immediately by the other (small number of) producers, producers may see
little point in reducing price. In conditions of oligopoly, competition tends
rather to focus on non-price competition. One of the main criticisms of EC
competition law is that it is ill-equipped to deal with market behaviour
characteristic of oligopoly.

If the model of perfect competition never exists in practice, it is just as   **2.91**
difficult to determine when a producer has sufficient market power to enable it
to reduce output and raise the price above the competitive level. The theory
requires isolating a single product market but in practice there may be other
products which can meet the same need. Even if a producer has a high market
share, demand may be elastic because an increase in price would cause
customers to turn to substitutes. Even if there are no existing substitutes, a
producer with 100% of the market will not be able to raise the price if this will
encourage others to enter the market. This leads to the question whether there
are barriers to this potential competition. One of the major recent debates on
the application of competition law is whether the authorities charged with
applying that law are overestimating the extent of barriers to entry in markets
which are in fact "contestable". In the case of the IT industry, the most
important barrier in practice may be the law itself. Thus, intellectual property
rights may give exclusive control over vital technology or exclusive rights may
be granted, for instance, to run the telecoms network. The interplay between
these exclusive rights and competition law is one of the most difficult areas of
EC IT law.

A further objection to the theory is that economists have yet to devise   **2.92**
reliable ways to measure market power. One reason for this failure is that, in
order to measure market power, we have to compare marginal cost (which
may be impossible to calculate) to the competitive price level (which is a
hypothetical price level).

In conclusion, great care must be taken in transposing theoretical models to   **2.93**
the real world. The position is complicated still further because the efficient

31

allocation of resources may be only one of the aims which the authorities charged with the application of competition rules may pursue. Indeed, competition law is easily hijacked for political motives. If the model of perfect competition is taken without qualification, it is easy to see how it can be argued that we should protect the small firm at the expense of big business in order to maximise choice. Even a brief consideration of criticisms of the theory shows that we may be protecting the small firm at the expense of efficiency. In other words, society is paying for choice. The European Commission (amongst others) has been accused of relying on competition law to protect the small firm at the expense of efficiency and competition.

2.94　　EC competition laws are also relied on to further the creation of the internal market. As early as 1966, the ECJ declared that Article 85 can apply to agreements which protect national markets from sources of supply elsewhere in the Community. In *Consten & Grundig* v *Commission* (Cases 56 & 58/64 [1966] ECR 299; [1966] CMLR 418), the German consumer electronics manufacturer, Grundig, agreed with its French distributor, Consten, not to supply other distributors in France and to ensure that distributors in other Member States could not sell into France. The ECJ held that Article 85 could apply to such an exclusive distribution agreement. It said

> "...an agreement between a producer and a distributor which might tend to restore the national divisions in trade between Member States might be such as to frustrate the most fundamental object of the Community. The Treaty, whose preamble and content aim at abolishing the barriers between States, and which in several provisions gives evidence of a stern attitude with regard to their reappearance, could not allow undertakings to reconstruct such barriers. Article 85(1) is designed to pursue this aim, even in the case of agreements between undertakings placed at different levels in the economic process" (para 17).

2.95　　There are a number of comments worth making about this extract. Firstly, the agreement in question was not the classic cartel type agreement between producers at the same level of the market (so-called "horizontal" agreements) but, instead, was an agreement between firms at different levels of the market, that is, a producer and a reseller (so-called "vertical" agreements). One of the central concerns at an EC level with vertical agreements is their propensity to maintain barriers to trade between Member States. Vertical agreements are not treated as strictly by competition laws in other jurisdictions which do not have such a concern with this type of barrier to trade.[34] Furthermore, in the Consten & Grundig case, the ECJ held that EC competition law can catch agreements which only affect competition in the same brand of products, in this case Grundig's consumer electrical products. This form of competition, known as "intra-brand" competition, is a concern again because the purpose of integrating the Community markets is to ensure that products cost the same throughout the Community. This would not be achieved if producers could protect national markets from supplies of their own products which had been

---

[34] See, *e.g.*, the US Supreme Court decision in *Continental TV* v *Sylvania* 433 US 36 (1977).

first sold in another Member State. The application of EC competition rules to vertical agreements and intra-brand competition is a recurring theme in EC competition law.

Articles 85 and 86 are a fundamental part of the Community tools for creating an internal market. This is reflected in the penalties for infringing those Articles. If an agreement infringes Article 85, the offending provisions will be invalid.[35] More importantly, for breach of either Article 85 or Article 86, the Commission can impose a fine of up to 10% of the firm's world-wide turnover.[36] The highest individual fine to date of 75 million ECU (about US$ 90m) was imposed in 1992 on Tetra Pak for breach of Article 86 (OJ 1992 L72/1; [1992] 4 CMLR 551).   **2.96**

The application of EC competition rules to conduct and transactions in the IT industry has raised some difficult issues. This section will briefly summarise EC competition rules so that subsequent chapters can focus in detail on specific IT issues.   **2.97**

(ii) Article 85(1): the prohibition

Theory tells us that society benefits if producers compete, that is, they decide autonomously on how to conduct themselves in the marketplace. However, we also know that combining resources can lead to efficiency. In the IT field, for example, there are few companies with the resources to launch a communications satellite. Banning others from combining resources in order to compete would either be at the expense of efficiency or just result in unnecessary mergers.   **2.98**

Reflecting this theory, Article 85 bans agreements but permits exemption under Article 85(3). An agreement will fall within Article 85(1) if (a) the agreement is between undertakings; (b) it is capable of affecting trade between Member States and (c) it has the object or effect of restricting competition.   **2.99**

(a) Agreement between undertakings

Article 85 applies not just to agreements but also to concerted practices. The latter have been defined by the ECJ as "... a form of cooperation between undertakings which, without having reached the stage where an agreement properly so called has been concluded, knowingly substitutes practical cooperation between them for the risks of competition" (*ICI* v *Commission* Case 48/69 [1972] ECR 619; [1972] CMLR 557 para 64).   **2.100**

Clearly, Article 85 covers not just formal, legally enforceable contracts but also "gentlemen's agreements". Indeed, it catches any form of coordinated behaviour. In this book, the term "agreement" will be used to refer to any cooperation sufficient to be caught by Article 85.   **2.101**

The agreement must be between "undertakings". This term is also widely defined to include "any body engaged in commercial activities" (*Polypropylene*   **2.102**

---

[35] Art 85(2). Whether the agreement as a whole survives depends on national law: *SVCB* v *Kerpen & Kerpen* Case 319/82 [1983] ECR 4173; [1985] 1 CMLR 511.

[36] Art 16 of Reg 17 OJ 1959-62 Spec. Ed. 87. For a recent discussion, see Reynolds (1992) EBLR 263.

OJ 1986 230/1; [1988] 4 CMLR 347 para 99). This extends all the way from individual inventors (*Vaessen/Moris* OJ 1979 L19/32; [1979] 1 CMLR 511) to State-owned telecoms administrations.[37]

2.103   Certain agreements may escape the control of Article 85 because the parties are treated as part of the same undertaking. Thus, Article 85 does not apply to arrangements between a parent and its subsidiary provided "the undertakings form an economic unit within which the subsidiary has no real freedom to determine its course of action on the market, and if the agreements or practices are concerned merely with the internal allocation of tasks as between the undertakings" (*Centrafarm* v *Sterling Drug* Case 15/74 [1974] ECR 1147; [1974] 2 CMLR 480 para 41).

2.104   Similar principles apply to agreements between employer and employee, at least during the employment. The principles could also extend to agency agreements (see para **3.74** *et seq*).

(b) Trade between Member States

2.105 This is the key jurisdictional limit to the application of EC competition law. In order for Article 85 to apply, the ECJ has held that "... it must be possible to foresee with a sufficient degree of probability on the basis of a set of objective factors of law or fact that it may have an influence, direct or indirect, actual or potential, on the pattern of trade between Member States" (*STM* v *Maschinenbau Ulm* Case 56/65 [1966] ECR 234; [1966] CMLR 357 para 10).

2.106   It is important to bear in mind that "The fact that an agreement has as its object only the marketing of products (or services) in a single Member State does not mean that trade between Member States cannot be affected" (*Eirpage* OJ 1991 L306/22; [1993] 4 CMLR 64).

(c) Restriction on competition

2.107 Agreements only fall within Article 85 if they have the object or effect of restricting competition. Although this concept is clearly central to competition law, it is perhaps the most difficult to explain. In principle, of course, the law should only catch agreements which conflict with the objectives of the law. Since we have seen that there may be a number of such objectives (which can conflict with each other), an understanding of the approach of EC competition law can only really be achieved by reviewing examples of various types of agreements which have been held to fall within Article 85. This book will do precisely this for typical transactions in the IT industry. A few introductory points can be made.

2.108   Firstly, the effect on competition must be appreciable. It is not enough that a firm is prevented or discouraged from acting as it otherwise would have done; this must have an appreciable effect on the market. Thus, the ECJ held in *STM* v *Maschinenbau Ulm* (Case 56/65 [1966] ECR 234; [1966] CMLR 357)

---

[37] *Italy* v *Commission* Case 41/83 [1985] ECR 873; [1985] 2 CMLR 368 on appeal from the Commission's decision in *British Telecommunications* OJ 1982 L360/36; [1983] 1 CMLR 457.

that an economic analysis of the market should be undertaken to assess whether an exclusive distribution agreement falls within Article 85.[38] The Commission's recognition of this principle is reflected in its Notice on Agreements of Minor Importance (OJ 1986 C231/2). This states the Commission's view that Article 85 will not apply provided the parties to the agreement have no more than 5% of the relevant market and the parties' combined group annual turnover is no more than 200m ECU (about US$ 240m).

As a qualification to the need to establish an effect on the market, it should **2.109** be noted that Article 85(1) refers to agreements "which have as their object or effect" the restriction of competition. In some cases, it seems sufficient that the object of the agreement is to restrict competition.[39] This principle may apply, for example, in the case of restrictions which are treated as very serious breaches of EC competition rules. One of the best examples is an agreement which seeks to stop a dealer from exporting to other Member States. Fines can also be expected for such *per se* breaches of EC competition rules.

We have seen that an exemption is available under Article 85(3) for **2.110** restrictive agreements if the negative effects on competition are outweighed by countervailing benefits. On a number of occasions, the ECJ has held that it may be appropriate for a balance to be made in determining whether an agreement falls with Article 85 at all—the so-called "rule of reason" approach. For example, in *Nungesser* v *Commission* (Case 258/78 [1982] ECR 2015; [1983] 1 CMLR 278), the ECJ held that Article 85 might not apply to an exclusive licence of intellectual property even if it restricted competition between the parties if the exclusivity was necessary to overcome the risk of market entry in the new territory. Moreover, in *Coditel* v *Ciné Vog* Case 262/81 [1982] ECR 3381; [1983] 1 CMLR 49, the ECJ held that an exclusive licence to show a film in Belgium may escape Article 85 given the special characteristics of the cinematographic industry.[40] Both these decisions may provide important analogies for arrangements in the IT industry.

The Commission has been criticised for not fully applying this jurisprudence **2.111** in its own decisions.[41] The danger in the Commission taking such an approach is that many agreements are caught by Article 85(1) because they restrict conduct rather than because they restrict competition. The result, in practice, is that innocuous or pro-competitive agreements are only enforceable if the Commission grants an exemption under Article 85(3). The Commission would argue that any balance of pro- and anti-competitive aspects of an agreement is better conducted in exercising its exclusive power to exempt agreements. It would argue that its block exemptions should relieve many agreements of the need to notify. These arguments can only fully be

---

[38] See more recently the ECJ's judgment in *Stergios Delimitis* v *Henninger Brau* Case C-234/89 [1991] ECR I-935; [1992] 5 CMLR 210, discussed by Korah (1992) EIPR 167.
[39] Bellamy & Child, *Common Market Law of Competition* (Sweet & Maxwell, 1993, 4th ed) para 2-100, 93.
[40] For the earlier *Coditel* case on free movement of services, see para 2.71.
[41] Professor Korah is one of the Commission's most fervent critics on this issue. See, *e.g.*, *EEC Competition Policy—Legal Form or Economic Efficiency* (1986) Current Legal Problems 85.

appreciated with an understanding of the availability of exemptions under Article 85(3).

(iii) **Article 85(3): exemptions**

2.112 An exemption may be available for an agreement which falls within Article 85 if the Commission grants an exemption following a request by the parties through the process of notification.[42] The parties have a further incentive to seek an exemption because notification confers immunity from fines.[43]

2.113 Article 85 lays down four conditions for the grant of an exemption. There are two positive conditions: first, the agreement must contribute to improving the production or distribution of goods or to promoting technical or economic progress and, second, consumers must be allowed a fair share of the resulting benefit. The other two conditions are negative: firstly, the agreement must not impose restrictions unless they are indispensable to attain the first two conditions and, secondly, the parties must not be given the possibility to eliminate competition in respect of a substantial part of the products in question. An example of an individual exemption in the IT field is the Commission's decision to exempt Computerland's franchise system (see para **3.87** *et seq*).

2.114 Only the Commission has the power to grant an exemption. Right from the beginning, the Commission has simply not had the resources to investigate the thousands of agreements notified to it. One method to which it has resorted in order partially to deal with the backlog is to exempt categories of agreements by a single regulation—the so-called "block exemption". Each regulation specifies the type of agreement which can benefit, lists aspects of the agreement which are either not caught by Article 85 or which are exempted ("white list") and lists those aspects of the agreement which will take the agreement outside the regulation ("black list").

2.115 The most important of these block exemptions for the IT industry are:

– Regulation 1983/83 on exclusive distribution agreements (OJ 1983 L173/1)
– Regulation 1984/83 on exclusive purchase agreements (OJ 1983 L173/5)
– Regulation 2349/84 on patent licences[44]
– Regulation 417/85 on specialisation agreements[45]
– Regulation 418/85 on research and development agreements[46]
– Regulation 556/89 on know-how licences[47]
– Regulation 4087/88 on franchise agreements (OJ 1988 L359/46)

---

[42] Under Reg 17/62 OJ 1959-62 Spec Ed 87. The parties send to the Commission a Form A/B giving details of the agreement and the market together with copies of the agreement.
[43] Art 15(5) of Reg 17 although the Commission can take a provisional decision under Art 15(6) removing that immunity.
[44] OJ 1984 L219/15, as amended by Reg 151/93 (OJ 1993 L21/8).
[45] OJ 1985 L53/1, as amended by Reg 151/93 (OJ 1993 L21/8).
[46] OJ 1985 L53/5, as amended by Reg 151/93 (OJ 1993 L21/8).
[47] OJ 1989 L61/1, as amended by Reg 151/93 (OJ 1993 L21/8).

NB: The patent and know-how block exemptions are to be replaced with effect from 1 January 1995 by the technology transfer block exemption.[48]

There are several points on this type of exemption which deserve mention. **2.116** Firstly, the Commission is itself partly responsible for the large number of agreements notified to it. As discussed above, on a number of occasions, the ECJ has indicated that a narrower, more flexible interpretation of Article 85 is appropriate. By failing adequately to take up this jurisprudence in its decisions, the Commission has contributed to the wide range of agreements which require exemption. Secondly, by laying down in advance the conditions under which an agreement will be automatically exempted, the Commission is encouraging businesses to tailor the terms of their agreements to a format which might not fully reflect needs but will avoid the cost and delay involved in a notification for an individual exemption. In other words, the block exemptions may themselves distort the efficient allocation of resources.

Finally, in the absence of a block exemption, in practice, firms may well take **2.117** the view that there is little point in notifying provided there is no significant risk of fines. It seems that, for one reason or another, this has happened in the IT sector and, for example, very few software licences have been notified to the Commission. This has not been wholly beneficial for the IT industry since it means that the Commission has been unable to get the necessary experience from granting individual exemptions to be able to formulate a block exemption.[49]

(iv) Article 86

Basic economic theory tells us that monopolies can result in the inefficient **2.118** allocation and use of resources. Article 86 is aimed at dealing with this problem. It controls firms which hold a dominant position. A monopoly in the sense of the theory described above is not necessary for a finding of dominance but some market power is required. We have seen that market power may arise as a result of economies of scale or other efficiencies. Thus, Article 86 does not prohibit the dominant position itself but only its abuse.

There are three conditions to the application of Article 86. There must be (a) a **2.119** dominant position (b) which has been abused and (c) that abuse must be capable of affecting trade between Member States:

(a) Dominant position

In the words of the ECJ, a dominant position is "a position of economic **2.120** strength enjoyed by an undertaking which enables it to prevent effective competition being maintained on the relevant market by allowing it to behave to an appreciable extent independently of its competitors and customers and

---

[48] Draft published OJ 1994 C178/3.

[49] *Cf.* Darbyshire, *Computer Programs and Competition Policy: A Block Exemption for Software Licensing* (1994) EIPR 374.

ultimately of consumers" (*Michelin* v *Commission* Case 322/81 [1983] ECR 3461; [1985] 1 CMLR 282 para 30).

2.121 How is this market strength determined? In theory, market strength depends on the actual and potential competition for the supply of the products in question and any substitutes. For example, even if a particular firm is the sole supplier of a particular product, it would not be able to raise its prices if customers could turn to a readily available alternative or, indeed, other firms could swiftly enter the market. Such an analysis does not require a final definition of the market. In practice, competition authorities tend to rely heavily on such definitions not least in order to encourage certainty. Community law is no different. Thus, the starting point for determining whether a dominant position exists is to identify the relevant market. This is discussed later in more detail (see para **2.135** *et seq*); suffice to say at this point that the relevant market includes the products in question and any substitutes.

2.122 Once the relevant market is identified, a number of factors are taken into account to determine the firm's strength in that market. Naturally, the most important of these factors is the size of the market share. The ECJ made the following comment in *AKZO* v *Commission* (Case C-62/86 [1991] ECR I-3359; [1993] 5 CMLR 215):

> "With regard to market shares the Court has held that very large shares are in themselves, and save in exceptional circumstances, evidence of the existence of a dominant position (judgment in Case 85/76 *Hoffmann-La Roche* v *Commission* [1979] ECR 461, paragraph 41). That is the situation where there is a market share of 50% such as that found to exist in this case" (para 60).

2.123 Of equal importance in theory but more contentious in practice is the extent of any barriers to entry. Barriers are very significant because the degree to which a firm with a large market share can act independently depends on the ease with which potential competitors can enter the market. The overriding importance given by the ECJ to market share can shift attention away from whether the market is in fact "contestable" as a result of potential competition.

2.124 Can Article 86 be used to control markets where no one firm is dominant but a few firms hold large market shares? We have seen that oligopolistic markets can raise concerns even in the absence of agreement between suppliers. The CFI has confirmed that Article 86 can apply to a dominant position held jointly by more than one independent undertaking where they are "united by some economic links" (*Société Italiano Vetro* v *Commission* Case T-68/89 [1992] ECR II-1403; [1992] 5 CMLR 302). It remains to be seen whether the powers at the Commission's disposal will allow it properly to control oligopolistic markets.[50]

(b) Abuse

2.125 Theory tells us that the concern over monopoly is that the rational producer will reduce output and raise price. Competition law may also be concerned

---

[50] See Whish and Sufrin, *Oligopolistic Markets and EC Competition Law* (1993) YEL 59.

with practices designed improperly to maintain or strengthen a position of dominance although it is not always straightforward to distinguish normal market behaviour. The starting point in EC law is the ECJ's definition in *Hoffmann-La Roche* v *Commission* (Case 85/76 [1979] ECR 461; [1979] 3 CMLR 211)

> "The concept of abuse is an objective concept relating to the behaviour of an undertaking in a dominant position which is such as to influence the structure of a market where, as a result of the very presence of the undertaking in question, the degree of competition is weakened and which, through recourse to methods different from those which condition normal competition in products or services on the basis of the transactions of commercial operators, has the effect of hindering the maintenance of the degree of competition still existing in the market or the growth of that competition" (para 91).

2.126 There is no exemption from Article 86 as there is from Article 85. Any justification for conduct which is alleged to be within Article 86 is taken into account in defining abuse. It also should be noted that just because an agreement benefits from an exemption under Article 85 does not mean that the agreement is protected from the application of Article 86 (*Tetra Pak Rausing* v *Commission* Case T-51/89 [1990] ECR II-309; [1991] 4 CMLR 334).

2.127 Like the concept of restriction on competition in Article 85(1), an understanding of the concept of abuse is best obtained by looking at examples and the most important examples for the IT industry are discussed in the subsequent chapters. Perhaps the most important category of potential abuses in the IT industry is the extension of power in one market to another market. An example often quoted is the *Télémarketing* case (*Centre Belge d'Etude de Marché-Télémarketing* v *Compagnie Luxembourgeoise de Télévision* Case 311/84 [1985] ECR 3261; [1986] 2 CMLR 558) where a TV broadcaster refused to allow advertising for telephone sales unless its phone number was given. The ECJ held

> "...an abuse...is committed where, without any objective necessity, an undertaking holding a dominant position on a particular market reserves to itself...an ancillary activity which might be carried out by another undertaking as part of its activities on a neighbouring but separate market, with the possibility of eliminating all competition from such undertaking" (para 27).

2.128 There are numerous examples of the application of this reasoning in EC competition law. The Commission seems now to be developing a theory which will require any firm which controls an essential facility to share that facility if required for competition in a separate market (*B & I Line* v *Sealink Harbours* Commission Press Release IP(92)478 [1992] 5 CMLR 255). This theory has been adopted from US law where it has not escaped criticism.[51] From the point of view of the IT industry, the key point is that exclusive rights are common whether specifically granted over a telecoms network or arising from

---

[51] For a summary, see Hovenkampf, *Federal Antitrust Policy* (West Publishing, 1994), 273.

intellectual property rights. However, great care has to be taken in applying the same reasoning to all forms of exclusive rights. As we will see, the purpose of granting exclusive rights over intellectual property will be different to the purpose for granting exclusivity over a telecoms network (see para **2.143** *et seq*).

(c) Trade between Member States

2.129   This is the equivalent jurisdictional requirement to Article 85. It represents "the boundary between the areas respectively covered by Community law and the law of the Member States" (*Hugin* v *Commission* Case 22/78 [1979] ECR 1869; [1979] 3 CMLR 345.)

(v) **Merger Regulation**[52]

2.130   In 1989, the Merger Regulation came into force giving the Commission the power to vet large mergers affecting the Community.[53] The Commission must be notified in advance of "concentrations" with a Community dimension, that is, where the aggregate world-wide turnover of all the undertakings concerned exceeds 5,000m ECU (about US$ 6,000m); the Community-wide turnover of at least two of the undertakings concerned exceeds 250m ECU (about US$ 300m); and the undertakings do not achieve more than two-thirds of their respective Community-wide turnover within one and the same Member State (Art 1).

2.131   The term "concentration" includes mergers and acquisition of control (Art 3(1)). It also covers "concentrative joint ventures", that is, a joint venture which performs on a lasting basis all the functions of an autonomous economic entity and does not give rise to coordination of competitive behaviour between the parents or between the parents and the joint venture (Art 3(2)). This is one of the more difficult issues under the Merger Regulation and yet, given that many notifications under the Merger Regulation have been joint ventures, applying the test has turned out to be very important in practice. If a joint venture is held to be cooperative (rather than concentrative), the Commission will deal with it under Articles 85 and 86.[54]

2.132   The purpose of the Commission's review is to determine whether the concentration is compatible with the common market, that is, whether it "creates or strengthens a dominant position as a result of which effective competition would be significantly impeded in the common market or a substantial part of it" (Art 2(3)). As a first step the Commission decides whether there are serious doubts to that effect. If so, it can undertake a full investigation. Its decisions under the Merger Regulation are subject to strict time limits.

2.133   In principle, the Commission has the exclusive right to vet concentrations with a Community dimension. In certain circumstances, national authorities may be involved.

---

[52] See, *e.g.*, Cook & Kerse, *EEC Merger Control* (Sweet & Maxwell, 1991) and Jones & Gonzalez-Diaz, *The EEC Merger Regulation* (Sweet & Maxwell, 1992).
[53] Council Reg 4064/89 on the control of concentrations between undertakings (OJ 1989 L395/1).
[54] See, *e.g.*, *BT/MCI* (OJ 1994 L223/36).

Full discussion of the Merger Regulation is outside the scope of this book but the points arising from Commission's decisions under the Merger Regulation on concentrations involving the IT industry are discussed particularly where they give guidance on the Commission's general approach to the application of competition law to the sector.   **2.134**

(vi) Market definition

Defining the relevant market is as difficult as it is important. It is necessary to identify market share not just to judge market strength for the purposes of Article 86 and for the Merger Regulation but also to determine whether an agreement can benefit from the Commission's Notice on Agreements of Minor Importance and a number of the block exemptions.[55] In addition, of course, the strength of a firm's position on the market will be important in answering the basic question under Article 85(1) of whether an agreement with that firm restricts competition appreciably.   **2.135**

The rationale for defining the market is to determine the market power held by a particular firm. If any rise in price will cause customers to turn to other products, then there is no market power and we should include the alternative supply in the definition of the market. In technical terms, we need to measure the "cross price elasticity of demand" to determine whether an increase in price for one product will cause a proportionately higher increase in the demand for another product. The starting point is to determine whether these other products perform the same function at a similar cost. The Commission's standard approach is to ask whether there are other products which are "identical or considered by users as equivalent in view of their characteristics, price and intended use."[56]   **2.136**

But this is not the whole story because market power may not exist due to the possibility of other producers meeting demand either by using spare capacity or by diverting resources from other tasks or, even, by setting up new capacity. Should we include this potential supply in the market definition? Although the ECJ has held that supply side competition must be taken into account in market definition under Article 86, the Commission tends only to take account of existing suppliers in defining the market leaving potential competition from new entrants to its consideration of dominance and, in particular, whether there are barriers to entry to the market. We have seen that the ECJ has also held that high market shares will lead to a conclusion of dominance save for exceptional circumstances. Unless the market definition properly reflects potential competition, there is a danger that firms will be held to be dominant even though they cannot act independently of competitors because the market is "contestable". In the case of Article 85, market definitions in, say, the block exemptions can also be criticised for failing adequately to take into account potential competition thereby overestimating market power.   **2.137**

---

[55] See, *e.g.*, the market share requirements in the R & D block exemption (OJ 1985 L53/5), as amended by Reg 151/93 (OJ 1993 L21/8).
[56] See, *e.g.*, Reg 1983/83 Art 3(a).

2.138   The process of market definition is particularly important in the case of products in the IT sector because in many cases high market shares are frequently quickly eroded through new entry. Until recently, there has been very little Commission guidance on this question although the position is starting to change as a result of a number of decisions of the Commission on IT mergers and joint ventures within the Merger Regulation. These decisions will be referred to in the discussion of market definition in the specific chapters on hardware, software, services and telecoms.

2.139   One factor which figures highly in the IT industry is the existence of intellectual property rights (IPRs). Perhaps the most important point to note is that the very existence of an IPR does not mean that the holder has a monopoly in the relevant product because there may be substitutes for the product (*Deutsche Gramophon* v *Metro* Case 78/70 [1971] ECR 487; [1971] CMLR 631 para 16). If there are no substitutes then the holder of the IPR may be held to have a dominant position if the holder does not license third party manufacture. The absence of substitutes is a common feature of aftermarkets. For example, if the supplier of a product holds IPRs over spare parts, it may be that no third party can produce alternative spare parts. In this case, since the supplier will have 100% of the spare parts market, there is a danger that this will be held to amount to dominant position.

2.140   But is it always true that a supplier can rely on the fact that his customers are locked into the primary product enabling the price for spare parts to be raised above the competitive level? In fact, it can be argued that competition for the primary product will constrain the ability of the supplier to exploit control over the market for spare parts. The argument is that customers for the primary product will take into account the cost of spare parts. If the supplier charged above the competitive price for the spare parts, customers would buy the primary product elsewhere. The argument depends on two points: firstly, that customers have access to adequate information about pricing for spare parts and, secondly, that there is in fact sufficient competition in the market for the primary product. This argument is discussed in more detail in **Chapter 5** (see para **5.38** *et seq*).

2.141   If a supplier is held to be dominant as a result of the existence of IPRs, the key question will be whether it is an abuse of that position either to refuse to supply those products to third parties or, indeed, to refuse to license third parties to exploit the IPRs themselves. These issues are introduced in the next section and discussed further on in more detail (see para **2.143** *et seq*).

2.142   Finally, when considering the nature of the relevant market, it is important to determine the geographic extent of that market. The basic test is that the market includes all areas where conditions of competition are the same (*United Brands* v *Commission* Case 27/76 [1978] ECR 207; [1978] 1 CMLR 429 para 44). The extent of the market may be very important. In *Alsatel* v *Novasam* (Case 247/86 [1988] ECR 5987; [1990] 4 CMLR 434), the ECJ held that the market for telephone installations extended to the whole of France so that Alsatel's high regional market share did not put it in a dominant position under Article 86.

(vii) **Competition law and intellectual property**

One of the important themes running throughout EC IT law is the debate over **2.143** how to resolve the apparent conflict between competition law and intellectual property protection. IPRs are conferred by the law, generally (but not exclusively) by statute. They give the right to one person to stop another pursuing a course of conduct. For example, a patent grants the right to stop use of inventive technology and copyright gives the right to stop copying. Assuming limited substitutes for the product protected by an IPR, the holder of that IPR may be able to act like a monopoly supplier, that is, the holder may be able to supply less and charge more than in a competitive market. This creates a tension between intellectual property law and the objectives of competition law. However, one of the main reasons why society accepts the efficiency lost because of an IPR is to encourage expenditure on innovation which may be a key factor in competitive markets. In other words, the difference between the competitive price and the actual price is the incentive given by the IPR in order to encourage innovation. So is there any justification for using competition law to delimit the circumstances in which reliance on an IPR is permitted?

A distinction can be drawn between two purposes for which competition law **2.144** might be used. Firstly, competition law could be applied to stop use of an IPR to distort the market further than simply taking the monopoly profits from the IPR in question. The typical concern is where the holder of an IPR uses that control to require the purchase of a further product or service which is not protected by the IPR. The traditional complaint in this case is that the IPR holder obtains a further monopoly profit in another market. In fact, we will see that this argument has been criticised by academics if not by the courts (see para **3.90** *et seq*) but, if there is an effect on another market, there are arguments that competition law should be used to control the situation.

Secondly, competition law could be invoked to reduce the incentive for **2.145** innovation when at a later date it is thought that the innovation does not merit the incentive. The problem in applying competition law in this type of case is that the principles of competition law do not necessarily point to a solution since a value judgment will invariably be involved in the process. In other words, the principles of competition law may be able to show that the IPR holder is exercising market power but cannot tell us whether society should encourage the development of the type of technology protected by the IPR in question. Thus, it can be argued that competition law alone should not be relied upon to force the holder of an IPR to license another to exploit that IPR. A further issue in the case of the application of EC competition law is that the EC Treaty itself limits the Community's intervention in the grant of IPRs (see para **3.50** *et seq*).

Even if we argue that, in some circumstances, competition law should be an **2.146** instrument available to control reliance on IPRs, in practice, we will see that, particularly in the IT industry, the IPR is unlikely to confer market power even in aftermarkets.

2.147   In what circumstances does EC competition law intervene to control the reliance on IPRs? A distinction can be made between restrictions in an IPR licence and refusals to license an IPR altogether. It is well established in EC competition law that Article 85 can apply in the first case. It is applied in order to control the extension of the IPR to markets for products or services which fall outside the scope of the IPR. For example, Article 85 has been applied to prevent the licensor of an IPR from requiring its licensee to purchase other products from the licensor over which the licensor has no IPR, at least where such a requirement cannot be justified, for example, for reasons of safety (*Vaessen/Moris* OJ 1979 L19/32; [1979] 1 CMLR 511).

2.148   EC competition law is not limited to catching those cases where the licensor relies on an IPR to extend control to other products. Article 85 can also catch licence provisions giving exclusive protection to the parties. For example, it may be contrary to Article 85 for a patent licensee to be prohibited from selling in the territory of another licensee.[57] It cannot be argued that this is an extension of the patent right; it is merely a reflection of the exclusivity conferred by a patent. The application of Article 85 in this type of situation circumscribes reliance on the IPR in order to achieve another aim, namely, dismantling barriers to intra-Community trade. We have seen that Article 30 is also applied to limit intellectual property protection for this same reason (see para **2.59** *et seq*).

2.149   More controversial is the question whether EC competition rules can apply to a refusal to license an IPR. If it is a unilateral refusal, it is only Article 86 which could apply. The first question is whether the owner of the IPR holds a dominant position. An IPR does not automatically confer market power because there will frequently be substitutes for the technology. However, an IPR is a barrier to entry and can give a supplier market power. We have seen that this is particularly an issue in the case of aftermarkets (see para **2.139**). In the IT industry, one key problem is the power that can be derived from control over a successful architecture, that is, the way in which products work together. In these cases, as we have seen, it can be argued that the exploitation of any market power is constrained by competition for the primary product (see para **2.140**).

2.150   Assuming market power can be shown, the vital question is whether a refusal to license the IPR will be an abuse of that dominant position. It has to be said that the current position under EC law is somewhat uncertain. It seems that the ECJ concedes that, at least in certain circumstances, Article 86 can be applied to a refusal to license.[58] The Commission has relied on this jurisprudence to force an IPR to be licensed. In the *Magill* cases, the Commission ordered a number of TV broadcasters to allow a third party to copy programme listings protected by copyright (OJ 1989 L78/43). The decision was upheld by the CFI (*RTE, BBC & ITP* v *Commission* Cases T-69,70&76/89 [1991] ECR II-485, 535 & 575; [1991] 4 CMLR 586, 669 & 745). The Advocate General has argued that the Commission's decision

---

[57] See, *e.g.*, *Velcro/Aplix* OJ 1985 L233/22; [1989] 4 CMLR 157.
[58] *Volvo* v *Veng* Case 238/87 [1988] ECR 6211; [1989] 4 CMLR 122. See para 3.51.

should be overruled although he admits that compulsory licences can be required on the basis of Article 86 in other circumstances (*RTE & ITP* v *Commission* Cases 241&242/91).[59]

The ECJ's judgment in the *Magill* cases is now awaited. It is unlikely that   **2.151** the judgment will resolve all outstanding issues but the ECJ will probably not rule out all possibility of the application of Article 86 to a refusal to license. The application of Article 86 in these types of situations is discussed in Chapter 3. The discussion is developed in Chapter 4 to deal with the question whether the application of Article 86 is affected by harmonisation of the underlying IPR. Chapters 5 and 6 address specific sectors in which the problem arises.

(viii) **Application of competition law in the IT sector**

In many ways, EC competition law applies the same rules to the IT industry as   **2.152** to other industry sectors. However, the law may be applied in a different manner as a result of the special position of the IT sector as a key EC industry together with the special industry environment characterised by technological advances in a highly competitive sector.

The application of EC competition rules is discussed: **2.153**

– for hardware in Chapter 3 para **3.37** *et seq*
– for software in Chapter 4 para **4.54** *et seq*
– for services in Chapter 5 para **5.31** *et seq*
– for telecoms in Chapter 6 para **6.41** *et seq*

6. **State involvement and Article 90**

One of the most important concerns of the authors of the EC Treaty was to   **2.154** ensure that the objectives of the Treaty were not prejudiced by State intervention. Article 5 EC provides that:

> "Member States shall take all appropriate measures, whether general or particular, to ensure fulfilment of the obligations arising out of this Treaty or resulting from action taken by the institutions of the Community. They shall facilitate the achievement of the Community's tasks. They shall abstain from any measure which could jeopardise the attainment of the objectives of this Treaty."

This general obligation in Article 5 is turned into specific requirements by   **2.155** Article 90. The wording of Article 90 is not without difficulty but essentially it has two functions. On the one hand, Article 90(1) requires Member States to respect the Treaty in their dealings with undertakings controlled by a Member State or put in a privileged position by a Member State. On the other hand, Article 90(2) protects undertakings which have been entrusted with providing

---

[59] Opinion of Advocate General Gulmann of 1 June 1994.

a public service from the application of the Treaty rules but only if those rules would stop them from performing that public service and provided the development of trade is not affected so as to be contrary to the interests of the Community.

2.156 The most important point about Article 90 is that it is concerned with the application of other provisions of the Treaty. Thus, Article 90(1) confirms that the usual Treaty rules apply also in the case of State-run organisations whilst Article 90(2) prescribes a limited exception. The provisions of Article 90 can be applied by national courts but Article 90(3) also gives the Commission a central role in its application.

2.157 Although in many respects the IT industry is free from State involvement, there are some important exceptions. In particular, the provision of telecommunications services is characterised throughout the Community and, indeed, the rest of the world, by State regulation. One of the main reasons invariably put forward for that role is the need to ensure universal service, that is, the availability of basic telephone services to everyone at a reasonable cost. In practice, State control has extended much further than would be necessary to achieve this goal. During the 1980s there was a growing realisation that this State involvement was protecting inefficient organisations as well as holding back the introduction of new technologies. Article 90 has played a key role in limiting this State involvement.

(i) Article 90(1)

2.158 This provision is directed at Member States. It obliges them to respect the Treaty rules in dealing with "public undertakings and undertakings to which Member States grant special or exclusive rights." Although the concept of public undertaking has not been exhaustively defined, the ECJ did reject a challenge to Commission Directive 80/723[60] which defines public undertakings for the purposes of the Directive as "any undertaking over which the public authority may exercise directly or indirectly a dominant influence by virtue of their ownership of it, their financial participation therein, or the rules which govern it" (Art 2).

2.159 There has been no significant need further to define "public undertaking" because Article 90(1) also covers undertakings to which special or exclusive rights have been granted—so-called "privileged undertakings". Thus, Article 90(1) would control the measures adopted by Member States in respect of privatised national telecoms providers, such as British Telecom, since, even after the privatisation, those undertakings still invariably benefit from special or exclusive rights.

2.160 One of the most important issues on the scope of Article 90(1) has been whether Article 90(1) enables a Treaty provision to override the general or exclusive rights themselves. In the *Terminal Equipment* case (*France* v *Commission*

---

[60] Commission Directive on the transparency of financial relations between Member States and public undertakings (OJ 1980 L195/35), upheld by the ECJ in *France v Commission* Case 188/80 [1982] ECR 2545; [1982] 3 CMLR 144.

Case C-202/88 [1991] ECR I-1223; [1992] 5 CMLR 552), the ECJ resolved
this issue by declaring that "even though [Article 90] presupposes the
existence of undertakings which have certain special or exclusive rights, it does
not follow that all the special or exclusive rights are necessarily compatible
with the Treaty. That depends on different rules, to which Article 90(1)
refers." (para 22).

The fact that the special or exclusive rights themselves can infringe the   **2.161**
Treaty means that the key question for the ECJ is whether those exclusive or
special rights are legitimate. This is only possible through the application of
Article 90(2).

(ii) **Article 90(2)**

Article 90(2) is directed at undertakings. Unlike Article 90(1), Article 90(2)   **2.162**
prescribes limited circumstances in which the Treaty rules, in particular, the
competition rules, do not apply. As an exception to the application of the
Treaty, it must be interpreted strictly (*BRT* v *SABAM* Case 127/73 [1974]
ECR 313; [1974] 2 CMLR 177 para 19).

Article 90(2) protects undertakings "entrusted with the operation of services   **2.163**
of general economic interest or having the character of a revenue producing
monopoly." Naturally, it is the former category which will be of greater
importance in the IT industry and, indeed, it is clear that telecoms
organisations do fall within this category.[61] However, it is also clear that the
strict conditions to the application of Article 90(2) mean that it will rarely be
applicable.

Firstly, Article 90(2) is unlikely to apply given that the approach of the ECJ   **2.164**
is to judge whether the infringement of the underlying rules is necessary to
achieve the task entrusted to it.[62] Secondly, the second sentence of Article
90(2) lays down a final proviso that "the development of trade must not be
affected to such an extent as would be contrary to the interests of the
Community." One question is whether national courts can apply this test. The
position seems to be that Article 90(2) can be applied by national courts to
determine whether the undertaking in question is entrusted with a task within
Article 90(2) and, if so, whether the Treaty rules obstruct that task (*ERT* v
DEP Case C-260/89 [1991] ECR I-2925; [1994] 4 CMLR 540). However, the
final proviso can probably only be applied by the Commission (subject to
review by the ECJ) rather like an individual exemption under Article 85(3).[63]

Recent cases show that, in applying Article 90(1) and 90(2), the ECJ will   **2.165**
look for an exclusive right which can be justified by Article 90(2) and, then, ask
how far that exclusive right should extend. In *Procureur du Roi* v *Corbeau* Case
C-320/91,[64] for example, the ECJ distinguished between basic postal services,
on the one hand, and further specific postal services, on the other. The national

---

[61] See, *e.g.*, *France* v *Commission* Case C-202/88 [1991] ECR I-1223; [1992] 5 CMLR 552.
[62] See, *e.g.*, *Procureur du Roi* v *Corbeau* Case C-320/91 Judgment of 19 May 1993. Not yet reported.
[63] See Wyatt & Dashwood, *European Community Law* (Sweet & Maxwell, 1993, 3rd ed) 566.
[64] Judgment of 19 May 1993. Not yet reported.

court was instructed to decide whether the further specific services were dissociable from the basic service and, then, whether extending exclusivity to the further services was necessary for the economic stability of the basic service. In other words, as the Advocate General recognised, in this type of case, the ECJ's approach is to apply its traditional reasoning on the extension of exclusive rights from one market to a derivative one (see para **2.127**).

(iii) **Article 90(3)**

2.166   Article 90 is concerned with the application of the normal Treaty rules in cases where there is some form of State involvement. In principle, then, the rules can be invoked before national courts, at least where the Treaty rules are directly effective (see para **2.47**). Further, the Commission can bring infringement proceedings against a Member State for failing to respect the Treaty. Article 90(3) supplements these remedies by empowering the Commission to address appropriate directives or decisions to Member States.

2.167   The Commission has relied on Article 90(3) to adopt individual decisions.[65] It has also relied on the Article to adopt legislation to liberalise the telecoms market. These steps are described in Chapter 6. All that need be said at this point is that in each challenge to the Commission's directives that the Member States have made, the ECJ has confirmed that the Commission does have a wide power to legislate under Article 90(3).

7. **The international picture**

2.168   The international picture is profoundly important to the IT industry as well as to EC law on IT. By virtue of Article 210 of the EC Treaty, the Community has the legal capacity to enter into international agreements. Whether it has the power to enter into a specific agreement depends on it having an express or implied power so to do. For example, Article 113 grants an express power to enter into international agreements for the purposes of the Community's common commercial policy. The draft Data Protection Directive is based in part on Article 113 (see para **7.5** *et seq.*).

2.169   The ECJ has held that the Community has an implied power to enter into agreements where necessary for proper exercise of an internal power (Opinion 1/76 [1977] ECR 741; [1977] 2 CMLR 295). The ECJ has also held that any international agreements to which the Community is a party form part of EC law and, indeed, can be directly effective (*HZA Mainz* v *Kupferberg* Case 104/81 [1982] ECR 3641; [1983] 1 CMLR 1).

2.170   Appying these principles, the ECJ has held that the Community is bound by the General Agreement on Tariffs and Trade (GATT) (*International Fruit*

---

[65] See, *e.g.* Commission Decision 90/16 (OJ 1990 L10/47) although this was in fact declared void by the ECJ in *Netherlands PTT* v *Commission* Cases C-48&66/90 [1992] ECR I-565.

Company v *Produktschap voor Groenten en Fruit* Case 21-24/72 [1972] ECR 1219 [1975] 2 CMLR 1). The Community also signed the Uruguay Round agreements which will replace GATT with the World Trade Organisation. One of the agreements within the package is the Agreement on Trade-Related Aspects of Intellectual Property Rights (TRIPs) which includes provisions on the protection of new technologies such as computer programs and semiconductor topographies. The ECJ has been asked to rule on the respective powers of the Community and the Member States.[66]

In 1991, the Commission signed an agreement on cooperation between the Community and the US on the application of competition law ([1991] 4 CMLR 823). The ECJ has since annulled the Commission's agreement because the Commission did not have the power to enter into it on behalf of the Community (*France* v *Commission* Case C-327/91).[67] The challenge to the agreement did not prevent cooperation between the EC and US competition authorities jointly to negotiate the settlement of the investigation of Microsoft (see para **4.54**).

    2.171

The Community has entered into more wide-ranging agreements such as the Treaty on the European Economic Area (EEA) which came into force in January 1994 and which extends many of the principles of EC law, in particular, competition law[68] to Iceland, Finland, Austria, Sweden and Norway. Since all but Iceland are scheduled to become full EC Member States in January 1995, the EEA Treaty will not be dealt with in any detail in this book.

    2.172

---

[66] Opinion 1/94 (OJ 1994 C218/20). Not yet decided.
[67] Judgment of 9 August 1994. Not yet reported.
[68] See Diem, *EEA Competition Law* (1994) ECLR 263.

Selected further reading on EC law

General texts

Weatherill & Beaumont, *EC Law* (Penguin, 1993)
Steiner, *EC Law* (Blackstone, 1994, 4th ed)
Kapteyn & Verloren Van Themat, *Introduction to the Law of the European Communities* (Kluwer, 1989, 2nd ed)
Wyatt & Dashwood, *European Community Law* (Sweet & Maxwell, 1993, 3rd ed)
Lasok & Bridge, *Law and Institutions of the European Communities* (Butterworths, 1991, 5th ed).

European Court

Brown & Kennedy, *The Court of Justice of the European Communities* (Sweet & Maxwell, 1994, 4th ed).

Treaty on European Union

O'Keefe and Twomey, Eds, *Legal Issues of the Maastricht Treaty* (Chancery, 1993).

Free Movement

Oliver, *Free Movement of Goods in the EEC* (European Law Centre, 1988, 2nd ed)

Competition

Goyder, *EEC Competition Law* (OUP, 1993, 2nd ed).
Whish, *Competition Law* (Butterworths, 1993, 3rd ed)
Bellamy & Child, *Common Market Law of Competition* (Sweet & Maxwell, 1993, 4th ed)
Kerse, *EEC Antitrust Procedure* (Sweet & Maxwell 1994, 3rd ed).
Cook & Kerse, *EEC Merger Control* (Sweet & Maxwell, 1991).
Jones & Gonzalez-Diaz, *The EEC Merger Regulation* (Sweet & Maxwell, 1992).
Fishwick, *Making Sense of Competition Policy* (Kogan Page, 1993).
Lipsey, *An Introduction to Positive Economics* (OUP, 1989, 7th ed).
Scherer & Ross, *Industrial Market Structure and Economic Performance* (Houghton Mifflin, 1990, 3rd ed).

Chapter 3
Hardware

1. Introduction

The focus of information technology law may have recently turned towards **3.1**
the software side of the industry but the hardware industry remains important.
Moreover, it was in the context of the hardware industry that many of the
issues now being discussed in relation to software were first aired such as the
need for special protection of new technologies and the interface of competition law and intellectual property.

2. Harmonisation legislation

There is a wide range of Community legislation which affects the IT hardware **3.2**
industry in the same way as it affects many other industries. For example,
many sectors will have been affected by the implementation at a Member
State level of the Product Liability Directive.[1] Many industries will be affected
by moves to harmonise intellectual property rights such as design rights[2] or by
the creation of rights at a Community level such as the Community Patent
Convention (if it ever comes into force) and, indeed, the proposed Regulation
on a Community design right.[3]

This book focuses on issues raised by Community legislation which are **3.3**
peculiar to the IT industry. Naturally, there are few items of legislation
specifically aimed at the hardware industry. This section will discuss two
different but illuminating measures to harmonise aspects of the hardware
industry at a Community level: first, the 1986 Semiconductor Chip Directive
and, then, the 1990 VDU Work Directive.

---

[1] Council Directive 85/374 on liability for defective products (OJ 1985 L210/29).
[2] Proposal for a European Parliament and Council Directive on the legal protection of designs (OJ
1993 C345/14).
[3] Proposal for a European Parliament and Council Regulation on Community design (OJ 1993
C29/20).

(i) **Semiconductor Chip Directive**[4]

(a) Background

3.4   The background to the adoption of the Semiconductor Chip Directive provides an interesting example of one possible approach to the international protection of those new technologies which do not fit easily into traditional intellectual property protection regimes. The story should start with a short description of the technical background.

3.5   Computers operate using digital processing—the manipulation of numbers represented in binary form, that is, a series of 1s and 0s. In the early days of commercial computing, the 1950s, valves (or vacuum tubes) were invariably used to create the "on" and "off" states which were required electronically to reproduce binary numbers. Even with the development of smaller valves, the powerful computers of the day were huge. In the space of a few decades, the computing power which once required a room full of hardware became available in a portable computer. How did this come about? A few key developments in hardware technology have allowed vastly increased computing power to be contained in ever smaller machines. The first major development was the replacement of the valve by solid state transistors using semiconductor materials. In turn, these transistors were integrated into chips. Finally, in 1971, Intel produced the first processor on a chip, the 4004. It contained 2,300 transistors and calculated 60,000 instructions per second. Improvements since then in the design and manufacture of these integrated circuits have enabled Intel, in a little over two decades, to reach the position where it can produce a Pentium chip which, in an area no larger than a thumbnail, contains over 3.3 million transistors and calculates 166 million instructions per second.

3.6   How are these amazing machines made?[5] The production of a semiconductor chip begins with a silicon wafer on which layers of other materials, such as aluminium and tungsten, are placed. On each layer of the chip, a pattern is produced by exposing the chip to light projected through a mask. Nowadays, lasers may be used instead of masks. The components of the processor, such as the transistor, are created by the interrelationship of the patterns on the various layers of the chip. A number of processors are made on each silicon wafer. For example, from a single 8-inch diameter silicon wafer Intel produces over 100 Pentium chips. At the end of the layering process, the microprocessors are cut out of the wafer into dies and packaged as chips.

3.7   Massive investment may be required to design a chip and yet that design can be copied relatively cheaply. As a result, the semiconductor industry, especially in the US, became concerned about the question whether chip designs fell within the scope of traditional intellectual property rights (IPRs). Although significant investment may be required to produce a chip design, the

---

[4] Council Directive 87/54 on the legal protection of topographies of semiconductor products (OJ 1987 L24/36). See Appendix A2.

[5] For a good description, see *Encyclopedia of Information Technology Law* (Sweet & Maxwell, 1990, looseleaf) 2.260 *et seq.*

technology used is not usually sufficiently inventive to satisfy the novelty requirement for a patent whilst, at least in some jurisdictions, copyright law did not extend to three-dimensional reproductions of drawings.

To overcome doubts in the US over the availability of IPRs to protect these **3.8** designs, in 1984, the Semiconductor Chip Protection Act was passed. Rather than fit the protection of designs into the existing system of intellectual property rights, the 1984 US Act created a specific *sui generis* right to control the exploitation of original "mask works", that is, the series of related images representing the patterns of the various layers of a chip (s 901(2)).

Since this was a new type of IPR, the existing international systems on, say, **3.9** patents and copyright were not applicable. This meant that the US could approach international protection in a different way. Instead of waiting for the negotiation of multilateral arrangements granting mutual national treatment, the protection of the 1984 Act was limited in the first instance broadly to those with a connection to the US. That protection can be extended to nationals of other countries in two cases: firstly, by Presidential proclamation if the third country establishes protection equivalent to the 1984 Act; or, secondly, if the third country and the US are parties to an international treaty dealing with such protection. In other words, the 1984 Act does not extend automatically to third countries. Rather, it requires reciprocity of treatment before it can be extended to nationals of third countries.

Some argue that reciprocity should not be the basis for international **3.10** protection of new types of IPRs for new technologies which may not fit easily into existing systems of international protection.[6] The reciprocity approach is compared to international arrangements such as the Berne Convention on copyright which requires signatories to grant protection to nationals of signatory States on the same basis as protection is granted to their own nationals. On the other hand, it could be argued that the two approaches—reciprocity or national treatment—lead to a similar result in the end, that is, an international system of protection where countries provide protection for foreigners if their countries comply with certain minimum criteria. Thus, the Berne Convention, for example, sets out fairly stringent rules with which national copyright law must comply and, in fact, the 1984 US Act, supposedly the paradigm case of reciprocity, itself provides for the possibility of international treaties to protect chip designs. Indeed, such a treaty has now been prepared—the 1989 WIPO Integrated Circuits Treaty (the Washington Treaty). Certain countries have not been willing to enter into the Washington Treaty but this may no longer be important in the light of provisions in the Uruguay Round Agreement on the Trade-Related Aspects of Intellectual Property Rights (TRIPs) which require signatories to protect "lay-out designs" of integrated circuits (Art 36 et seq.).

In terms of the end result, then, it might seem that there may not be a great **3.11** difference between the multilateral negotiated approach to national treatment and the approach of the US in requiring reciprocity. However, the

---

[6] See, *e.g.*, Cornish, *The Canker of Reciprocity* (1988) EIPR 99.

method by which that end result is achieved is very different and this will affect the final result. Thus, the 1984 US Act could be seen as an aggressive, unilateral approach to set up an international system based on the US model. On the other hand, what has to be taken into account is that the US only succeeded because of the perceived need on the part of the international community, particularly the European Community and Japan, to obtain protection under the US system for their own nationals. This would surely also have influenced the result of any negotiation for an international treaty. Moreover, it could be argued in defence of the US approach in this case that international protection was obtained more quickly than if national law had awaited international accord.

3.12   The US 1984 Act provided for the possibility of interim protection. The Secretary of Commerce can extend the Act to nationals, domiciliaries and sovereign authorities of a foreign nation if:

- the foreign nation is making good faith efforts and reasonable progress towards entering into an international treaty to which the US is party or enacting legislation giving equivalent protection to the US legislation, and
- the nationals, domiciliaries and sovereign authorities of that foreign nation are not engaged in the misappropriation, or unauthorised distribution or commercial exploitation, of mask works, and
- an order by the Secretary of Commerce would promote the purposes of the 1984 Act and international comity with respect to the protection of mask works (s 914(a)).

3.13   To ensure this interim protection for Community nationals, in December 1986, the Council adopted the Semiconductor Chip Directive which required Member States to establish exclusive rights over topographies of semiconductor chips by 7 November 1987, although not all Member States implemented the Directive in accordance with this timetable. As we have seen, the result of the US acting first in the field combined with the perceived need for protection in the US market led international reaction to the 1984 Act to follow closely the US model of intellectual property protection for semiconductor chip designs.[7]

3.14   The Semiconductor Chip Directive is restricted to laying down "certain basic principles" leaving the Member States considerable freedom on a number of issues. The Directive deals with four principal issues: what is protected and the extent, beneficiaries and duration of that protection.

(b) What is protected?

3.15   The Directive requires topographies of semiconductor products to be protected. Topographies are the equivalent of mask works in the US Act, although, unlike the 1984 Act, the Directive does not require the topography to be fixed in a semiconductor chip before protection is granted.[8] A

---

[7] For a comparison of the UK, EC and US provisions, see Hart (1988) CL&P 151.
[8] See definitions in Art 1(1) and compare s 902(a)(1) of the US Act.

topography only benefits from the Directive in so far as "it is the result of the creator's own intellectual effort and is not commonplace in the semiconductor industry" (Art 2(2)). The topography can incorporate commonplace "elements" provided the two originality conditions are satisfied "as a whole." Protection does not extend to "any concept, process, system, technique or encoded information embodied in the topography other than the topography itself" (Art 8). The Directive does not oblige Member States to lay down any formalities to be fulfilled for protection although Member States are allowed to establish a national registration system (Art 4).

(c) Extent of protection

The Directive requires the grant of the exclusive right to control reproduction **3.16** of a protected topography as well as commercial exploitation or importation of the topography or a semiconductor chip manufactured using the topography. Article 5(5) incorporates the rules of Community exhaustion (see para **2.59** *et seq*) so that the exclusive right to control commercial exploitation does not apply "after the topography or the semiconductor product has been put on the market in a Member State by the person entitled to authorise its marketing or with his consent."

One of the most fascinating substantive issues raised by the Directive **3.17** concerns the reverse engineering exception. It is common industry practice for chips to be analysed by third parties to discover the design techniques. This might be done, for example, with a view to designing chips which could work in tandem with the first chip. On the other hand, it is also the method by which the chip design can be purely and simply copied. The US 1984 Act contained the following exception:

"...it is not an infringement of the exclusive rights of the owner of a mask work for—
(1) a person to reproduce the mask work solely for the purpose of teaching, analyzing, or evaluating the concepts or techniques embodied in the mask work or the circuitry, logic flow, or organization of components used in the mask work; or
(2) a person who performs the analysis or evaluation described in paragraph (1) to incorporate the result of such conduct in an original mask work which is made to be distributed" (s 906(a)).

So the US Act allows not only reproduction for the purpose of examining the **3.18** chip's design but also the use of the information obtained to produce a second chip. How does the EC Directive deal with the issue? Again, the reverse engineering exception is divided into two parts. Article 5(3) states that the exclusive rights granted by the Directive "shall not apply to reproduction for the purpose of analyzing, evaluating or teaching the concepts, processes, systems or techniques embodied in the topography or the topography itself."

Article 5(4) goes on to deal with the use of the results obtained through this **3.19** process. It states that "The exclusive rights referred to in paragraph 1 shall not extend to any such act in relation to a topography meeting the requirements of

Article 2(2) and created on the basis of an analysis and evaluation of another topography, carried out in conformity with paragraph 3."

3.20   In other words, Article 5(4) permits the results of reverse engineering carried out in accordance with Article 5(3) to be used to create a new topography provided that new topography is the result of the creator's own intellectual effort. It has been argued that this means that the designer of the second chip can copy parts of the original topography.[9] The debate seems to hang on what is meant by the Article 2(2) requirement that the topography is the result of "the creator's own intellectual effort." Comparisons with the US position are not straightforward because, in the US Act, the requirement is that the mask work is original which may be interpreted in a different way to the Article 2(2) requirement. It could be argued that Article 5(4) limits the reverse engineer to the use of the results referred to in Article 5(3) and these results do not include the design itself. In other words, Article 5(4) could be argued to be simply confirmation in the context of reverse engineering of Article 8 which excludes from the protection of the Directive "any concept, process, system, technique or encoded information." The position is by no means free from doubt. Although the technical background is different, this issue of the scope of legislative permission for reverse engineering will crop up again in the context of the Software Directive (see para **4.29** *et seq*).

3.21   Another issue which is important for intellectual property protection of new technologies is the extent to which competition law can intervene to force the holder of the right to license a third party to exploit the technology. The basic arguments on this issue have already been aired (see para **2.143** *et seq*). One argument is that the legislation establishing the right should deal with the balance of intellectual property protection against competition and, if that legislation contains no provision for compulsory licences, competition law should not fill the lacuna. It is interesting that Article 6 of the Semiconductor Chip Directive stops Member States from granting compulsory licences "for the sole reason that a certain period of time has elapsed, automatically, and by operation of law." Otherwise, the recitals add that national law can determine to what extent compulsory licences can be granted. It follows that Member States can permit the grant of compulsory licences on the basis of competition law. This is the position in the UK where the Secretary of State has the power to order a licence of right if the Monopolies and Mergers Commission finds that a refusal to grant licences on reasonable terms is against the public interest.[10] It is also worth noting that Article 37(2) of TRIPs would permit compulsory licensing of the lay-out design right "to remedy a practice determined after judicial or administrative process to be anti-competitive."[11]

3.22   It could also be argued that the Directive would not stop the application of EC competition law to force the licence of a topography right granted by virtue of Member State implementation of the Semiconductor Chip Directive.

---

[9] Hart, *High Technology "Reverse Engineering": The Dual Standard* (1987) EIPR 139.
[10] Copyright Designs and Patents Act 1988, s 238, together with the Design Right (Semiconductor Topographies) Regulations 1989.
[11] See Art 37(2) in combination with Art 31(c).

The application of EC competition in these circumstances is discussed further on in this chapter (see para **3.48** *et seq*).

(d) Beneficiaries of rights

In the first instance, it is the creator who obtains the rights granted by the **3.23** Directive (Art 3(1)). There are two qualifications. Firstly, where the creator is an employee, national law can provide that the rights accrue directly to the employer (subject to contractual provision to the contrary) (Art 3(2)(a)). National law may establish a similar position for commissioned works (Art 3(2)(b)). Secondly, the rights only accrue to natural persons who are Member State nationals or residents or, in addition, where rights accrue to employers or commissioners, companies or other legal persons which have a "real and effective industrial or commercial establishment" in a Member State. Where there is no beneficiary according to these rules, the rights can accrue to a natural or legal person satisfying the Community test who carries out the first commercial exploitation in the Community with the exclusive authorisation to exploit the topography throughout the Community. These are complicated provisions. Essentially, Article 3 only grants rights to persons with a connection to the Community.

Article 3 goes on to deal with extension of these rights to non-Community **3.24** persons. The Directive allows Member States to extend protection to a non-Community country subject to giving time to the Council to adopt a decision requiring all Member States to extend protection to that non-Community country. So far as the US is concerned, the current position is that the US benefits from temporary protection until 1 July 1995 pending the implementation of TRIPs.[12]

(e) Term of protection

Where the rights have been commercially exploited, protection ends ten years **3.25** from such exploitation (or, where national law requires registration, from such registration). If the rights are not exploited commercially, protection ends 15 years from the first fixation or encoding of the topography.

(f) Appraisal

The Directive is addressed at a very specific problem in the IT sector and, **3.26** consequently, is somewhat technical. The Directive, though, is of wider interest because of the way in which the US approached the international position concerning the protection of a new technology. This is reflected in the fact that the provisions of the Directive follow closely the provisions of the US 1984 Semiconductor Chip Protection Act with the objective of ensuring equivalent protection to that Act. The Directive is also interesting in how it balances the need to stop piracy and reward innovation against the fear of stifling the development of the industry. There are clear parallels on all these

---

[12] Council Decision 94/373 (OJ 1994 L170/34).

issues in the Commission's approach to other IPRs for new technologies not least in the case of software and databases.

(ii) **VDU Work Directive**[13]

3.27 Harmonisation of standards is vital to the removal of barriers to trade within the Community. There may be other ways in which EC law can have an impact on standards in the IT hardware industry. An example of the latter which is often overlooked is the VDU Work Directive adopted on basis of Article 118a (in the EC Treaty's chapter on social provisions). Given the growing awareness of the risks of repetitive strain injury (RSI), it is bound to receive more attention in the future. The concern over RSI (and potential legal liability) is illustrated by the recent announcement that a number of manufacturers are to post warnings on keyboards about health and safety.[14] The Directive also illustrates the wide reach of EC law.

3.28 The VDU Work Directive is based on the framework Directive 89/391 concerning improvements to working conditions (OJ 1989 L183/1). The Directive lays a number of obligations on employers to protect employees who work at workstations with VDUs.

(a) Beneficiaries

3.29 The Directive is concerned with those who work at workstations. A workstation is "an assembly comprising display screen equipment" (Art 2). The term includes all the immediate working environment such as keyboard, telephone and work chair. It even includes the software which determines the operator/machine interface.

3.30 The Directive refers to employees as workers. A worker is only protected by the Directive if that worker "habitually uses display screen equipment as a significant part of his normal work" (Art 2).

3.31 There are a number of exceptions to the Directive such as portable systems not in prolonged use at a workstation (Art 1).

(b) Employers' obligations

3.32 The Directive lays down a number of obligations on the employer. They include the obligation to analyse workstations in order to evaluate the safety and health implications. The employer must take "appropriate measures" to remedy any risks found.

3.33 The Annex to the Directive lays down the requirements which all workstations must satisfy. They cover everything from screen and keyboard tilt facilities to lighting and radiation levels. As we have seen, they also cover

---

[13] Council Dir 90/270 on the minimum safety and health requirements for work with display screen equipment (fifth individual Directive within the meaning of Art 16(1) of Directive 89/391) (OJ 1990 L156/14). See Appendix A3.

[14] *Computer Weekly* 25 August 1994, 1.

the operator/computer interface although the obligations on the employer are less strict in this case and only require certain principles to be taken into account in selecting software and designing tasks using display screen equipment.

These requirements apply to workstations put into service after 31 **3.34** December 1992 (Art 4). Those put into service before that date must comply by 31 December 1996 (Art 5). If the Directive were not properly implemented within these time limits, national courts might be required to apply the provisions of the Directive itself although only as against public bodies. However, if an employee in the private sector could prove that they were injured as a result of the failure of a Member State to implement correctly the VDU Work Directive, there may be a claim for damages directly against that Member State (see para **2.47** *et seq*).

There is an obligation to inform workers about health and safety relating to **3.35** their workstations. There are also provisions on consultation and participation with workers and/or representatives. Workers must be trained in the use of the workstation. The employer must plan the worker's activities to allow breaks in work with display screens. Finally, the employer must arrange free eye and eyesight tests.

(c) Appraisal

The VDU Work Directive falls within the so-called social dimension of **3.36** Europe. Once fully implemented, it will have a fundamental impact on the approach of employers to the large and growing number of employees who cannot do their jobs without significant use of desktop terminals. Even though primarily concerned with the working environment, the Directive will also have a major impact on IT manufacturers as they strive to provide employers with the products which they require to fulfil the obligations laid down in the Directive.

3. **Competition law issues**

The analysis of competition law in this book is not intended to be **3.37** comprehensive. Rather, it will pick out for discussion those issues which are raised by typical transactions or conduct in the IT industry. These issues are not always dealt with in sufficient detail by basic texts on competition law.

This section on competition law will begin with the problem of defining the **3.38** relevant market and then consider the application of competition law to conduct and transactions typical of the IT industry.

(i) **Market definition**

The basic theory has already been described (see para **2.135** *et seq*). It should be **3.39** emphasised that defining the relevant market is important not only to determine dominance under Article 86 but also for such purposes as calculating market share figures for block exemptions, for example, Regulation 418/85 on research and development agreements.[15] The adoption of the Commission's proposal for a technology transfer block exemption will increase the importance of market definition (see para **3.68**).

3.40　　How does the basic theory apply in the case of hardware? The first point is that just because there is intellectual property protection does not automatically mean that the owner of the intellectual property right (IPR) holds a dominant position. There may well be substitutes for the product protected by the intellectual property. One factor in the IT industry which may affect this analysis is that products will often be components of a larger system. If the customer has already invested in a particular type of hardware or software, that customer may in practice have a limited choice in replacing components because the alternative might involve scrapping the entire system. The way in which EC competition law should deal with this question is addressed in the Commission's decision in *Hilti* which has now been upheld by both the CFI and the ECJ.[16] Hilti's customers had bought nail guns. To use the nail gun, a nail had to be inserted into a cartridge (or strip of cartridges) over which Hilti had certain IPRs. Hilti used its control over the supply of cartridges to force customers to buy its nails. Hilti argued that there was one market for powder activated fastening (PAF) systems which included the nail guns together with consumables (the cartridges and nails). The Commission disagreed. It held that there were three separate markets: nails guns, cartridges and nails. Since Hilti was the only source of cartridges, owners of Hilti nail guns were forced to buy cartridges from Hilti. The Commission held that Hilti was dominant in this market and had abused that dominance by tying the sale of nails to cartridges. Both the CFI and ECJ upheld the Commission's decision.

3.41　　The principles which can be derived from the *Hilti* case are of wide ranging importance. For example, if a manufacturer holds IPRs over spare parts and, as a result, is the sole source of those parts, the manufacturer may be held to have a dominant position in the market for spare parts. One argument that can be put forward in these cases is that any market power over spare parts or consumables cannot be exercised to the detriment of consumers if there is competition in the primary market. Thus, it can be argued that competition in the market for nail guns would prevent Hilti from raising the price of cartridges because customers would take this into account in deciding whether to buy a Hilti nail gun. This argument could also be used to show that tying nails to cartridges should not be a concern for competition policy. In fact, in the *Hilti* case, the Commission found Hilti to be dominant in the primary market for nail guns. It remains to be seen how receptive the Commission and the ECJ will be to the argument that competition in the primary market precludes abuse of high market shares in the aftermarket. Previous jurispru-

---

[15] OJ 1985 L53/5, as amended by Reg 151/93 (OJ 1993 L21/8).
[16] Commission Decision OJ 1988 L65/19. Upheld on appeal *Hilti* v *Commission* Case T-30/89 [1991] ECR II-1439; [1992] 4 CMLR 16 (CFI) and Case C-53/92P [1994] ECR I-667; [1994] 4 CMLR 614 (ECJ).

dence suggests that they will not be receptive to this argument. These issues are discussed in more detail in Chapter 5 (see para **5.38** *et seq*).

These principles are very relevant to the IT hardware market. There are **3.42** clear indications that the Commission will use the *Hilti*-type reasoning to find narrow market definitions and strong market power. For example, in its statement of objections in the *IBM* case, the Commission alleged that IBM was dominant in the supply of CPUs and basic software for the IBM 360 and 370 type computer systems. Why did the Commission not take into account other types of large systems? It must be because, once customers had elected to install software and hardware based on IBM's 360 or 370 architecture, the cost of moving to another system would be prohibitive in practice. Consequently, customers would not move to a non-IBM architecture. So, in defining the market, the Commission did take into account suppliers of "plug-compatible" hardware but it did not take into account suppliers of other hardware which could not work within an IBM system.

More recently, the Commission has followed a similar reasoning in its **3.43** decision on the AT&T/NCR merger (Case IV.M050 [1992] 4 CMLR M41). The Commission took the view that the UNIX operating system represents a market of its own (para 16). This conclusion must be based on the argument that, once the customer has invested in a UNIX-based system, the cost of moving to another architecture will force the customer to buy only hardware and software which work in the UNIX environment. This is not exactly the same situation as the *Hilti*-type aftermarket case where the supplier of the primary product is the sole source of supply for consumables protected by IPRs. The *AT&T* case concerned an operating system which is an "open system" precisely because AT&T's policy was to license the UNIX source code to all major computer manufacturers under generally irrevocable, paid up licences (para 18). What the Commission seemed to be concerned about in the *AT&T/NCR* case was the fact that AT&T owned the copyright in the source code and could change its policy. In the end, the Commission thought this unlikely (para 21) but the case does show the way in which the Commission may deduce market definition and power from control over architecture.

Within a particular system architecture, there may be still narrower **3.44** markets. For example, in its decision in *Digital/Kienzle* (Case IV.M057 [1992] 4 CMLR M99) the Commission identified the following markets as separate: personal computers for professional and private use (but excluding pure games systems); small computers (costing up to US$ 100,000); medium sized computers (within the range of US$ 100,000 to US$ 1m); and workstations. The Commission added that:

> "The differences between PC's and small and medium multi-user computers as well as workstations with respect to characteristics, price and intended use indicate the existence of distinct product markets for each of these computer systems. Even though it may be appropriate in certain cases to further break down these product groups with regard to distribution channels and/or special

commercial and industrial market firms, it would not seem justified to do this for the purposes of the present case."[17]

3.45   It is interesting that the Commission focuses on price as a key factor in the choice of market definition. There is an argument in the IT hardware field that mainframe prices have fallen as a result of moves to distributed computing or client/server technology. This would undermine the Commission's definition of the market according to unit price. It also indicates how market definition can change over time.

3.46   In *ICL/Nokia Data* (Case IV.M105), the Commission looked again at the market for personal computers and terminals. It defined the former as "general purpose, single user computer systems for professional use" (excluding pure game systems) (para 10). It stated that "Terminals consist of a screen, processor and a keyboard. They allow the user to enter data and retrieve information but without access to the function of the application" (para 12). The Commission did not reach any firm conclusion in the case, however, on market definition.

3.47   The market for semiconductors was discussed by the Commission in its decision under the Merger Regulation on the acquisition of control of SGS-Thomson (*CEA Industrie/France Télécom/Finmeccanica/SGS-Thomson* Case IV.M216). The transaction did not lead to any increase in market share and the Comission decided that it was not likely to create or strengthen a dominant position. It also mentioned the following factors concerning the market:

> "—an essential characteristic of this sector is the rapidity of change. Every three years, a new technological generation is implemented. Integrated circuits with high technological intensity are on the increase.
> —certain markets such as the Japanese market (40% of the world market) are largely captive markets because the manufacturers of semi-conductors are part of highly vertical integrated groups where the parent company meets up to 85% of its needs via its semi-conductor subsidiary" (para 17).

(ii) Refusal to license/supply

3.48   If a firm refuses to supply products to another, can EC competition rules apply? The first point is that Article 85 cannot apply unless the refusal is part of an agreement with another firm.[18] If not, the refusal can only be caught by Article 86 which only applies where the firm in question holds a dominant position. In practice, the cases on refusal to supply tend to concern situations where the complainant is dependent on a sole source of supply. This may be because there is only one source of a raw material.[19] More relevant to the IT

---

[17] Para 11. See also *Digital/Philips* Case IV.M129 para 9.
[18] However, see *Ford v Commission* Case 25&26/84 [1985] ECR 2725; [1985] 3 CMLR 528 where an apparently unilateral refusal to supply motor cars to dealers was found to be part of an arrangement with other dealers.
[19] See *Commercial Solvents v Commission* Cases 6&7/73 [1974] ECR 223; [1974] 1 CMLR 309.

industry is where the reason for the single source is intellectual property protection. This may give rise to two problems. Firstly, the owner of the right may refuse to sell the product to the third party. This is what happened in the *Hugin/Liptons* case where a cash register manufacturer was held by the Commission to be dominant in the supply of spare parts. The Commission decided that Hugin had abused that dominant position by discontinuing the supply of spare parts to an independent repairer of Hugin machines. This issue is discussed in detail in relation to the supply of spare parts to third party maintainers in Chapter 5 (see para **5.38** *et seq*).

Secondly, the owner of the intellectual property right may refuse to license third parties to manufacture the product in question. This raises the difficult issue of the interface of competition rules and intellectual property protection. The issue could arise in the hardware field. For example, we have seen that the Semiconductor Chip Directive does not exclude the possibility of compulsory licences based on competition grounds. The basic arguments on the issue have been set out already (see para **2.143** *et seq*).   **3.49**

How has the ECJ dealt with the possible conflict of competition rules and IPRs? The starting point is the existence/exercise distinction. This is the cornerstone of the ECJ's jurisprudence on the application of Article 30 to IPRs (see para **2.63**) but was in fact first aired in a competition case (*Consten & Grundig* v *Commission* Cases 56 & 58/64 [1966] ECR 299; [1966] CMLR 418). Indeed, it probably better describes the way in which competition law applies. Unlike Article 30 which has the effect of excising one part of an IPR, in principle, competition rules are applied on a case-by-case basis and do not preclude reliance on the IPR in circumstances where the conditions for the application of Article 86 are not fulfilled.   **3.50**

What are the circumstances in which Article 86 can be applied to the refusal to license IPRs? In *Volvo* v *Veng* (Case 238/87 [1988] ECR 6211; [1989] 4 CMLR 122) the ECJ was asked to consider whether it was unlawful for a car manufacturer to rely on IPRs to stop third parties from manufacturing replacement car panels. The ECJ said: **3.51**

"8. It must also be emphasised that the right of the proprietor of a protected design to prevent third parties from manufacturing and selling or importing, without its consent, products incorporating the design constitutes the very subject-matter of his exclusive right. It follows that an obligation imposed upon the proprietor of a protected design to grant to third parties, even in return for a reasonable royalty, a licence for the supply of products incorporating the design would lead to the proprietor thereof being deprived of the substance of his exclusive right and that a refusal to grant such a licence cannot in itself constitute an abuse of a dominant position.

9. It must however be noted that the exercise of an exclusive right by the proprietor of a registered design in respect of car body panels may be prohibited by Article 86 if it involves, on the part of an undertaking holding a dominant position, certain abusive conduct such as the arbitrary refusal to supply spare parts to independent repairers, the fixing of prices for spare parts at an unfair level or a decision no longer to produce spare parts for a particular model even

though many cars of that model are still in circulation, provided that such conduct is liable to affect trade between member states".

3.52 It is abundantly clear from this extract that the ECJ is reluctant to allow Article 86 to be relied upon to interfere with an IPR so as to require the owner to license a third party, in particular, because the right to control reproduction is part of the "very subject matter" of the right. The concept of specific subject matter is used in the context of Article 30 to resolve the conflict between free movement rules and the barriers to trade caused by IPRs (see para **2.64**). It is not clear how it helps in the context of compulsory licences since the ECJ does seem to concede that there may be circumstances when such a licence could be required under Article 86. There is considerable uncertainty over precisely how to apply the examples of additional abusive conduct set out by the ECJ.

3.53 The CFI has since relied on the judgment in the *Volvo* case to uphold a Commission decision that TV companies had abused Article 86 by refusing to license a third party to reproduce their programme listings information in a comprehensive weekly TV guide.[20] If the ECJ approves the CFI's decision, the principle would allow significant intervention by the Commission in the exploitation of IPRs. The decision in the *Magill* cases has been criticised in the academic literature[21] and the Advocate General has since argued that the ECJ should overturn the CFI judgment and the Commission decision on the basis that a licence should not be ordered under EC competition law unless the IPR owner does not itself supply the product protected by the IPR.[22] The issue will be returned to in the context of the application of Article 86 to software (see para **4.62** *et seq*).

(iii) **Mergers**

3.54 Significant restructuring of the hardware side of the industry took place in the 1980s reflecting the changing nature of the market place. Merger activity seems now to have moved rather to the software and telecoms side of the industry. However, there have been a number of mergers within the hardware sector since the Merger Regulation came into force in September 1990 (see para **2.130** *et seq*). Commission decisions under the Regulation are useful indicators of the Commission's approach to determining the relevant market. They are also important in deducing its attitude to the general application of competition law in this sector of the IT industry, especially the question of market definition.[23]

---

[20] *RTE, BBC & ITP* v *Commission* Cases T-69,70&76/89 [1991] ECR II-485, 535 & 575; [1991] 4 CMLR 586, 669 & 745. Under appeal to the ECJ: *RTE & ITP* v *Commission* Cases 241&242/91(OJ 1991 C307/5).

[21] See, *e.g.*, Reindl *The Magic of Magill: TV Program Guides as a Limit of Copyright Law?* (1993) IIC 60. See also the articles cited at para 26 of Advocate General Gulmann's Opinion.

[22] Advocate General Gulmann's Opinion of 1 June 1994.

[23] For a discussion of the US approach to high tech mergers, see Reback & Wright, (1992) The Computer Lawyer Vol 9 No 6, 1.

One of the most important mergers which fell within the Regulation was the 3.55
acquisition by AT&T of NCR (Case IV.M050 [1992] 4 CMLR M41). The
Commission's main concern focused on the combination of NCR's "fairly
strong position on the financial and retail workstation market" and AT&T's
control over the UNIX operating system software. Thus, AT&T could
improve NCR's position by easing NCR's access to UNIX. However, given
AT&T's open licensing policies, the Commission concluded that the merger
did not raise serious doubts as to compatability with the common market.
Nonetheless, the decision shows the Commission's concern that ownership of
standards for key products can give significant power in the market.

The Commission made some points about the market for financial 3.56
workstations in its decision on the acquisition by a subsidiary of Digital
Equipment of Philips' Information System Division (Case IV.M129 [1992] 4
CMLR M4). The Commission stated that:

> "High market shares on high growth markets involving modern technology are
> not extraordinary, and they do not necessarily indicate market power. In fact the
> development of the market shares of the three leading companies over a period of
> time shows the dynamic nature of this market. There has been constant change
> including a change of market leadership" (para 18).

Digital Equipment was involved in another merger falling within the Merger 3.57
Control Regulation when it agreed to acquire control of the computer system
business of Mannesmann Kienzle transferred to a new company, Digital
Kienzle Computersystems Gmbh (Case IV.M057). In clearing the merger,
the Commission emphasised the lack of barriers to entry in the workstation
market:

> "...barriers to entry are relatively low for other computer systems manufac-
> turers, especially for those who sell PCs and small multi-user computers. Market
> entry seems to be feasible even for companies on adjacent markets. Sony and
> Matsushita are apparently potential, if not already actual, competitors on the
> workstation market" (para 21).

The Commission also commented that "High market shares on a new 3.58
developing market are not extraordinary, and they do not necessarily indicate
market power" (para 20).

In conclusion, the Commission seems to be well aware of the changing 3.59
nature of the IT hardware market and the ease of entry into new markets. Its
key concern is control over standards. This concern is a common theme in its
application of competition law throughout the IT industry as well as its
approach to IPRs over new technologies.

(iv) Joint ventures

Joint ventures are becoming more common as technological advances become 3.60
too expensive for one firm to undertake or exploit alone and as differing

technologies combine. Perhaps the most well-known recent IT hardware joint venture is the Apple, IBM and Motorola arrangement to bring the RISC-based PowerPC to the market.

3.61   Advising on the application of EC competition law to joint ventures is never easy. As the Commission points out in its Notice on joint ventures (OJ 1993 C43/2; [1993] 4 CMLR 401) "In view of the variety of situations which come into consideration, it is impossible to make general comments on the compliance of JVs with competition law" (para 5).

3.62   In fact, the Notice makes no specific reference to the IT industry at all. Advising on joint ventures concerning hardware is made all the more difficult by the dearth of Commission decisions on specific joint ventures. Some positive points can be made in relation to such joint ventures. First, certain block exemptions may be applicable. For example, in the case of joint research and development, Regulation 418/85[24] may automatically exempt the arrangement as well joint exploitation of the results and, subject to satisfying a lower market share test, joint marketing.[25] Moreover, the patent and know-how licence block exemptions have recently been amended to apply to such agreements entered into in the context of a joint venture.[26] These block exemptions are now to be replaced by a single technology transfer block exemption.[27]

3.63   Secondly, in its decision exempting the joint venture between Olivetti and Canon to develop, design and manufacture copying machine products, laser beam printer products and facsimile products (OJ 1988 L52/51; [1989] 4 CMLR 940), the Commission commented that:

> "The joint venture enables a transfer of the benefit of advanced technology to Olivetti, a Community undertaking, in markets where technology is of crucial importance. An important part of the transferred technology comes from an undertaking, Canon, which is a leader of innovation and whose policy is R&D-oriented.... It is reasonable to expect that a combination of this technology with that of an also R&D-oriented EEC undertaking will contribute to improving the technological patterns of the EEC industry and ultimately its competitivity. This will result in improving production and distribution and technical progress" (para 54).

3.64   Thirdly, in considering an individual exemption, the Commission will look favourably at joint ventures involving "the development of new or improved products and processes which are marketed by the originator or by third parties under licence. In addition measures opening up new markets, leading to sales expansion of the undertaking in new territories or the enlargement of its supply range by new products."[28]

---

[24] OJ 1985 L53/5, as amended by Reg 151/93 (OJ 1993 L21/8).
[25] The change was introduced by Reg 151/93 (OJ 1993 L21/8).
[26] Again, this change was introduced by Reg 151/93 (OJ 1993 L21/8).
[27] Draft published OJ 1994 C178/3.
[28] Commission Notice, para 55.

These factors seem to have influenced the Commission's favourable   **3.65**
approach to a joint venture between Fujitsu and Advanced Micro Devices
(AMD) to set up a joint venture to produce a new generation of semiconductor
chip: flash memory (OJ 1994 C153/11). The Commission noted the expected
massive increase in demand due to "explosive growth in markets for products
requiring this technology such as cellular phones, computer disk drives, mobile
and desktop personal computers." A number of hardware manufacturers had
entered into joint ventures in order to compete for this anticipated demand.
These factors were also taken into account by the Commission in its decision
under the Merger Regulation on the change in control of SGS-Thomson, a
concentrative joint venture for the manufacture and sale of semiconductors
(*CEA Industrie/France Télécom/Finmeccanica/SGS-Thomson* Case IV.M216).

At the end of 1993, the Commission indicated that it would take a   **3.66**
favourable view of an arrangement whereby Digital Equipment was to
acquire 8% of Olivetti's share capital and Olivetti agreed to adopt Digital's
Alpha AXP RISC architecture for all its non-Intel based computers (OJ 1993
C276; [1994] 4 CMLR 499). The Commission set out the parties' arguments
that the agreement exclusively to adopt a third party's RISC architecture
should not be considered to restrict competition because Olivetti was unlikely
to develop its own RISC architecture and was unlikely to use more than one
such architecture. In other words, it was argued that the parties were not
potential competitors and that the exclusivity was inherent in the arrangement. The Commission's notice is not a final decision and, unfortunately, does
not say whether the Commission's view was that the arrangement fell outside
Article 85 or would benefit from an individual exemption. It seems that Digital
and Olivetti have now gone their separate ways.[29]

Finally, it is worth noting that the Commission has adopted a number of   **3.67**
decisions concerning joint ventures in the telecoms field. The principles
followed in those decisions may well be relevant to hardware joint ventures.
They are discussed in **Chapter 5** (see para **6.46** *et seq*).

(v) **Licensing**

IPRs over hardware technology are a fundamental part of the industry. For   **3.68**
example, in 1993, IBM was awarded the highest number of US patents.[30]
Naturally, technology licence agreements are a common feature of the IT
industry. Unlike licences of software, the block exemptions on patent and
know-how licences apply to hardware technology as they do to licences of
other forms of technology. Ensuring that the requirements of the block
exemptions are satisfied does raise complicated issues but those issues tend to
be the same in the IT field as in other industries. The patent licence block
exemption expires at the end of 1994. The Commission is planning to combine
the patent and know-how block exemptions in a single regulation to be

---

[29] *Computer Weekly* 1 September 1994, 6.
[30] *Financial Times*, 13 January 1994.

finalised by the end of 1994 (OJ 1994 C178/3). Its current draft has been criticised for the addition of market share tests for agreements to benefit from exemption ((1994) EIPR 259). Given uncertainty over market definition in the IT industry, this is likely to be a real problem in that industry.

3.69　　One specifically IT-related point on the existing regulations as well as the proposed replacement is that licences of rights over topographies are not generally covered. It is probable that the Commission would follow similar principles, though, in dealing with this form of licence.

(vi) **Distribution**[31]

3.70　　Hardware manufacturers have resorted to a number of different methods for the distribution of their products influenced in particular by the needs of the customers to whom sales are targeted. The advent of the personal computer in the 1980s led to increased reliance on independent distributors and dealers. Although personal computers are now sufficiently familiar to many users to be sold by mail order, there is still a significant dealer channel to cater for those customers who require a dealer experienced in the relevant field. Indeed, the dealer may well need to incorporate software and other hardware to create a specific customer solution.

3.71　　How are these various methods of distribution treated by EC competition law? One preliminary observation is that the Commission's reliance on block exemptions has led to a tendency to establish categories of agreements. Within a particular category, say, franchising, the rules may be straightforward and fair but it is sometimes difficult to see why there is such a difference in treatment from one category to the next. In practice, problems can arise from the fact that advisors will generally feel more comfortable with an agreement which complies with the well-known criteria for a particular type of agreement. Unfortunately, those devising IT distribution channels may well not think in terms of the Commission's various categories of agreement and many of these channels fit uneasily into those categories. For example, one key (and as yet unanswered) question concerns the treatment of value added resellers (VARs). Like many other IT industry terms, this is not a term of art but a VAR is generally taken to mean a reseller who is obliged to add other hardware and/or software before resale of the product. Typically, the question arises whether this obligation will remove the benefit of protection for a selective distribution system (see para **3.38** *et seq*).

3.72　　Before looking at how EC competition law deals with the various types of distribution agreement, it is worth emphasising an overriding concern of EC law. It has already been pointed out (see para **2.94**) that one function of EC competition law is to further the creation of the internal market. This results in a sensitivity to vertical agreements and restrictions on intra-brand competition. This is reflected in the seriousness with which any ban on export is dealt

---

[31] See, generally, Goyder, *EC Distribution Law* (Chancery, 1992) and Korah & Rothnie, *Exclusive Distribution—EEC Competition Rules* (Sweet & Maxwell, 1992, 2nd ed).

with under EC law. Although in certain cases dealers may be restricted from pursuing an active sales policy outside of their territory (an "active" sales ban), this can never extend to an absolute ban on sales (a "passive" sales ban). Indeed, the Commission has frequently fined firms for imposing the latter type of restriction. For example, in a 1991 decision, the Commission fined Toshiba Europa 2m ECU (about US$ 2.4m) for including an export prohibition in agreements with its exclusive distributors (*Viho/Toshiba* OJ 1991 L287/39; [1992] 5 CMLR 180).

(a) Direct sale

One way to escape Article 85 is to avoid entering into an agreement with an   **3.73**
independent firm (see para **2.100**). The current move to sale of personal computers by mail order clearly avoids the need for a distribution agreement. There will, of course, still be agreements with the end-user, discussed below (see para **3.89**).

(b) Agency

One way to retain control over distribution is to sell through an agent. This is   **3.74**
more common for larger systems. To begin with the Commission took a lenient attitude to these arrangements. In its 1962 Notice on Exclusive Agency Agreements (OJ 1962 2921), the Commission stated that agreements with commercial agents fell outside Article 85. The key question is to determine what is to be considered a commercial agent. The test in the 1962 Notice was based on whether the agent took on any financial risk. If not, the agreement would not be caught by Article 85. Subsequent case-law of the Commission and the ECJ has introduced another test based on the other activities carried out by the agent. Thus, in *Suikerunie* v *Commission* (Case 40/73 [1975] ECR 1663; [1976] 1 CMLR 295), the ECJ held that an agency agreement with a firm could fall within Article 85 if the firm performed the same function for other principals.[32] In other words, even if the agent carries no financial risk, the agreement may fall within Article 85 if the agent is not economically dependent on the principal. This approach may mean that agency agreements for hardware sale do not escape Article 85 since agents may well act in a similar capacity for other suppliers.

The Commission has proposed a revised Notice which also reflects this   **3.75**
approach. The draft Notice distinguishes between integrated and uninteg-rated agents. An integrated agent is one which either acts solely for the principal or has limited additional activity. If the agent deals in competing products or the agency agreement accounts for less than one third of its activity, it will be an unintegrated agent. The interesting point about the draft Notice is that the Commission does not take the view that agreements with unintegrated agents fall outside Article 85 altogether but rather only that the principal is allowed to exert more control over the agent through the agency agreement. It seems that not even an integrated agent can be prohibited from

---

[32] See also the Commission's decision in *Pittsburg Corning Europe* OJ 1972 L272/35; [1973] CMLR D2.

meeting unsolicited orders outside its territory. The proposed revised Notice has never been officially published and the lapse of time since it was made available for preliminary comment suggests that the Commission may well have changed its mind.

(c) Exclusive distribution

3.76   If an independent dealer is appointed, it is common for the supplier to agree not to appoint other dealers within a specified territory. In *Société Technique Minière* v *Maschinenbau Ulm* (Case 56/65 [1966] ECR 235; [1966] CMLR 357), the ECJ held that such an exclusive distribution agreement does not automatically fall within Article 85. Instead, the agreement has to be appraised in the light of its factual and legal context. However, given that the Commission has adopted a block exemption on these forms of agreement, there is a clear incentive to comply with the conditions laid down in that exemption. If the conditions of the exemption are fulfilled, there is no need to rely on economic arguments to defend the agreement.

3.77   Regulation 1983/83 (OJ 1983 L173/1) exempts "agreements to which only two undertakings are party and whereby one party agrees with the other to supply certain goods for resale within the whole or a defined area of the common market only to that other" (Art 1).

3.78   The reseller can be obliged to employ staff having practical or technical training and to provide customer and guarantee services (Art 2(3)). However, the block exemption only applies to goods supplied "for resale". The block exemption will not apply where the reseller adds significant value before supplying the goods itself. In its Guidelines on the block exemption (OJ 1984 C101/2), the Commission states that "only a slight addition in value can be taken not to change the economic identity of the goods."[33] Thus, if the dealer installs valuable software before resale, the block exemption may not apply. In such a case, though, an individual exemption may be available.[34]

3.79   The Commission has also suggested that the block exemption may not apply to an OEM arrangement. In *ICL/Fujitsu* (OJ 1986 C210/3; [1986] 3 CMLR 154), Fujitsu supplied large computers for resale by ICL under its own trade marks. The Commission took the preliminary view that the block exemption could not apply because ICL was "not holding itself out as a distributor of the Fujitsu M-380/M-382 and SB-2 systems but were buying them to sell as ICL's own Atlas range of computer systems" (para 13). This is a restrictive interpretation of the Regulation given that Article 2(3) specifically permits an obligation on the reseller "to sell the contract goods under trademarks or packed and presented as specified by the other party."[35]

3.80   A further reason why the block exemption may not be available is the restriction on exclusive distribution agreements between competitors. Article

---

[33] Guidelines, para 10.
[34] See, *e.g.*, the OEM type arrangements in *VFA/Sauer*, XVth Competition Report (1985) para 78.
[35] See Vajda, *The Application of Community Competition Law to the Distribution of Computer Products and Parts* (1992) ECLR 110 at 111.

3(a) states that the block exemption does not apply where "manufacturers of identical goods or of goods which are considered by users as equivalent in view of their characteristics, price or intended use enter into reciprocal exclusive distribution agreements between themselves in respect of such goods."

The equivalent provision in the earlier Regulation 67/67 (OJ 1967 10) was relied on by the Commission in the case of *Siemens/Fanuc* (OJ 1985 L376/29; [1988] 4 CMLR 945) where it was held that the block exemption did not apply to an arrangement between Siemens and Fanuc, a subsidiary of Fujitsu, under which Siemens had the exclusive right to distribute Fanuc's numerical controls (NCs) in Europe and Fanuc had the reciprocal exclusive right to distribute Siemens's NCs in Asia. Indeed, the Commission imposed a fine of 1 million ECU (about US$ 1.2 million) on each party.

Article 3(b) also removes the protection of the block exemption from a **3.81** non-reciprocal exclusive distribution agreement unless one of the parties has a total annual group turnover of no more than 100 million ECU (about US$ 120 million).

(d) Exclusive purchase

The exclusive distribution block exemption permits an obligation on the **3.82** reseller to obtain the contract goods for resale only from that other party. What if that obligation is imposed on a reseller who is not also granted an exclusive territory? Such an exclusive purchase agreement may be covered by Regulation 1984/83 (OJ 1983 L173/5). The exclusive purchase obligation is only permitted for a fixed term of five years (Art 3(d)). Furthermore, the block exemption does not apply "where the exclusive purchasing obligation is agreed for more than one type of goods where these are neither by their nature nor according to commercial usage connected to each other" (Art 3(c)). This block exemption, again, only applies to goods supplied "for resale". It also contains similar provisions to Article 3 of Regulation 1983/83 on agreements between competitors.

(e) Selective distribution

It is common for certain types of hardware to be sold through dealers who have **3.83** to satisfy certain criteria in order to be appointed as dealers. The dealers are then prohibited from supplying unauthorised dealers. There is now a considerable body of case-law both of the Commission and the ECJ in this area. Basically, a selective distribution system is permitted provided that the product is one for which selective distribution is necessary and provided that the criteria for appointment of dealers are qualitative rather than quantitative. In other words, the supplier is entitled to require the reseller to attain certain standards of quality in relation to the premises, staff and after-sales service but the supplier cannot limit the number of dealers by refusing to admit to the network resellers who fulfil these quality criteria. In practice, the distinction between qualitative and quantitative criteria is not always obvious.

In 1984, the Commission considered IBM's selective distribution system for **3.84**

PCs.[36] The Commission held that IBM personal computer products did justify a selective distribution and the system complied with the requirements laid down by the ECJ so that the system fell outside Article 85 altogether and did not even need to be exempted. It commented that

> "This conclusion is based on the present situation in this market in which new highly technical products are being sold mainly to inexperienced users who have not enjoyed the education in computers that is now being offered in many schools and colleges" (para 15).

It may well be that the Commission could take a different view given developments over the last ten years.

3.85 The Commission permitted the following terms in the dealer agreement:

(i)   a dealer is appointed for three years, renewable; a dealer may terminate the agreement without reason at any time; IBM may terminate only if IBM decides to cease completely distribution through dealers (this at one year's notice to all dealers) or for breach of contract by the dealer, duly reasoned and notified;

(ii)   the dealer is specifically free to fix its own prices without any reference to or influence from IBM;

(iii)   IBM may only refuse a dealer's order if out of stock;

(iv)   a dealer must submit its advertisements (but not including any advertised prices or conditions) for IBM's approval;

(v)   a dealer must maintain a record of customers' names and addresses, serial numbers of purchases and dates of delivery, for the purposes of repairs under warranty, and make the record available to IBM in the event of any necessary safety changes;

(vi)   within the warranty period, a dealer must provide service under warranty for any machine whether originally supplied by it or by IBM or any other authorised dealer within Western Europe (which includes the whole of the Community); IBM pays dealers for warranty services performed;

(vii)   a dealer is free to sell competing products, and has an obligation to describe IBM and competing products to prospective customers fairly;

(viii)   a dealer may nominate other prospective dealers; IBM undertakes to process such nominations within two months (the time they take to process direct applications and train applicants' staff) and appoint if the prospective dealer is qualified.

3.86 One key question in the IT industry is whether a system of sale through VARs will comply with the rules for selective distribution. If this were the case, then there would be no need to notify the agreement for an exemption. There is as yet no Commission decision permitting an obligation on a dealer to add value before resale. The first point is that the Commission tends to find that Article 85 does apply to restrictions on resale. For example, in *Bayo-n-ox* (OJ 1990

---

[36] OJ 1984 L118/24; [1984] 2 CMLR 342, noted Klemens (1985) *Journal of Law and Commerce* 505.

L21/71; [1990] 4 CMLR 930),[37] the Commission held that a ban on simple resale of a raw material contravened Article 85. On the other hand, there is some support in the case-law for allowing different channels of distribution[38] so it may be that Article 85 could be avoided provided VARs were free to deal between themselves in the product but it would be dangerous to assume this. Article 85 would catch customer allocation.[39]

(f) Franchising

One of the few Commission decisions on transactions in the IT industry concerned the Computerland franchise (OJ 1987 L 222/12). This was one of the decisions from which the Commission gained the necessary experience to adopt Regulation 4087/88, the block exemption for distribution franchises (OJ 1988 L359/46). **3.87**

The Computerland franchisees sell numerous different brands of microcomputer products (hardware, software and peripheral products). In 1986, there were 85 stores in the Community covering all but one Member State but representing less than 1% of the 10,000 authorised microcomputer dealers in Western Europe. The largest market share in any one Member State was only about 4%. Nonetheless, the Commission held that the franchise agreement was caught by Article 85. Following the judgment of the ECJ in *Pronuptia* (Case 161/84 [1986] ECR 353; [1986] 1 CMLR 414), the Commission held that provisions in the franchise agreement designed to control the know-how and other assistance provided to the franchisee did not fall within Article 85. On the other hand, the restrictions on opening further stores and on sales to anyone except end-users and other franchisees brought the agreement within Article 85(1). These restrictions on competition within the network were, however, exempted because the Computerland system improved the distribution of microcomputer products and the restrictions were necessary to protect the franchisee's investment and to channel their efforts into retail sales. **3.88**

(vii) **Sale**

Simple sale agreements can fall within Article 85 provided the agreement has sufficient impact on competition and trade between Member States (*SVCB* v *Kerpen & Kerpen* Case 319/82 [1983] ECR 4173; [1985] 1 CMLR 511). **3.89**

One common practice in the IT field is to supply a product with a number of attachments whether software or hardware. Does this raise a problem under EC competition law? The question is whether such a practice would be considered to be an illegal tie. A tie is where the supplier requires the purchaser of one product (tying product) to take another product (tied product). Traditionally, the principal concern over a tie was that, if the supplier had **3.90**

---

[37] On appeal to CFI *Bayer* v *Commission* Case T-12/90 [1991] ECR II-219; [1993] 4 CMLR 30 and on appeal to ECJ Case C-195/91P.
[38] See, *e.g.*, *Villeroy & Boch* OJ 1985 L376/15; [1988] 2 CMLR 461. See also Vajda, *The Application of Community Competition Law to the Distribution of Computer Products and Parts* (1992) ECLR 110 at 115.
[39] *Cf.* Guidelines (OJ 1984 C101/2) para 29.

power in the market for the tying product, this power could be transferred to the market for the tied product and would allow the supplier to reap monopoly profits from another market. The concern over "leverage" has been criticised although, in certain cases, tying can cause concern if it creates barriers to entry, forecloses the market or enables the supplier to price discriminate.[40] What is clear is that many ties are efficient. No one would think it right to require a shoe manufacturer to sell right and left shoes separately for the occasion when a customer wanted a single shoe. The cost of making individual shoes available for the occasional customer would increase the price of the shoes for everyone else.

3.91　　What is the position under EC competition law? Both Articles 85 and 86 refer expressly to ties and have been so applied.[41] The key problem in advising on the legality of ties in the IT industry is that it is not clear if, and to what extent, the Commission and, indeed, the ECJ have accepted the criticisms described in the previous paragraph. Nonetheless, it is generally accepted that the supplier must have market power in the tying product market. Tying allegations often relate to aftermarkets, for example, tying maintenance to spare parts. These issues are discussed in Chapter 5 (see para **5.38** *et seq*); suffice to point out at this stage that there is an argument that competition in the primary market will constrain the supplier from deriving any monopoly profit from the aftermarket.

3.92　　The classic example of an allegation of a tie with the IT industry is the IBM case. As we have seen, the Commission alleged that IBM was dominant in the market for System/370 compatible computers.[42] One of the Commission's allegations was that IBM had abused that dominant position by supplying CPUs together with main memory (so-called "memory bundling"). In the settlement of the proceedings IBM undertook:

> "Without prejudice to IBM's freedom to design its CPUs, upon the announcement of a new System/370 CPU which is to be supplied within the EEC, IBM will offer within the EEC and, upon application of a customer, will supply that CPU at IBM's option either without any main memory capacity or with only such capacity of main memory as is strictly required in order that reasonable tests of the CPU can be effected. IBM reserves the right to offer any System/370 CPU with main memory in such other capacity or increments thereto as IBM may determine." ([1984] 3 CMLR 147 at 153)

3.93　　So far as end-user sales are concerned, the *Tetra Pak II* case[43] may contain lessons for the IT industry. The Commission imposed a record fine on Tetra Pak which was found to be dominant on the market for aseptic packaging machines as well as having a strong position on the market for non-aseptic

---

[40] See, *e.g.*, Bowman, *Tying Arrangements and the Leverage Problem* (1957) Yale LJ 19.
[41] For an example of the application of Art 85, see *Vaessen/Moris* OJ 1979 L19/32; [1979] 1 CMLR 511. There are a number of cases on the application of Art 86, *e.g.*, *Tetra Pak II* OJ 1992 L72/1; [1992] 4 CMLR 551. On appeal to CFI Case T-83/91 *Tetra Pak v Commission*.
[42] See *IBM v Commission* Case 60/81 [1981] ECR 2639 at 2642.
[43] OJ 1992 L72/1; [1992] 4 CMLR 551. On appeal to CFI Case T-83/91 *Tetra Pak v Commission*.

packaging machines. The Commission condemned customer obligations which were not connected to the purchase and, indeed, were inconsistent with a sale such as a prohibition on adding accessory equipment to the original machine, a prohibition on modifying the machine, a prohibition on moving the machine and the obligation to obtain Tetra Pak's consent to sale. The Commission also condemned a number of ties such as the obligation to obtain spare parts, cartons and maintenance services from Tetra Pak (paras 107 and 123). It added that even the free supply of maintenance services was an abuse of Article 86 because "the client has no right to refuse the services offered by Tetra Pak even though he owns the machine" (paras 108, 109 and 116 et seq.)

(viii) **Leasing**

There are two points which should be made in relation to leasing. First, it is of **3.94** course permissible to impose additional obligations in a lease agreement to protect the product. On the other hand, if additional obligations are imposed, the Commission will investigate to ensure that, in economic terms, the arrangement is a lease rather than a sale. It is worth quoting in full a paragraph of the Commission's decision in *Tetra Pak II* which covers both these points:

> "The clauses intended to ensure respect for the machine's integrity form part of the attribution of ownership and do not therefore in themselves constitute abuses within the meaning of Article 86 when they are imposed on a leaseholder by an undertaking in a dominant position. In the case in hand, however, any assessment of these clauses in relation to Article 86 must also take account of the clauses on rental payments, or else those concerning the term of the lease (Italy), which in fact make leasing equivalent in economic terms to sale. To this extent, Tetra Pak is guilty of an abuse in maintaining ownership rights whilst, in economic terms, it must be considered that it relinquishes its property to the leaseholder because the latter must pay an amount not only equivalent to almost all present and future rental payments combined but moreover roughly the same as, and sometimes even higher than, selling prices" (para 131).

These comments are equally applicable to the IT hardware industry, although **3.95** there is always the argument that the supplier is not dominant in the first place.

(ix) **Pricing**

The application of competition rules to pricing in the IT industry raises **3.96** complex issues. The principles, though, are essentially the same as those applicable in other sectors. Further, there are no Commission or ECJ decisions on pricing in the IT hardware field. Pricing has raised specific questions for the software industry and for telecoms (see para **4.94** *et seq* and para **6.52** *et seq*).

Chapter 4
Software

1. Introduction

The previous chapter on hardware demonstrates that the IT industry does **4.1**
raise specific issues for the application of the EC Treaty's basic rules as well as
creating a need for specific Community legislation, albeit in that case in
response to moves in the US. The software side of the industry is no different.
The unique characteristics of software combined with its economic importance have prompted the Community to legislate. The application of
competition rules also raises difficult, specific issues. One futher issue is the
impact which Community legislation may have on the application of
competition rules.

2. Harmonisation legislation

(i) Software Directive[1]

The Software Directive must occupy a central position in a work devoted to **4.2**
EC information technology law. Not only will it have a significant impact on
industry practices but it is also the first Directive to be adopted on the basis of
the Commission's Green Paper on Copyright and the Challenge of Technology (COM(88) 172 of 7 June 1988). The importance of the Software Directive
is reflected in the unprecedented scale of lobbying of Community institutions
during the legislative procedure and in the growing number of works devoted
to the Directive and its implications both at a Community and a national
level.[2] The current state of incorporation of the Directive into national law is
summarised in a table at the end of this chapter.

(a) Background

The basic aim of the Directive was to resolve the debate in the Community **4.3**
over the nature of protection to be accorded to software. This was not a
straightforward issue. Patents do not protect much software, not least because
it is not usually sufficiently inventive. Nevertheless, vast amounts of time and
resources may be required to produce software; yet not only can software be

---

[1] Council Dir 91/250 on the legal protection of computer programs (OJ 1991 L122/42). See Appendix
A4.
[2] See, *e.g.*, Czarnota & Hart, *Legal Protection of Computer Programs in Europe* (Butterworths, 1991) and
Lehmann & Tapper, Eds, *A Handbook of European Software Law* (Clarendon Press, 1993, looseleaf).

cheaply and easily copied but the copies are as good as the original. Software piracy is a major concern in the industry. Estimates put the lost value of the black market in billions of US dollars.[3] If piracy were to be outlawed, copyright seemed to many the appropriate form of protection. In any event, software actually looks like one of the traditional subjects of copyright protection, a literary work, at least when the software is represented in human readable form.

4.4   Opting for copyright protection was not the end of the story. Questions then had to be answered over the extent of copyright protection. Firstly, software is different in nature to many works protected by copyright. In particular, unlike a book, it is often purely functional. Moreover, software often incorporates code to connect to other software or hardware. Should copyright protection be limited in order to prevent control over the development of interconnecting products? Secondly, there is a well developed international system of copyright protection. Was it appropriate to comply with the rules laid down in that system in order to avoid the effort which would be required to set up another international system specifically devoted to software?

4.5   At this early stage, naturally, there is still a lot of speculation over the interpretation of the Directive. This uncertainty can only be resolved finally by guidance from the ECJ which is unlikely to be forthcoming for many years.

(b) Computer programs

4.6   Although commonly referred to as the Software Directive, in fact, the Directive covers the protection of "computer programs" and does not extend to the materials which invariably accompany programs such as manuals. Those materials may, of course, benefit from protection under other provisions of national law.

4.7   The term "computer program" is not defined. The Commission considered in its Green Paper that enacting a definition would carry the risk of failing to cover future technological advances.[4] The Green Paper put forward a simple working definition: "A computer program is a set of instructions the purpose of which is to cause an information processing device, a computer, to perform its functions."[5] Clearly, this is a broad definition. It is very similar to the definition in the US Copyright Act.[6]

4.8   Article 1(2) confirms that the Directive applies to computer programs regardless of the form in which they are expressed. The Recitals add that this includes programs incorporated into hardware which would include so-called "firmware" (see para **2.5**).

4.9   Article 1(1) provides that the term "computer program" does include preparatory design material although the Recitals add the condition that the

---

[3] *Computer Weekly* 14 April 1994, 88.
[4] See Explanatory Memorandum to the original proposal (COM(88) 816 of 5 January 1989), para 1.1.
[5] Green Paper on Copyright and the Challenge of Technology (COM(88) 172 of 7 June 1988), para. 5.1.1 170.
[6] "A 'computer program' is a set of statements or instructions to be used directly or indirectly in a computer in order to bring about a certain result" s 101, US Copyright Act.

materials must be such that a computer program can result at a later stage. It is important to bear in mind the inclusion of preparatory material when analysing the Directive's provisions.

(c) Nature of protection

The key issue which the Directive had to resolve was the nature of the **4.10** intellectual property rights (IPRs) which should attach to programs. Under the European Patent Convention, patent protection is not available for programs "as such",[7] although a patent can extend to programs which have a technical impact on the functioning of hardware provided they are sufficiently inventive. This excludes most software from patent protection.[8] The importance of patent protection in some cases is demonstrated by the successful claim in the US by Stacker against Microsoft for infringement of a patent covering data compression software. The court awarded Stacker damages of US$ 120m on this claim.[9]

The alternative to patent protection was protection either by copyright or **4.11** by a similar specific right. In choosing between protection by an existing intellectual property right, such as copyright, and devising a new *sui generis* right, one factor was the international position. Trade in software could be hampered if countries did not extend national intellectual property protection to foreign authors. Copyright is the subject of an international system based on the Berne Convention which dates back to 1886.[10] The Convention has developed over the last 100 years, most recently with the Paris Revision of 1971, and there are now more than 100 countries which are party to the Convention.[11] It is administered by the World Intellectual Property Organisation (WIPO).

The Convention requires parties to establish copyright protection for **4.12** "literary and artistic works" and lays down certain criteria with which that protection must comply. National copyright protection must extend to nationals and residents of other signatory States as well as to authors of works first published in a signatory State. Thus, the two basic principles underlying the Berne Convention are, on the one hand, relatively stringent conditions governing national copyright law and, on the other hand, national treatment. Some countries were not willing to change their law to comply with the conditions laid down in the Convention, for example, the US did not become a party until 1989. As a result, UNESCO sponsored another less demanding multilateral treaty, the Universal Copyright Convention (UCC).

There are doubts whether computer programs fall within the definition of **4.13** literary works in the Berne Convention. Even if they do not, protecting

---

[7] Art 52 of the Convention.
[8] See, *e.g.*, Sherman (1991) EIPR 85 and Von Hellfeld (1993) CL&P 18.
[9] *Computer Weekly* 3 March 1994, 12. Noted Vinje (1994) EIPR 364.
[10] For an introduction, see Cornish, *Intellectual Property* (Sweet & Maxwell, 1989, 2nd ed), 249 *et seq*. For more detail, see Ricketson, *The Berne Convention on the Protection of Literary and Artistic Property: 1886-1986* (Kluwer, 1987).
[11] A Council Resolution notes that Member States which are not yet party to the Paris Revision have undertaken to become parties by 1 January 1995 (OJ 1992 C138/1).

computer programs by copyright which complied with the Convention would inevitably facilitate international accord. The drawback with this approach was that the Berne Convention was not drafted with computer programs in mind and its provisions might constrain choice on the scope of protection. Thus, the duration of protection of at least 50 years after the author's death might seem excessive. In addition, the Convention limits the extent to which protection can be qualified. Article 9(1) establishes the exclusive right to control reproduction. Article 9(2) adds:

> "It shall be a matter for legislation in the countries of the Union to permit the reproduction of such works in special cases, provided that such reproduction does not conflict with a normal exploitation of the work and does not unreasonably prejudice the legitimate interests of the author."

4.14 If the conditions laid down by the Berne Convention were not followed, there would certainly have been greater freedom to deal with the special problems to which computer programs give rise. On the other hand, there would have been no existing international system to tap into. The issue would then arise whether the legislation establishing a *sui generis* right should grant national treatment or whether protection for foreigners should be dependent on their home country establishing reciprocal protection. This was the approach taken by the US in its 1984 legislation on protection for semiconductor chips (see para **3.8**). It is also the position proposed for the unfair extraction right in the draft Database Directive (see para **5.23** *et seq*).

4.15 Following trends both in the Member States[12] as well as further afield,[13] the Directive opted for the copyright approach. Thus, Article 1 states that computer programs shall be protected "as literary works within the meaning of the Berne Convention." Of course, EC law cannot amend the Convention and it remains to be seen whether computer programs are, in fact, within the Convention. Steps are now under way within WIPO to negotiate a protocol under Article 20 of the Berne Convention which would deal with the question of computer programs. Moreover, the Uruguay Round Agreement on Trade Related Aspects of Intellectual Property Rights (TRIPs) states that "Computer programs, whether in source or object code, shall be protected as literary works under the Berne Convention (1971)" (Art 10).

There is an equivalent provision in TRIPs to Article 9(2) of the Berne Convention (Art 13).

4.16 One issue that had led to a different approach in Member State law was the extent to which a program had to be original to benefit from protection. Under UK law, this is set at a comparatively low level—a work is original if it is not a copy. By contrast, the requirement was held to be at a much higher level in Germany.[14] The Directive opts for a low requirement. Article 1(3) states that

---

[12] In 1985, Germany, France and the UK had all introduced legislation confirming that programs would benefit from copyright protection: Green Paper para 5.3.9, 178 and the Explanatory Memorandum to the original proposal (COM(88) 816 of 5 January 1989), para 2.9.

[13] *e.g.*, in 1980, US law had been altered to confirm copyright protection for computer programs.

[14] See Lehmann, *The Legal Protection of Computer Programs: A Summary of the Present Situation* (1988) IIC 473 discussing, in particular, the judgment of the Federal Supreme Court in *Inkasso-Programm* Case No IZR 52/83 1985 GRUR 1041.

the only requirement for protection is for the program to be "original in the sense that it is the author's own intellectual creation". The Recitals add that "no tests as to the qualitative or aesthetic merits of the program should be applied". By Article 9(2), this test applies to existing programs, although "without prejudice to any acts concluded and rights acquired before that date." It remains to be seen how this qualification will be applied but Article 9 will protect programs which did not benefit from protection in Germany as a result of the level of originality required by national law.

One important point is that the Directive specifically preserves the right for Member States to provide protection for computer programs by other means. This saving for protection through, for example, trade secrets law may undermine the Directive in certain respects since software licences sometimes impose confidentiality obligations, if not for object code then invariably for source code.

4.17

(d) Beneficiaries of protection

Article 3 refers to national law to determine the beneficiaries of protection. Since all Member States are parties to the Berne Convention, the beneficiary will be the author of the computer program. Article 2, in turn, states that the author will be the natural person who created the program. There are some further issues. Firstly, the Directive does not deal with the increasingly common situation where a computer itself generates a work, for example, using fourth generation languages. It follows that this must be a question for national law provided that the national approach is compatible with the Directive's requirement that the natural person "creates" the program.[15]

4.18

Secondly, it is common nowadays in the light of the complexity of many software products for a team of programmers to be involved in designing and writing a program. It is possible that a programmer will write an original work individually which is then incorporated into the final product. However, if a work is genuinely created by more than one person, Article 2(2) provides that the rights will be held jointly.

4.19

Thirdly, again, it may well be that programmers will be employed. Article 2(3) seems to provide that the copyright vests in the employer. If the employer is a company, by Article 2(1), it is a question of national law whether a legal person can hold copyright. Moral rights, where they exist, will vest in the employee. The application of these provisions may have an impact on the duration of protection laid down in Article 8.

4.20

(e) Scope of protection

Many of the difficult questions of interpretation will no doubt focus on the complicated provisions dealing with the extent to which the owner of copyright in a program can control the exploitation of that program. Essentially, Article 4 describes the acts which the owner of the copyright has

4.21

---

[15] The UK Copyright (Computer Program) Regs 1992 implementing the Directive have not amended the Copyright, Designs and Patents 1988, s 9(3), which grants copyright in computer-generated works to "the person by whom the arrangements necessary for the creation of the work are undertaken".

the exclusive right to control. These rights are subject to the qualifications set out in Article 5 as well as the highly complex Article 6. A number of issues arise:

(a) Running

4.22 Unlike most copyright works, the use of a computer program may involve copying the program without a separate work being available for sale. Thus, reading a book clearly does not involve the creation of a second copy. However, in order to run a program, a computer may well have to reproduce in a temporary memory (or RAM) part or all of the program actually recorded in a more permanent form on another medium such as on hard disk or on a diskette. Is this form of copying an infringing act requiring the consent of the copyright holder? The Directive does not resolve this issue. It does say that temporary reproduction is a restricted act and that, if running does necessitate reproduction, this will be a restricted act (Art 4(a)). Is the answer to this question important? At first sight, it seems not because Article 5(1) does allow such an act if "necessary for use of the computer program by the lawful acquirer in accordance with its intended purpose, including for error correction." It would seem, then, that the question whether running is a restricted act would appear to be academic. The position may not be so straightforward. Article 5(1) is expressed to be subject to "specific contractual provisions." Not only does this seem inconsistent with the purpose of the remainder of Article 5(1) but Recital 18 also states clearly that the running of a program and error correction "may not be prohibited by contract." It may be that this Recital could be relied on by the ECJ to confine the right to vary the position by contract to the other acts referred to in Article 5(1). One difficulty with this approach is that it appears to conflict with the anti-avoidance provision in Article 9(1) which does not refer to Article 5(1). Moreover, even if contractual restriction is not permitted, a licensor may well be able to draft licence terms to define restrictively the intended purpose referred to in Article 5(1). The end result seems to be that a licensor will be able to rely on copyright to restrict the use of a program, for example, to a single CPU or site.

(b) Maintenance

4.23 The position as to maintenance is similarly unclear. Article 5(1) allows error correction but again only if this is necessary in accordance with the program's intended purpose and subject to specific contractual provision. It is important to note that the common definition of maintenance includes more than just error correction and would normally include software enhancement and upgrade. The Directive seems to leave a large measure of control here in the hands of the licensor. This may have an impact on the application of the competition rules (see para **4.91**).

(c) Non-literal copying

4.24 Straightforward copying of a program is, of course, a restricted act requiring the consent of the rightholder. More difficult is the question whether a new program can be written which performs a similar function to the original program without infringing the copyright in the original program. This question can have enormous practical significance. If a software product becomes successful, it may well be difficult for a competing product to establish a market position without a certain degree of similarity to the successful product.

There have been a number of cases in the US on this question. The starting **4.25** point in US law is their Copyright Act which draws a distinction between ideas (which are not capable of protection) and expression (which is capable of copyright protection) (s 102 (b)). This distinction can be criticised on the basis that it does not itself provide an answer but only an *ex post* justification. Whatever the merits of the distinction, it is clear that it gives a large measure of discretion to the court in determining the extent of copyright protection.

By according a particularly narrow scope to the concept of idea, one US **4.26** court went so far as to hold that copyright extended to a program's "structure, sequence and organisation" (*Whelan* v *Jaslow* [1987] FSR 1). Subsequent cases in the US have taken different and more narrow approaches to the scope of copyright protection.[16] However, some courts are still reaching the conclusion that copyright can extend to non-literal elements such as the user interface. For example, in 1992, in *Lotus Development* v *Borland*,[17] a court accepted copyright could extend to certain aspects of the graphical user interface (GUI) of the well-known spreadsheet program, Lotus 1-2-3.

The Directive follows the US approach inasmuch as Article 1(2) states that **4.27** ideas and principles are not protected by the Directive. However, the fact that the Directive incorporates the idea/expression dichotomy does not necessarily mean that a Member State court or, indeed, the ECJ would follow decisions of US courts on the scope of copyright protection against non-literal copying. In one recent case in the UK, the judge expressly doubted the usefulness in this context of comparisons from abroad (*Ibcos Computers* v *Barclays Mercantile* (1994) FSR 274 at 302). What is clear, though, is that the extent of copyright protection has an impact on competition. There is no doubt that exclusive rights over a popular user interface can hinder the entry of other products. Those who become used to the Lotus 1-2-3 GUI may be less likely to move to a product which has a different interface. A number of commentators have suggested that the (protected) expression of a computer program should be limited given its functional characteristics.[18] It is argued that this can be achieved by use of traditional principles of copyright law. It will be for the courts to resolve the issue in interpreting the Software Directive. As in the US, we can expect a lot of disagreement over a number of years before the issue is resolved. On this particular issue, we can only wait and see.

This debate is another example of the difficulties involved in balancing **4.28** intellectual property against competition. On the one hand, we want to encourage firms to bring new products to the market, including improved user interfaces. On the other hand, we do not want this to stifle competition

---

[16] In particular, *Computer Associates* v *Altai* 23 USPQ 2d 1241 (2nd Cir 1992).

[17] 799 F Supp 203 (Dt Mass 1992). On appeal to the First Circuit Court of Appeals (No. 93-2214).

[18] See, *e.g.*, Karjala, *Recent United States and International Development in Software Protection* (1994) EIPR 13 (Part 1) and 58 (Part 2).

excessively. Should the balance of intellectual property protection involved in legislation and, in this case, its interpretation, be the final word? If a user interface, for example, does become so popular that the supplier is dominant in that market, one way to deal with the problem would be to require that interface to be licensed to third party competitors. The extent to which EC competition law can apply to require software to be licensed is discussed later in this chapter (see para **4.62** *et seq*).

(d) Decompilation right

4.29   As in the case of non-literal copying, the extent to which a user can decompile a computer program can have significant consequences for competition. Unlike non-literal copying, this issue is dealt with in some detail in the Directive. The Commission's original proposal left the issue for resolution by competition law alone and, in fact, the Commission appended to its original proposal its thoughts on the application of EC competition rules.[19] Following lobbying on an unprecedented scale of both the Community institutions as well as national governments, the European Parliament proposed an amendment dealing with the question of decompilation and the final version of the Directive incorporates a complex provision on the issue.

4.30   An understanding of this aspect of the Directive is not possible without a basic understanding of the technical aspects. A computer program is worth nothing unless it makes something else work. Indeed, the very definition of a program requires it to "cause an information processing device, a computer, to perform it's functions."[20] Just as important nowadays is that programs have to be able to talk to other programs. It is more efficient to have a set of programs which controls the hardware—the operating system software—while the user's specific needs are fulfilled by other software—applications software—which interacts with the operating system when it wants the hardware to do something. The links between software, on the one hand, and other software or hardware, on the other, are known as technical interfaces. As we have seen, there is a second type of interface between the applications program and the human operator - the user interface.

4.31   The following diagram shows the interfaces in a typical word processing package running on a microcomputer:

UI: User Interface

TI: Technical Interface

---

[19] Commission conclusions on the occasion of the adoption of the Commission's proposal for a Council Directive on the legal protection of computer programs (OJ 1989 C91/16). See Appendix A5.

[20] This is the working definition in the Green Paper on Copyright (COM (88) 172 of 7 June 1988) para. 5.1.1, 170. There is no definition in the Directive itself.

In the same way that the screen display and user interface must be in a   **4.32**
language and format which the user can understand, so the software and
hardware must talk to each other according to the same rules in order to
function together as intended. If these rules are in some way protected by
copyright, it may be possible for the owner of that copyright to control the
creation of software and hardware which interfaces with that owner's product.
In other words, in the above diagram, if the supplier of the operating system
held copyright which protected the technical interface between the operating
system and the word processing package, that supplier might be able to control
the market for word processing packages which work with that operating
system. The operating system supplier would also be able to stop third parties
from creating other operating systems which interfaced in the same way as its
own. This raises the spectre of copyright extending so far as to stifle
competition excessively.

Two observations are worth making at this stage. Firstly, control over an   **4.33**
interface is only important from the point of view of competition if the interface
is used by software with an appreciable share of the market. There is no market
strength if no-one is interested in the principal product! The second point is
that it may be disputed whether control over the interface does give real
market power in practice. It could be argued that those who want to achieve a
strong market position will be forced to allow third parties to use the relevant
interfaces. In other words, a strong market position may only have been
achieved by an open interface licence system. It is interesting to note that the
Commission has described Microsoft's operating system MS-DOS as an open
system.[21] This does not mean that there is no ownership of the relevant
interfaces but rather that the interfaces have been made widely available to
ensure the supply of a wide range of applications software which works with
MS-DOS. It is this range of applications software which has contributed to the
incredible success of MS-DOS as an operating system.

If the technical issues on interfaces are difficult, what of the legal position?   **4.34**
The first issue which arises is whether copyright in a program extends to the
interface. A further distinction has to be made at this stage. An interface will be
reflected in program code because the way in which that code is written will be
determined by the interface rules or specification. For example, the interface
specification might state that data must be sent at a particular speed or to a
particular place. The interface specification does not necessarily have to
dictate the actual code which is required to implement the interface.

Article 1(2) of the EC Directive states that "Ideas and principles which   **4.35**
underlie any element of a computer program, including those which underlie
its interfaces, are not protected by copyright under this Directive."

It can be argued that this means that the interface specification is not
protected by copyright. What about the code that implements that specification? Although this could be argued to be expression of an idea, it can also be
argued that a further rule applies—the "merger doctrine"—which denies

---

[21] In its decision approving the IBM France/CGI merger (Case IV.M336).

copyright protection for expression when that expression is the only way to express an idea. It follows that, if an interface specification can only be implemented by code in one way, then it is not protected by copyright because of the merger doctrine. At this stage, it is not clear how the Software Directive will be interpreted on this point.[22]

4.36   Even if the interface is not protected by copyright, there is a second legal issue which results from another peculiar feature of software. Software is traditionally written in human-readable code ("source code"). This code is not generally included in the software licensed to a customer. Rather, the source code is "compiled" into machine-readable code ("object code") which is recorded on a medium such as a diskette before being released to the public. It may well be that a third party cannot obtain access to the interface without decompiling the licensed object code into human-readable source code. The legal issue that arises is whether this act of decompilation may amount to a translation of the original (or target) program thereby infringing copyright in the target program.[23]

4.37   It follows that (in one way or another) the owner of copyright in a computer program may have the right to control the use of any technical interfaces whether by stopping access to the interface or use of it. As we have seen, this raises important issues of both intellectual property and competition law. How is the issue dealt with by the Software Directive?

4.38   Article 6 establishes an exception from the restricted acts listed in Article 4. Essentially, a lawful user has a right to obtain and use interface information for use in the creation of an independent program. This decompilation right cannot be excluded by contract (Art 9(1)). However, the right is hedged about with a number of important checks and balances. Firstly, there is no right to decompile where the information necessary to achieve interoperability is readily available (Art 6(1)(a)). In other words, a software supplier can effectively remove the right to decompile by making the interface information available. The Directive does not say whether payment can be demanded by the supplier of the interface information. In the settlement of the *IBM* case, IBM reserved the right to charge a licence fee or royalty as well as to require payment for reasonable costs of reproduction and dissemination of information.[24] This suggests that it would at least be open to the provider of information under Article 6 to require reasonable compensation for the cost of providing the information.

4.39   Secondly, the program which results from the use of interface information obtained must not infringe copyright (Art 6(2)(c)). This means that, if copyright does extend to the interface code, use of that code could infringe copyright in the target program. The way in which the courts approach

---

[22] See, *e.g.*, Karjala, *Copyright Protection in the United States and Japan Part 1* (1991) EIPR 195 at 199 but see Sherwood-Edwards, *Seven Degrees of Separation: the Software Directive and UK Implementation* (1993) CL&P 169 at 173.

[23] The restricted acts listed in Art 4(b) include "translation, adaptation, arrangement and any other alteration of a computer program".

[24] Paras 4 and 7 of Appendix B to IBM's undertaking [1984] 3 CMLR 147 at 161.

copyright protection for interfaces, for example, their approach to the merger doctrine, will determine to a large extent how the decompilation right will operate in practice.

Thirdly, the right is limited to those parts of the program necessary to achieve interoperability (Art 6(1)(c)). This would not stop the use of the information to prepare a competing product but, as we have seen, the competing product must not infringe copyright in the target product. Again, the extent to which a competing product can emulate the user interface will depend on how the courts approach the extent of copyright protection. **4.40**

Fourthly, Article 6(2)(a) provides that information obtained under Article 6 can only be used "to achieve the interoperability of the independently created computer program." At first sight, this might suggest that Article 6 cannot be relied upon in order to design hardware which interfaces with the target program. On the other hand, the relevant Recitals refer to interfaces between software and both other software and hardware. It is likely that the Directive will be interpreted in line with the Recitals. Article 1 states that computer programs are protected under the Directive regardless of their form and the Recitals confirm that this would include a program incorporated into hardware. This definition seems wide enough to cover the configuration of hardware. If so, there would be no reason why the decompilation right should not be available to decompile a program whenever necessary for the purposes of interoperability and whether the information is obtained to design hardware or software.[25] If the right were held not to be available to a hardware designer in these circumstances, there may be an argument that the competition rules could be relied upon. Reliance on competition rules for the purposes of decompilation is discussed further on in this chapter (see para **4.62** *et seq*). **4.41**

The limit set out in Article 6(2)(a) does make it clear that the decompilation right is not available for the purpose of maintaining software. Again, the key question here is whether competition law can be relied on to make up for the limited right in the Directive. This is discussed in Chapter 5 (see para **5.45** *et seq*). **4.42**

Finally, Article 6(3) contains an overriding limitation included to ensure that the Directive is consistent with Article 9(2) of the Berne Convention (see para **4.13**). It is difficult to predict how a court would approach this qualification to Article 6 given the delicate process which is already explicit in its terms.[26] **4.43**

The decompilation right is a fascinating example of the difficulties inherent in fashioning an IPR so that adequate protection is granted to encourage investment whilst not hindering competition. One way to conduct this balance is by specific qualification to the legislation. It is interesting to note that other jurisdictions may reach a similar position through reliance on the traditional **4.44**

---

[25] The same conclusion seems to be reached in Czarnota & Hart, *Legal Protection of Computer Programs in Europe* (Butterworths, 1991) 85.
[26] See Cornish, *Computer Program Copyright and the Berne Convention* in Lehmann & Tapper, Eds, *A Handbook of European Software Law* (Clarendon Press, 1993, looseleaf) 199.

principles of copyright. For example, in *Sega Enterprises* v *Accolade* (977 F.2d 1510 (9th Cir. 1992)), the US Court of Appeals (Ninth Circuit) concluded that:

> "...where disassembly is the only way to gain access to the ideas and functional elements embodied in a copyrighted computer program and where there is a legitimate reason for seeking such access, disassembly is a fair use of the copyrighted work, as a matter of law. Our conclusion does not, of course, insulate Accolade from a claim of copyright infringement with respect to its finished product" (at 1527).

4.45   Thus, the court relied on the traditional common law doctrine of fair use[27] to permit decompilation subject to conditions which are similar to those laid out in the Software Directive. It is also worth noting that the requirement in TRIPs to protect computer programs as literary works under the Berne Convention does not mention decompilation. Presumably, such a right can be justified on the basis of Article 9(2) of the Berne Convention (see para **4.13**).

(e) Secondary infringement

4.46   Perhaps the least controversial (but, in practice, the most important) aspect of copyright protection is the need for adequate remedies against straightforward copying and piracy. Article 7 requires Member States to provide "appropriate remedies" for possession or marketing of an infringing copy if the offender knew or had reason to believe that it was an infringing copy. Article 7 also covers the sale of devices to circumvent software copy protection.

(f) Exhaustion of rights

4.47   Even before the Directive was adopted, Article 30 prevented reliance on national copyright law to stop the import of a product marketed in another Member State by the copyright holder or with his consent (see para **2.59** *et seq*). The Software Directive now requires Member States to incorporate this position in national law. Once implemented, there should no longer be a need to rely on Article 30. One particular difficulty over Article 4(c) is what the Directive means by sale. Since copyright in computer programs marketed to the public is invariably licensed rather than sold, Article 4(c) will presumably apply when the medium on which the program is recorded is sold. This seems to follow from the ECJ's judgment in *Warner Bros* v *Christiansen* (Case 158/86 [1988] ECR 2605; [1990] 3 CMLR 684) (see para **2.64**) where Article 30 was considered in principle to be applicable to the import of a video.

4.48   As we have seen, the ECJ in the *Warner Bros* case held that Article 30 did not stop reliance on a rental right even where the product had been sold in a Member State where no such rental right existed. Article 4(c) now establishes such a right for computer programs. The Rental Right Directive does not affect the operation of Article 4(c).[28]

---

27 Now embodied in s 107 Copyright Act 1976
28 Council Dir 92/100 on rental right and lending right and on certain rights related to copyright in the field of intellectual property (OJ 1992 L346/61) Art 3.

If software is not sold, the question whether IPRs are exhausted will depend **4.49** on the application of the principles in the ECJ's judgment in *Coditel I* (*Coditel* v *Ciné Vog* Case 62/79 [1980] ECR 881; [1981] 2 CMLR 362) (see para **2.71**).

(f) Duration of protection

Article 8 of the Directive lays down a term of copyright protection of 50 years **4.50** from the end of the year in which the author dies or the year in which the program is first marketed in the case of anonymous or pseudonymous works or where the author is a legal person. When the Duration Directive comes into force, the original Article 8 will be repealed and, instead, the term of protection will be based on a period of 70 years.[29]

(g) Effect on national law

Article 10 of the Directive requires Member States to implement the Directive **4.51** by the end of 1992. The current state of implementation is summarised in the table at the end of this chapter. The Directive gives some options to Member States in implementing the Directive.[30] Moreover, there are a number of difficult questions of interpretation which can only be finally resolved by the ECJ. What is the position if the Directive is incorrectly implemented? The first point is that the Commission has the power under Article 169 to take proceedings before the ECJ for a declaration that a Member State has not implemented the Directive properly. If the Member State does not comply with the ECJ's judgment, Article 171 (as amended by the TEU) now gives the ECJ power to fine that Member State.

But can an individual rely on the terms of the Directive before a national **4.52** court before the Directive has been properly implemented? This would only be possible as against a Member State which is relying on provisions of national law which are inconsistent with the Directive. However, the ECJ has recently recognised the possibility of claiming damages against a Member State if loss is suffered as a result of failure to implement a directive (see para **2.48**).

(h) Appraisal

The Software Directive is very significant for EC information technology law **4.53** and, consequently, for the industry itself. The success of the Directive in creating a level playing field in the Community will depend on proper implementation at a national level as well as consistent interpretation by national courts. This may require guidance from the ECJ and it could be years before such guidance is given. One fascinating aspect of the Directive is the way in which the authors have sought to comply with international agreement on copyright protection whilst ensuring that intellectual property protection cannot be relied on to stifle competition excessively. The arguments over the decompilation right illustrate the difficulties inherent in the need to balance

---

[29] Council Dir 93/98 on the term of protection of copyright and certain related rights (OJ 1993 L290/9) Art 11.
[30] See, *e.g.*, Art 2(1) on whether a legal person can hold copyright and Art 7(3) on seizure for secondary infringement.

competition against the exclusivity of IPRs. These issues are closely tied up with the application of competition law. The effect of the Software Directive on the application of competition law is discussed in the next section of this chapter as well as in Chapter 5 (see para **5.45** *et seq*).

3. Competition law issues

(i) Introduction

4.54 One of the most important recent events for the application of competition law to the software industry was the settlement of the investigation of Microsoft by both the US Department of Justice (DoJ) and the European Commission. Complaints were originally made to the Federal Trade Commission (FTC) about certain practices, in particular, the obligation on PC manufacturers to pay for a copy of Microsoft's operating system, MS-DOS, for each PC supplied, whether or not that manufacturer had in fact loaded MS-DOS on that PC. The FTC could not agree on whether to take action and, in August 1993, the DoJ took over the investigation. In June 1993, Novell complained to the European Commission about Microsoft's practices. On 15 July 1994 both these investigations were settled by undertakings in similar form given by Microsoft both to the DoJ and to the European Commission.[31]

4.55 The Commission made the following comment on the settlement:

> "This undertaking is very significant at least in two respects. It is the most important case in the software industry until now. It opens up the market for the operating system software which is at the heart of the estimated 150 million computers in use worldwide and is of strategic importance to the development of some of the fastest growing sectors of the Information Technology industries. Furthermore, the negotiation of the undertaking was a historic and unprecedented piece of co-operation between the EC Commission and the United States Department of Justice. It serves as an important model for the future, as it shows how the two authorities can combine their efforts to deal effectively with giant multinational companies. The success of this joint approach sends a strong signal to all multinational companies, including those in other sectors."[32]

The terms of the settlement will be discussed at the appropriate points in this section.

4.56 Applying the general rules of EC competition law to transactions involving software is hardly ever straightforward. The Microsoft settlement will not have much impact mostly because it is only a settlement. It is still the case that there are hardly any Commission decisions addressing the issues involved. Moreover, Commission decisions involving other sectors may not be applicable by simple analogy because software products are unlike other products, even those protected by copyright. Thus, unlike a book, simple use of software may

---

[31] See Appendix A10.
[32] Commission Press Release IP/94/653.

involve copying and, further, software is often a functional rather than an artistic creation. For this reason, it may not be appropriate to apply by analogy the Commission's comments on copyright licences.

Although the Software Directive answers some questions, it raises many **4.57** more, in particular, the effect of the Directive on the application of the general competition rules to software transactions. This latter issue will be addressed in connection with the analysis of unilateral refusals to license under Article 86. Then, the issues raised by the different types of software licences will be discussed in relation to Article 85. First, though, it is necessary to consider the vexed question of how to define the relevant market. This is vital under Article 86 to determine dominance but is also important under Article 85, for example, to determine whether an agreement can benefit from the application of the Notice on Agreements of Minor Importance (OJ 1986 C231/2) or those block exemptions which contain market share criteria, for example, Regulation 418/85 on research and development agreements[33] and the proposed replacement of the know-how and patent licence block exemptions by the technology transfer block exemption.[34]

(ii) **Market definition**

Defining the relevant market for the purposes of Articles 85 and 86 can be **4.58** complex. It is no different in the case of software. Indeed, the absence of authoritative decisions makes it even more difficult to settle on a conclusive opinion. Naturally, the starting point will be the same for software as for other products, that is, the relevant market will contain the product in question and all reasonably substitutable products (see para **2.135** *et seq*).

There is one Commission decision which addresses the market for software. **4.59** In 1987, the Commission exempted Computerland's franchise system for the distribution of microcomputer products including software (OJ 1987 L222/12). Unfortunately, the legal assessment does not discuss the market definition. In its general description, the Commission does give some estimates of the sales of Computerland stores by reference to retail sales of microcomputer products. This is certainly an indication of the strength of a retailer but cannot be relied on in determining the market share of a manufacturer.

Perhaps the most important factor to be considered in market definition in **4.60** the case of software is that software has to work with other products (both hardware and software). It follows that the market may have to be defined by reference to those customers who have products which are compatible with the software in question. As far as applications software is concerned, this means that the market will be the installed base of operating systems with which the applications software can operate. Similarly, the market for operating systems depends on the market for hardware which runs the operating system. Thus, a specialist operating system which can only run a limited range of applications

---

[33] OJ 1985 L53/5, as amended by Reg 151/93 (OJ 1993 L21/8).
[34] Draft published OJ 1994 C178/3.

software will limit the choice of the purchaser. If there are only a limited number of products compatible with that specialist operating system, the suppliers may be held to have large market shares. At the extreme, this could lead to a finding of dominance.[35] If that strong market position were maintained by a refusal to license interface information to third parties, then the principles discussed in the next paragraphs could be relevant.

4.61   It has already been mentioned that one argument in this kind of case is that the firm which controls the interface may not derive any market power because of competition in the primary market (see para **3.91**). For example, if Microsoft were to rely on its control of the Application Programming Interface (API) of Windows to charge excessively for access so as to raise the price of applications programs, customers would take this into account in their initial choice of operating system. This competition would constrain the price of the applications programs. This argument was not given much weight in the *Hilti* case but, in that case, the supplier was in fact dominant in the supply of the primary equipment.[36] It may be that the Commission would take a similar view of Microsoft's position in the market for operating systems. This is clearly suggested by the investigation of Microsoft although that investigation was not based exclusively on Article 86. The issue is discussed in more detail in Chapter 5 together with the way in which the Commission distinguishes between the markets for software and services (see para **5.32** *et seq*).

(iii) **Refusal to license software**

4.62   One issue in the IT industry is the extent to which control over an architecture will give excessive control of the market place. The first question is whether access to and use of the technical interfaces which make up an architecture can be controlled by a single supplier. The Software Directive clearly plays a role here since the decompilation right prevents copyright in a computer program from being relied on to stop access to and use of information necessary for interoperability. The limits to the right may mean that competition rules still have a role to play.

4.63   Firstly, the Software Directive is expressed to be without prejudice to national laws on trade secrets. Could these laws be relied on to hinder access to and use of interface information? Although it is only a settlement, the *IBM* case supports the application of Article 86 to this type of situation. As we have seen, IBM was alleged to hold a dominant position in the supply of products compatible with the System/370 architecture (see para **3.42**). In the settlement, IBM undertook "to disclose sufficient interface information to enable competing companies in the EEC to attach hardware and software of their design to System/370" ([1984] 3 CMLR 147, para 11).

The settlement does permit IBM to impose certain conditions on this disclosure. The proposed Information Disclosure Agreement required a

---

[35] *Cf.* the discussion of *IBM* settlement at para 3.42.
[36] For discussion, see para 3.40 *et seq*.

commitment to pay reasonable costs for reproduction and dissemination of information. In addition, "Any competing undertaking seeking interface information from IBM must be prepared to disclose corresponding information to IBM on the same terms."[37]

The Commission relied on the reasoning in the *IBM* case in deciding not to include a decompilation right in its first draft of the Software Directive. It said that

> "...the ability of a competing manufacturer to write an independent but compatible program often depends on his possibility to have access to the target program or to certain information relating to it. Access to information is not a matter of copyright law. Article 86 always applies where a dominant company abusively refuses access to such information or restricts unreasonably such access" (OJ 1989 C91/16. See Appendix A5).

4.64

As we have seen, the final version of the Software Directive does include a decompilation right (see para **4.29** *et seq*). Does this mean that Article 86 can no longer be applied to force a firm to disclose confidential information? Since a Directive is secondary legislation and cannot amend the Treaty, the better view is that Article 86 can still apply. This is supported by the Recitals which state that "the provisions of this Directive are without prejudice to the application of the competition rules if a dominant supplier refuses to make information available which is necessary for interoperability as defined in this Directive."

4.65

The second limit to the decompilation right which raises the question whether the competition rules will still play a role is the possible interpretation of the decompilation right to the effect that there is no right to decompile for the purpose of designing hardware. The more likely interpretation is that the decompilation right will be available in these circumstances (see para **4.41**). A similar issue, though, has to be addressed in determining whether a third party maintainer (TPM) can get access to information necessary to maintain software. Again, it can be argued that the limits on the decompilation right in the Directive will not foreclose the application of Article 86 in this type of case (see para **5.45**).

4.66

Finally, the decompilation right does not apply if information is used "for the development, production or marketing of a computer program substantially similar in its expression, or for any act which infringes copyright" (Art 6(2)(c)).

4.67

We have seen that it can be argued that copyright should not extend to the implementation of an interface specification (see para **4.35**). At the moment, the situation is by no means free from doubt. If a court were to take an expansive view of copyright, could Article 86 apply? This issue would also arise if it were held that copyright extended to a popular user interface.

The Commission's view was put forward at the time it issued the first draft of the Software Directive:

4.68

---

[37] Appendix B to the settlement.

"...companies in a dominant position must not abuse that position within the meaning of Article 86 of the Treaty. For example, under certain circumstances the exercise of copyright as to the aspects of a program, which other companies need to use in order to write compatible programs, could amount to such an abuse. This could also be the case if a dominant company tries to use its exclusive rights in one product to gain an unfair advantage in relation to one or more products not covered by these rights" (OJ 1989 C91/16. See Appendix A5).

4.69 Of course, Article 86 can only apply if the holder of the copyright holds a dominant position. In the first place, the simple fact of an IPR does not confer such a position. In any event, it is important to take into account in this type of case the fact that any market power over a secondary market may be constrained by competition for the primary product (see para **4.61**). In addition, Article 86 cannot apply unless there is an abuse of that dominant position. The ECJ seems to accept the possibility that a refusal to license can in certain circumstances amount to an abuse (see para **3.51**). The CFI has upheld a Commission decision requiring TV broadcasters to license a third party to publish TV programme listings which were protected by copyright.[38] As we have seen, there is an argument that the principles of competition law alone cannot tell us when an IPR incentive should be limited (see para **2.145**). The *Magill* cases are a good illustration because there is little doubt that the Commission was influenced in its decision by its view that programme listings were not worthy of copyright proctection.

4.70 The reasoning in the *Magill* cases could allow extensive intervention in the exploitation of IPRs in the IT industry. The only limit to the principle seems to be that the market into which the third party seeks entry must be a derivative market. Thus, even the reasoning in the *Magill* cases would not allow a compulsory licence of a popular user interface. The Advocate General in the *Magill* cases has argued that the CFI's judgment should be overturned because Article 86 should not apply if the holder of the copyright itself supplies a product protected by the copyright in question.[39] It is to be hoped that the ECJ will clarify the situation in its judgment.

4.71 One argument in the case of copyright is that it would be inconsistent with international agreements for Article 86 to apply to a refusal to license. We have seen that Article 9(2) of the Berne Convention limits the situations in which the exclusive right of reproduction can be qualified. The better view is that the case-by-case application of competition rules does not infringe Article 9(2).[40]

(iv) **Mergers and joint ventures**

4.72 There are few decisions of the Commission on mergers and joint ventures in the software industry. Reflecting industry moves away from supplying hardware and software to providing solutions, many transactions are better analysed

---

[38] *RTE, BBC & ITP v Commission* Cases T-69,70&76/89 [1991] ECR II-485, 535 & 575; [1991] 4 CMLR 586, 669 & 745. Under appeal to the ECJ: *RTE & ITP v Commission* Cases 241&242/91(OJ 1991 C307/5).

[39] Opinion of 1 June 1994, para 112.

[40] See the Advocate General's Opinion, para 166.

under services. The principles which the Commission will apply are well illustrated by its decision in *Dräger/IBM/HMP* (Case IV.M101) which involved a concentrative joint venture to develop and market computerised intensive health care and patient data management solutions for public and private hospitals. The parties argued that these solutions were different from existing systems and would "ultimately create a market of its own." The Commission decided that, however narrow the market definition, there was no risk of the creation of a dominant position because of potential competition from about 20 other firms developing or marketing the existing systems. The Commission's decision is a good example of a case where 100% market share does not equate with dominance because of potential competition.

Other decisions show that the key concern of the Commission in the case of **4.73** software mergers and joint ventures is control of interface specifications and other standards. The AT&T/NCR merger has already been discussed (see para **3.43**). Another case involving the UNIX operating system is the Commission's decision to exempt the X/Open Group which had been set up by a number of major IT companies in order to develop a common application environment for the UNIX System V operating system (OJ 1987 L35/36; [1988] 4 CMLR 542). The objective of the Group was to standardise the UNIX interface in order to avoid the problem of many different versions of UNIX. In the X/Open decision, the Commission notes that there were 30 to 35 different commercial versions (para 5). In the *AT&T/NCR* decision, it said that there were about 100 so-called "UNIX derivatives" (Case IV.M050 [1992] 4 CMLR M41 para 18).

The arrangements in the *X/Open* case were held to fall within Article 85 **4.74** because membership was not open to all and non-members would have no say in the definition of the common application environment. An exemption was granted because these restrictions were necessary to achieve the benefits of an open system.

(v) **Software licensing**[41]

It has been pointed out already that there are no ECJ cases nor Commission **4.75** decisions dealing with the application of competition rules to software licences. However, there are a number of ECJ cases and Commission decisions which, it could be argued, should be applied by analogy. Care must be taken here because, firstly, software is different in nature to other products which are protected by copyright. In particular, software is cheaply and easily copied and the copy is as good as the original so the licensor must be able to control copying in order to calculate the price per copy. A further reason why it may not be appropriate to apply Commission decisions to software licences is that there are a variety of economic purposes for which software licences may be agreed. The fact that there are different types of software licences from an economic point of view will be especially relevant in determining the extent to

---

[41] See, *e.g.*, Forrester, *Software Licensing in the Light of Current EC Competition Law Considerations* (1992) ECLR 5; Vinje, *Compliance with Article 85 in Software Licensing* (1992) ECLR 165; and Darbyshire, *Computer Programs and Competition Policy: A Block Exemption for Software Licensing* (1994) EIPR 374.

which the know-how block exemption (and its forthcoming replacement) can be applied by analogy.

4.76   A broad distinction can be drawn between three sorts of licences: licences to develop, distribute and use. Of course, particular transactions may involve a combination of some or all or these purposes.

(vi) Licence to develop

4.77   It is common nowadays for expensively developed software to be used as a building block for further software products. If a third party is involved, this will invariably involve access to the human-readable source code. What sort of restrictions can be imposed on the use of this code?

4.78   The first point is that the ECJ has held that agreements can be more restrictive without falling foul of Article 85 where the subject matter of the agreement so requires. In *Erauw-Jacquery* v *La Hesbignonne* (Case 27/87 [1988] ECR 1919; [1988] 4 CMLR 576), the ECJ even upheld an export ban where this was necessary to allow special control by the licensor, in this case over "basic seed" which embodies the licensed technology for plants. This case could be relied upon to defend confidentiality and other restrictions on the use of source code.

4.79   Secondly, there is a strong argument in the case of a licence of this form of software for the application by analogy of Regulation 556/89[42] which grants a block exemption for know-how licences. The Regulation itself cannot apply because Article 5(1)(4) provides that it does not apply to licences of computer software "...except where...the software is of assistance in achieving the object of the licensed technology and there are no obligations restrictive of competition other than those also attached to the licensed know how and exempted under the present Regulation."

4.80   This is clearly a very restrictive qualification to the broad exclusion. Of course, a block exemption applied by analogy does not automatically exempt the agreement but an individual exemption would be likely. Even if the agreement was not notified, it is unlikely that the Commission would impose a fine although the need for the restriction to be enforceable may mean that the licence would have to be notified, at least before enforcement proceedings were initiated.

4.81   The know-how block exemption permits a number of restrictions which would be common in a development agreement including a confidentiality obligation (Art 2(1)(1)), a post term use ban[43] and access to improvements on a non-exclusive reciprocal basis (Art 2(1)(4)). In addition, the Regulation allows the licensor to restrict the licensee to one or more technical fields of application or to one or more product markets (Art 2(1)(8)). This may give a software licensor useful control over the activities of the developer.

---

[42] OJ 1989 L61/1, as amended by Reg 151/93 (OJ 1993 L21/8).
[43] Art 2(1)(3), provided the know-how is still secret (Art 3(1)).

Similar provisions to the above are included in the draft technology transfer **4.82**
block exemption which is to replace the know how block exemption on 1
January 1995 (OJ 1994 C178/3).

Development agreements are also discussed in Chapter 5 (see para **5.51** *et
seq*).

(vii) **Licence to resell**

As for hardware, there are numerous methods chosen to market software. **4.83**
Indeed, the same distribution network may market both hardware and
separate software. The *Computerland* decision (OJ 1987 L222/12; [1989] 4
CMLR 2597) (see para **3.87**), for example, involved a franchise system for
microcomputer products including hardware and software. Some of the issues
discussed in relation to hardware distribution apply to software as well.
However, there are some specific issues which arise in the case of the
distribution of software.

Perhaps the most important issue in practice is whether an exclusive **4.84**
distribution agreement for software can benefit from either of the relevant
block exemptions, that is, Regulation 1983/83 on exclusive distribution or
Regulation 1984/83 on exclusive purchase. Each of these exemptions only
applies to agreements for the resale of goods, thus raising the familiar problem
of whether software can ever be treated as goods.[44] This issue has already been
aired (see para **4.47**). There are now arguments that, at least in some cases,
software can indeed be treated as goods for the purposes of these Regulations.
Firstly, in *Warner* v *Christiansen* (Case 156/86 [1988] ECR 2605; [1990] 3
CMLR 684) (see para **2.64**), the ECJ applied Article 30 to the sale of video
cassettes. The nature of video cassettes is clearly very similar to "off the shelf"
software since that software is only licensed while the medium on which the
software is recorded is sold. Furthermore, Article 4(c) of the Software Directive
refers to the "sale" of a computer program. This presumably means sale of the
medium because invariably the software itself will be licensed rather than sold.

If a distribution agreement does concern goods, the block exemption will **4.85**
only apply if those goods are for "resale." The exemptions do not apply where
the distributor adds significant value before reselling. As in the case of
hardware distribution, this may exclude agreements with value added resellers
(VARs) (see para **3.78**). If one of the Regulations is relied upon, restrictions in
an ancillary software licence agreement with the distributor could remove the
benefit of the Regulation.[45]

If the distribution of software was held to be a service rather than goods, **4.86**
there may be an argument any exclusivity fell outside Article 85 on the basis of
the principles laid down by the ECJ in *Coditel II* (*Coditel v Ciné Vog* Case 262/81
[1982] ECR 3381; [1983] 1 CMLR 49) (see para **2.110**).

---

[44] Reg 4087/88 on distribution franchises (OJ 1988 L359/46) applies to both goods and services so the
problem does not arise.
[45] Art 2(2) of Reg 1983/83 and Art 2(2) of Reg 1984/83.

4.87   One of the issues in the Microsoft investigation concerned the terms of licences to PC manufacturers and assemblers (OEMs) to resell operating systems by loading one on to a PC before supply. One complaint was that Microsoft charged for a copy of its operating system whether or not the OEM in fact loaded that system before sale. In other words, if the OEM loaded a non-Microsoft product, the OEM would pay two royalties. In its settlement with the US Department of Justice and the European Commission (see Appendix A10), Microsoft undertook not to enter into any licence with an OEM which prohibited or restricted the OEM's licensing, sale or distribution of any non-Microsoft operating system. Microsoft also undertook not to use any "Lump Sum Pricing," that is, a royalty which does not vary with the number of copies of the MS-DOS or Windows product. It also undertook not to enter into any "Per Processor License," that is, a licence under which the OEM has to pay a royalty for all PCs sold. Furthermore, it undertook not to include a minimum royalty commitment independent of actual sales. Microsoft also agreed not to enter into any licence for a duration of more than one year.

(viii) Licence to use

4.88   Article 85 can apply to simple end-user agreements,[46] although it can be argued that there is insufficient impact on competition.[47] There are a number of restrictions common in end user software licences which need to be analysed to see if Article 85 can apply.

(a) Single CPU

4.89   It is not unusual for a licensee to be restricted to running software on a single, specified CPU. Although it is not beyond doubt, it seems that running a computer program will generally be a restricted act within Article 4(a) of the Software Directive (see para **4.22**). The traditional starting point for considering restrictions based on IPRs is the ECJ's distinction between existence and exercise. The ECJ has held that Article 85 may apply if the exercise of an IPR "manifests itself as the subject, means or the result of a restrictive practice" (*Sirena* v *Eda* Case 40/70 [1971] ECR 69; [1971] CMLR 260). This would not be the case if the restriction was included in order to delimit use for the purpose of calculating royalties. In *Coditel I* (Case 26/79 [1980] ECR 881; [1981] 2 CMLR 362) (see para **2.71**), the ECJ held that this could justify an exclusive licence. Although that case concerned the free movement rules, in *Coditel II* (Case 262/81 [1982] ECR 3381; [1983] 1 CMLR 49) (see para **2.110**), the ECJ held that the specific characteristics of the

---

[46] *SVCB* v *Kerpen & Kerpen* Case 319/82 [1983] ECR 4173; [1985] 1 CMLR 511. See also the Commission's decision in *Bayo-n-ox* OJ 1990 L21/71; [1990] 4 CMLR 930. On appeal to CFI *Bayer* v *Commission* Case T-12/90 [1991] ECR II-219; [1993] 4 CMLR 30 and on appeal to ECJ Case C-195/91P.

[47] On the basis of the Notice on Agreements of Minor Importance or the principles laid down by the ECJ in *Stergios Delimitis* v *Henninger Brau* Case C-234/89 [1991] I ECR 935; [1992] 5 CMLR 210. See para **2.108**.

market could justify exclusivity. It is the specific characteristics of software which justify the single CPU provision. However, if the purpose of the contractual restriction was to limit the licensee to a specific brand of machine, there may be a tie contrary to Article 85. In practice, the licensor can avoid this result by permitting use of the software on another CPU subject to a requirement that only one copy of the software is used at any time and that the licensee notify the licensor of any new location.[48]

(b) Decompilation

The Software Directive itself outlaws a restriction on the right to decompile set out in Article 6 (Art 9(1)). It may be that the licensor could restrict decompilation in situations not covered by Article 6. Thus, it seems that Article 6 does not apply to facilitate access to and use of interface information with a view to maintaining the software. Presumably, a similar result would be achieved as that discussed in relation to Article 86 (see para **5.45**).   **4.90**

(c) Maintenance

A licensor may wish to require the licensee to obtain maintenance from the licensor. The first point is that Article 5(1) of the Software Directive allows the licensee to reproduce and translate a computer program if necessary for use of the program "in accordance with its intended purpose, including for error correction." This would allow the licensee to decompile in order to correct errors. It is not clear whether it would extend to updating the program. Article 5(1) is also subject to "specific contractual provision", although Recital 18 states that error correction "may not be prohibited by contract." It seems likely that this conflict will be resolved in favour of the Recital.[49] We return to the issue of maintenance in Chapter 5 (see para **5.38** *et seq*).   **4.91**

(d) Sublicensing/assignment

In principle, a restriction on an end user from reselling a product may be caught by Article 85.[50] At least in the case of "off-the-shelf" software, a restriction on assignment may be caught if the effect is to prevent resale by the end-user or licensee. It has been seen that this type of software may well be treated as goods.[51] On the other hand, a restriction on sublicensing may be intended to prevent the creation of additional copies which presumably would be a legitimate exercise of copyright. The principles to apply are the same as those discussed above in relation to a restriction to use on a single CPU.   **4.92**

---

[48] Vinje, *Compliance with Article 85 in Software Licensing* (1992) ECLR 165 at 168.
[49] Vinje (1992) ECLR 165 at 169.
[50] *SVCB* v *Kerpen & Kerpen* Case 319/82 [1983] ECR 4173; [1985] 1 CMLR 511. See also the Commission's decision in *Bayo-n-ox* OJ 1990 L21/71; [1990] 4 CMLR 930. On appeal to CFI *Bayer v Commission* Case T-12/90 [1991] ECR II-219; [1993] 4 CMLR 30 and on appeal to ECJ Case C-195/91P.
[51] See Art 4(c) of the Software Directive. *Cf. Warner Bros* v *Christiansen* Case 158/86 [1988] ECR 2605 [1990] 3 CMLR 684. See para **4.84**.

(e) Confidentiality

4.93   Such an obligation will generally be perfectly acceptable for source code, as discussed in relation to a licence to develop (see para **4.78**). However, source code is unlikely to be made available in a typical licence to use. If a confidentiality obligation has the effect of preventing resale, it could also fall within Article 85 in the same way as a restriction on sublicensing.

(ix) **Pricing**

4.94   Perhaps the most complicated area of EC competition law concerns the rules applicable to pricing decisions. Although the calculations may be more difficult, in principle, the same rules apply to pricing of software products. Thus, a dominant firm may not discount unless the discount is justified on the basis of cost savings (*Michelin* v *Commission* Case 322/81 [1983] ECR 3461; [1985] 1 CMLR 282). Applying this rule to software pricing is extremely difficult. This is because the expense of producing the software may be almost entirely taken up with development, so that there may be almost no additional cost from the sale of one more software product.

4.95   The Microsoft settlement also concerned pricing. As we have seen, it was alleged that Microsoft had charged a royalty for each PC sold whether or not a copy of the Microsoft product had been loaded. Clearly, this made it more expensive for a PC manufacturer to load a non-Microsoft product because the manufacturer would have to pay two royalties. As we have seen, Microsoft undertook not to engage in practices which would have the effect of requiring a manufacturer to pay except where it had loaded a copy of the relevant Microsoft product on the PC sold. Although the settlement is based on Articles 85 and 86, it is only if a firm has some market power that this practice would cause a concern from the point of view of competition law.

Opposite

The following *Comparative Table of Implementation* concerning the EC Software Directive (pages 105–112) shows the status of implementation in the Member States of the EU and EFTA as at October 1994. The Table was compiled by the international law firm, Baker & McKenzie, and is reproduced with their kind permission.

EU MEMBER STATES

	United Kingdom	Ireland	Netherlands	Belgium
1. Formal implementation of Directive?	Yes	Yes	No NB. Commission proceedings initiated.	No NB. Commission proceedings initiated.
2. National implementing legislation or proposed implementing legislation (if any)?	Copyright (Computer Programs) Regulations 1992 (SI 3233/92) amending Copyright, Designs and Patents Act 1988	EC (Legal Protection of Computer Programs) Regulations 1993 (SI 26/93)	Proposed amendment to Copyright Act Bill No. 22531 (1991/1992)	Copyright Bill pending, to replace existing Copyright Law. (Note; Computer programs already protected under copyright law). Doc. Senate No. 145, SA/BZ 1991–1992
3. Date from which national implementation legislation effective or proposed timetable for implementation?	1 January 1993	31 December 1992	Implementation expected late 1994	Implementation expected during 1994
4. Apparent inconsistency between Recital 18 and Article 5.1 addressed?	No—Article 5.1 of Directive implemented.	No—Article 5.1 of Directive implemented.	Yes—Bill largely adopts Recital 18.	No—Article 16 of Bill echoes Article 5.1.
5. Following implementation of the Directive, does national Copyright Law provide for seizure as permitted under Articles 7.2 and 7.3?	Yes—provisions for seizure under existing copyright law.	Yes—provisions for seizure under existing copyright law.	Yes—provisions for seizure under exisiting law.	Yes

EU MEMBER STATES

	United Kingdom	Ireland	Netherlands	Belgium
6. Features of (proposed) legislation which warrant or have attracted attention?	Submissions were made regarding wording of the draft Regulations—in particular, ambiguity in drafting, and deviations from wording of the Directive. Nonetheless, Regulations were ultimately passed without substantial change, and it remains to be seen how issues will be resolved. Regulation 11, for example, introducing a new s. 296A(1)(c) into the copyright legislation, fails to limit permitted observation, study or testing of a program's functioning to such actions performed in the course of permitted acts of loading, displaying, running the program etc, as Article 5.3 of the Directive provides.	Continued discussion expected flowing from: (1) Retrospective effect of Regulations, implemented on 1/2/93, to 31/12/92—despite proviso that nothing in Regulations will have effect of making unlawful any acts not lawful at date of commission; (2) Absence of definition in Regulations (and in Directive) of "computer program" (although Regulations incorporate provision in Directive that "computer program" includes design materials used for preparation of such program); (3) Other specific issues arising from deviations from wording of the Directive in the Regulations.	Use of vague terms (largely replicating Directive), such as "error correction", "intended use" of software, "interoperability". Also, less than faithful implementation of Directive into Bill.	Language of Directive largely not repeated, although meaning largely preserved. Proposed provisions implementing Articles 4(c), 6 and 7 criticised for deviaitons from Directive.
7. Unresolved issues arising from (proposed) implementing legislation?	See Item 6 above	See Item 6 above	Issues arising from inconsistency between Recital 18 and Article 5.1 as well as items referred to in 6. above, are being discussed.	N/A

EU MEMBER STATES

	France	Italy	Spain	Portugal	Greece	Germany
1. Formal implementation of Directive?	No	Yes	Yes	No NB. Commission proceedings initiated.	Yes	Yes
2. National implementing legislation *or* proposed implementing legislation (if any)?	Implementing legislation Draft Law No. 2953 (amending French Code on intellectual property) adopted.	Amendment to Copyright Law by Legislative Decree No. 518 of 29 December 1992	Act 16/1993 of 23 December 1993	Implementing legislation currently being finalised.	Intellectual Property Act Law 2121/1993	Second Act amending Copyright Act dated 9 June 1993 BGBI1 S.910
3. Date from which national implementation legislation effective *or* proposed timetable for implementation?	Implementation expected during 1994	15 January 1993	24 December 1993	Implementation expected late 1994	4 March 1993.	24 June 1993
4. Apparent inconsistency between Recital 18 and Article 5.1 addressed?	Yes—Article 5.1 of Directive implemented (but see Item 7 below).	No—Article 5.1 of Directive implemented.	No—Article 5.1 of Directive implemented.	N/A	No—Article 5.1 of Directive implemented	No—Article 5.1 of Directive implemented
5. Following implementation of the Directive, does National Copyright Law provide for seizure as permitted under Articles 7.2 and 7.3?	Yes—provisions under existing law.	Yes	Yes	N/A	Yes	Yes

EU MEMBER STATES

	France	Italy	Spain	Portugal	Greece	Germany
6. Features of (proposed) legislation which warrant or have attracted attention?	—Definition of "computer program" differs from that under French law (latter including documentation associated with the program and necessary for its use). —Implementing legislation provides for creation of pledges over copyright in computer programs, provided evidenced in writing and registered with French Intellectual Property Office.	No	No	N/A	Amount of compensation payable for reproduction of work for private use by means of technical media.	No—Directive has been implemented more or less literally into national law, although with retrospective effect.
7. Unresolved issues arising from (proposed) implementing legislation?	—Legislation, whilst acknowledging the justification put forward by the Commission for the prima facie contradiction, nonetheless gave effect to the language of Article 5.1.	No	No—New legislation supersedes relevant provisions of Intellectual Property Act 1987.	N/A	No	Yes—In view of retrospective effect of implementing legislation, position under existing software licence agreements need clarification, especially regarding use restrictions.

	EU MEMBER STATES		EFTA MEMBER STATES	
	Denmark	Luxembourg	Sweden	Switzerland
1. Formal implementation of Directive?	Yes	No NB. Commission proceedings initiated.	Yes	Yes
2. National implementing legislation or proposed implementing legislation (if any)?	Act No. 1010 of 1992, amending Copyright Act.	Bill to amend Copyright Act currently being finalised.	Act (1992:1687) dated 17 December 1992, amending Copyright in Literary and Artistic Works Act (1960:729).	Federal Law on Copyright and Neighbouring Rights of 9 October 1992; and Ordinance on Copyright and Neighbouring Rights of 26 April 1993.
3. Date from which national implementation legislation effective or proposed timetable for implementation?	1 January 1993	Implementation expected by end 1994	1 January 1993	1 July 1993
4. Apparent inconsistency between Recital 18 and Article 5.1 addressed?	No—Wording of relevant implementing provision (Section 11(a)) is perhaps ambiguous on this point, but accompanying Ministry comments clarify intention to implement Article 5.1.	No—Bill implements Article 5.1.	No—Article 5.1 effectively implemented.	Not addressed.

EU MEMBER STATES

EFTA MEMBER STATES

	Denmark	Luxembourg	Sweden	Switzerland
5. Following implementation of the Directive, does national Copyright Law provide for seizure as permitted under Articles 7.2 and 7.3?	No—Article 7.3 *not* implemented. Articles 7.1(b) and 7.2 felt to be already accommodated in s. 57 of Copyright Act, providing for seizure, destruction etc, of illegal copies following court judgment. Items covered by Article 7.1(c), however, addressed by introduction of fines (only) as remedy.	Yes—provisions for seizure under existing law.	No, but relevant provisions of Criminal Code and Code of Procedure will apply.	Article 77 empowers the Customs authorities to inform the rights owners of suspect imports and, upon request, to temporarily seize allegedly infringing products at the border. Relevant provisions of criminal Code and Code of Procedure will also apply.
6. Features of (proposed) legislation which warrant or have attracted attention?	Professional body of software suppliers made additional proposals regarding sanctions, including ex parte injunctions and seizure during injunction application. These proposals to be considered in course of general deliberations and consultation on Copyright Act (although this is not imminent).	As existing Copyright Law already provides general software protection, necessity of further legislation has been questioned.	Issue of unauthorised copying of software for private use without penalty.	N/A
7. Unresolved issues arising from (proposed) implementing legislation?	See Item 6 above	No	See Item 6 above.	N/A

EFTA MEMBER STATES

	Iceland	Norway	Finland	Austria	Liechtenstein
1. Formal implementation of Directive?	Yes.	Yes.	Yes.	Yes.	No
2. National implementing legislation *or* proposed implementing legislation (if any)?	Act No. 57/1992 amending Copyright Act.	Act No. 128/1992 amending Copyright Act.	Amendment to Copyright Act.	Amendment to Copyright Act.	Amendment to existing law under consideration.
3. Date from which national implementation legislation effective *or* proposed timetable for implementation?	22 June 1992	1 January 1994	1 January 1994	1 March 1993.	Likely implementation date unknown.
4. Apparent inconsistency between Recital 18 and Article 5.1 addressed?	Act provides for any licence to include right to alter and use program in accordance with purpose for which licence is granted.	No—Article 5.1 implemented	No—Article 5.1 implemented.	No—Article 5.1. implemented.	N/A

EFTA MEMBER STATES

	Iceland	Norway	Finland	Austria	Liechtenstein
5. Following implementation of Directive, does National Copyright Law provide for seizure as permitted under Articles 7.2 and 7.3?	Yes—provisions under existing law.	Yes, provisions under existing law.	Yes—provisions under existing law.	Yes. Express implementation of most of Article 7 considered unnecessary.	Yes—provisions under existing law.
6. Features of (proposed) legislation which warrant or have attracted attention?	Language of Directive not repeated, although meaning preserved.	No—Directive closely followed.	None—Basic principles of Directive already reflected in existing law; otherwise, Directive closely followed.	Some dispute as to whether implementation of Article 7 necessary.	N/A
7. Unresolved issues arising from (proposed) implementing legislation?	N/A	N/A	N/A	N/A	N/A

CONTENTS OF CHAPTER 5

Chapter 5
Services

1. Introduction

The provision of services has developed into a significant sector within the IT **5.1** industry. It has been estimated that services and maintenance accounted for 41% of the European IT market in 1993.[1] Revenue from services accounts for a major part of the profits of many of the main players in the industry. There is a continuing growth in firms devoting to niche services such as on-line information services. The Commission recently commented that "Of central importance to the development of the European information society is the need to safeguard the free circulation of services across our internal frontiers."[2]

In this chapter, we deal first with an important proposal for legislation on **5.2** databases. Although this draft Directive, if adopted, will not just have an impact on services, it is included in this chapter because one of its objectives is to facilitate the provision of cross-border on-line information services. One of the EC Treaty provisions on which it is based is Article 66 which gives the Council the power to adopt legislation to ensure the free movement of services (see para **2.68** *et seq*). This chapter goes on to deal with competition law and services and, in particular, the principal issues generated by the application of competition law to the activities of third party maintainers (TPMs).

2. Legislation

(i) Draft Database Directive[3]

The Commission's current proposal for a Directive on databases has some **5.3** parallels in the Software Directive. Most importantly, both are concerned with addressing a need for intellectual property protection arising from new technology. Both deal specifically with the danger of excessive intellectual property protection having the effect of stifling competition. In the Software Directive, this is achieved by limiting copyright protection. In the draft Database Directive, the Commission proposes achieving a similar result by establishing a novel *sui generis* right which lasts for a considerably shorter

---

[1] *Computer Weekly* 24 March 1994, 14.
[2] Commission Communication on Europe's Way to the Information Society: An Action Plan COM(94)347 of 19 July 1994, 3.
[3] Amended proposal for a Council Directive on the legal protection of databases (OJ 1993 C308/1). See Appendix A6.

period than the usual copyright term and which, in certain circumstances, is subject to compulsory licences.

5.4   It will be recalled that one factor in the choice of copyright as the appropriate intellectual property right (IPR) for computer programs was to take advantage of the existing well-developed international copyright system. This meant that the Directive had to fulfil the conditions laid down in the Berne Convention including national treatment. A *sui generis* right is not subject to any such constraint so the Commission was free to propose limiting protection to Community nationals whilst empowering the Council to enter into international agreements to extend protection to those who come from a non-Community country. This would enable the Council to require equivalent protection to the Directive echoing the stance taken by the US in the 1984 Act on semiconductor chip protection (see para **3.8**). It remains to be seen whether the Community approach will provoke the US into the speedy response with which the Community reacted to the semiconductor chip legislation.

5.5   Overall, the proposal is probably even more complex than the Software Directive, particularly from a technical point of view. One result of this complexity will no doubt be even greater uncertainty over interpretation.

(a) Background

5.6   Many arguments over the draft Directive can only be understood with some knowledge of the background to the proposal. In its Green Paper on Copyright and the Challenge of Technology, the Commission devoted a chapter to databases.[4] It pointed out that there were a number of different types of databases. First, there are collections of materials where those materials are literary works in themselves, for example, a collection of poems by a living author or a collection of recent newspapers. In this case, consent would generally be required to place the materials in a database as well as to extract them from the database (subject to arguments in some jurisdictions that screen outputs are too transitory to infringe copyright). In addition to the copyright in the materials, the Berne Convention also requires copyright protection for the collection itself. Article 2(5) states: "Collections of literary or artistic works such as encyclopaedias and anthologies which, by reason of the selection and arrangement of their contents, constitute intellectual creations shall be protected as such, without prejudice to the copyright in each of the works forming part of such collections."

5.7   There is a second type of database where the contents are not protected by copyright. This would include collections of materials which are in the public domain, for example, a collection of poems written in the 16th century. It would also cover factual databases such as a list of names and addresses. Information technology enables massive collections of data to be compiled and searched with incredible speed and ease. Given that there may be considerable investment in compiling the database and maintaining it, should these

---

[4] COM(88)172 of 7 June 1988, Chapter 6.

databases be protected by copyright? Before looking at the Commission's approach, it is worth looking at the existing position in the Community and in the US.

In 1991, the US Supreme Court was faced with the question of the extent of **5.8** copyright protection for factual databases. In *Feist Publications* v *Rural Telephone Service* ((1991) 113 L.Ed. 2d 358), Rural had compiled a telephone directory made up of an alphabetical list of names together with addresses and telephone numbers. When Rural refused to license Feist to use the list to produce a telephone directory including the same area, Feist used Rural's list to compile its own directory. Rural found out about the copying because Feist copied some fake names and addresses included in Rural's directory in order to detect copying. The Supreme Court held that factual databases could be protected by copyright provided the selection, coordination or arrangement of the facts was original. This condition is similar to that laid down by Article 2(5) of the Berne Convention. The Court made it clear that facts could not be protected by copyright. It said:

> "Facts, whether alone or as part of a compilation, are not original and therefore may not be copyrighted. A factual compilation is eligible for copyright if it features an original selection or arrangement of facts, but the copyright is limited to the particular selection or arrangement. In no event may copyright extend to the facts themselves" (at 372).

How do we determine whether a selection or arrangement is original? The **5.9** Supreme Court held that, in determining originality, it was not sufficient that effort had been expended in compiling the list. Thus, it rejected the so-called "sweat of the brow" test. The test was set out as follows: "Original, as the term is used in copyright, means only that the work was independently created by the author (as opposed to copied from other works), and that it possesses at least some minimal degree of creativity" (at 369).

The Supreme Court added that: "Presumably, the vast majority of compilations will pass this test, but not all will. There remains a narrow category of works in which the creative spark is utterly lacking or so trivial as to be virtually nonexistent" (at 377).

The Supreme Court held that Rural's directory was insufficiently creative **5.10** to satisfy this test. It followed that Feist had not infringed copyright by using Rural's list in compiling its own. The case is helpful in providing at least one example of a compilation which is not protected. However, the case is less helpful in explaining how the test should be applied to other types of selection and arrangement.[5]

The requirement for originality is probably even more stringent in those **5.11** continental European legal systems which grant protection to factual databases.[6] This may be contrasted with the existing position in the UK where

---

[5] See Schwarz, *Copyright in Compilations of Facts* (1991) EIPR 178 at 181.
[6] Porter, *The Copyright Protection of Compilations and Pseudo-literary Works in EC Member States* (1993) JBL 1.

a compilation is protected as a literary work provided only that it is original in the sense that it is the author's own work and involves some labour and skill.[7]

5.12   What should be the extent of protection? As in the case of arguments over the extent of protection to be granted by the Software Directive, it is a question of balancing two competing interests: on the one hand, encouraging and rewarding the effort involved in establishing new databases and, on the other hand, avoiding stifling competition by allowing the first to compile a new database control over latecomers. Some argue that the UK has adopted the best position since it is under this regime that the UK has developed a strong position on the database market.[8] Others prefer a stricter requirement of originality.[9] There are still others who would prefer a different type of right altogether.[10]

5.13   How does the proposed Database Directive deal with the balance? Broadly, if adopted, it will require Member States to grant copyright protection to electronic databases where the selection or arrangement is original. Some databases will fall outside this test but Member States will also have to establish a *sui generis* right to control unauthorised use of electronic databases even if the selection or arrangement is not original.[11] The existence of two forms of IPR makes the proposal somewhat complicated.

(b) Databases within the draft Directive

5.14   By Article 1(1):

> "'database' means a collection of works or materials arranged, stored and accessed by electronic means, and the materials necessary for the operation of the database such as its thesaurus, index or system for obtaining or presenting information; it shall not apply to any computer program used in the making or operation of the database."

5.15   A few points should be noted. Firstly, the proposal only covers electronic (basically, computer-based) databases. Secondly, it does not cover computer programs. This should exclude database software products such as Borland's dBase IV software. But the proposal states that the term "database" does include "materials necessary for the operation of the database."[12] This is not very helpful. If this covers the commands for accessing a specific database, it is difficult to see why those commands should not be protected as computer programs under the Software Directive.[13] Finally, copyright protection under the draft Directive applies whether or not the materials contained in the database are themselves protected by copyright (Art 2(4)).

---

[7] Porter (1993) JBL 1 at 15.

[8] Hall, *New Thoughts on Databases: The Proposed EC Directive* (1992) ICCLR 275 at 276.

[9] Thorne, *The Infringement of Database Compilations: A Case for Reform?* (1991) EIPR 331 at 332.

[10] Metaxas, *Protection of Databases: Quietly Steering in the Wrong Direction?* (1990) EIPR 227.

[11] Similar to the right advocated by Metaxas (1990) EIPR 227.

[12] The original proposal referred to "electronic" materials. It is difficult to see what the deletion was intended to achieve given the reference in Art 5 to "electronic material".

[13] Pattison, *The European Commission's Proposal on the Protection of Computer Databases* (1992) EIPR 113 at 115.

What about the key criterion of originality? By Article 2(3): **5.16**

"A database shall be protected by copyright if it is original in the sense that it is a collection of works or materials which, by reason of their selection or their arrangement, constitutes the author's own intellectual creation. No other criteria shall be applied to determine the eligibility of a database for their protection."

Again, a number of points are worth noting. Firstly, as we have seen, it is the **5.17** selection or arrangement which must be original rather than the contents but it remains to be seen how courts will approach this test. Presumably an alphabetical telephone directory would not be arranged originally but could the selection be original? It is very difficult to predict how the courts will deal with this major issue. What we can look forward to is a period of uncertainty before the issues are finally resolved. This may well require guidance from the ECJ which would take some years.

It has also been pointed out that it is odd to judge originality on the basis of **5.18** the way in which the database is arranged in the storage medium.[14] Database software does not store information in a human-readable format. The data may be scattered all over the storage medium. Surely this is not the criterion for originality. Could the test be applied to the database as printed in human readable form? In fact, a database may never be printed out in full. Another possibility is that the arrangement is determined by the electronic materials for access and, indeed, this is probably why they are included within the definition in Article 1(1). However, this is open to the further criticism that command procedures can be altered over time.[15] It should be noted that, even if the test is satisfied, copyright only lies in the selection or arrangement. Thus, copying the entire contents but changing the arrangement could prevent a claim for breach of copyright. The conclusion must be that the intention behind the Directive is that, in many cases, access to databases will not infringe copyright either because the database is not eligible for protection or because that protection is not very extensive. This brings us to other limits to the extent of protection.

(c) Extent of protection

Copyright lasts for the same period as for literary works. This period is to be **5.19** harmonised throughout the Community by the Duration Directive to 70 years from the death of the author.[16] A "substantial change to the selection or arrangement of the contents of a database" will give rise to a new copyright with a full new period of protection (Art 9(2)). The usual rights attached to copyright in literary works apply. Thus, under Article 5, the author has exclusive rights to stop temporary or permanent reproduction as well as translation and adaptation and "any communication, display or performance

---

[14] See Pattison (1992) EIPR 113 at 116.
[15] See Pattison (1992) EIPR 113 at 116.
[16] Council Directive 93/98 on the term of protection of copyright and certain related rights (OJ 1993 L290/9).

of the database to the public." The author also has the exclusive right to control distribution to the public. Like the Software Directive, this right is exhausted on first sale in the Community but the right to control rental remains intact (Art 5(d)). If the database is provided as a service rather than sold, exhaustion will depend on the principles in the *Coditel I* case (*Coditel* v *Ciné Vog* Case 62/79 [1980] ECR 881; [1981] 2 CMLR 362) (see para **2.71**).

5.20   We have seen that a database's contents may be made up of materials protected by copyright. If they are not, the proposal makes it clear that, if copyright is granted by virtue of the Directive, this does not confer copyright protection on the contents.

5.21   Where copyright does exist in the underlying materials, naturally, the draft Directive does not remove that protection. Clearly, if use of a database involves copying those materials, there may be a claim for breach of copyright. It is worth noting, however, that Article 7(1) will require Member States to extend fair use type exceptions, such as brief quotations, to the contents of databases.

(d) Copyright: conclusion

5.22   In conclusion, the proposed Directive is drafted so as to exclude from copyright protection at least some electronic databases. Even if copyright protection is available, this may not provide the author with protection against access to the database. The Commission has attempted to plug these gaps with the "right to prevent unauthorised extraction."

(e) Right to prevent unauthorised extraction

5.23   By Article 10(2) of the proposed Directive:

> "Member States shall provide for a right for the maker of a database to prevent the unauthorised extraction or re-utilization, from that database, of its contents, in whole or in substantial part, for commercial purposes. This right to prevent unfair extraction of the contents of a database shall apply irrespective of the eligibility of that database for protection under copyright. It shall not apply to the contents of a database where these are works already protected by copyright or neighbouring rights."

5.24   This is fairly self-explanatory. Some comments are worth making. Firstly, the right to prevent unauthorised extraction protects the contents of the database but only if those contents are not protected by copyright. However, it does not matter whether or not the database itself is protected by copyright by virtue of the Database Directive.

5.25   The right to prevent unauthorised extraction is a *sui generis* right and is not a form of copyright. Consequently, the authors of the proposal did not need to take into account the conditions for copyright laid down in the Berne Convention. For example, the duration of the right is limited to 15 years (Art 12(1)), although a "substantial change to the contents of a database" will start a new period of protection (Art 12(2)). In addition, the proposal includes provision for compulsory licences. Thus, Article 11 requires a fair and non-discriminatory licence to be granted where the contents of the database "cannot be independently created, collected or obtained from any other source." This does not apply where the contents are not available "for reasons such as economy of time, effort or financial investment." In addition, Article 11(2) provides for compulsory licences by public bodies whose function is to provide information or by other entities "enjoying monopoly status by virtue of an exclusive concession by a public body." These provisions may have an impact on the application of competition rules to situations where a firm holds a strong position on the market by virtue of rights arising from implementation of the Database Directive. This issue is discussed in the next section of this chapter (see para **5.38** *et seq*).

Since the right to prevent unauthorised extraction is a *sui generis* right, there **5.26** was no obligation on the Commission to extend the right to non-Community nationals. The proposal limits the right to Community nationals unless the person claiming the right comes from a country which has entered into an agreement with the Council extending protection to that country. This could be used by the Council to limit protection to those countries which have equivalent protection. This move from national treatment towards reciprocity has been discussed (see para **3.10**). We have seen that it is the approach taken by the US in 1984 in protecting topographies of semiconductor chips. It remains to be seen whether the adoption in this form of the Database Directive would prompt equally hurried moves in the rest of the world to establish equivalent protection. We have seen that the protection of computer programs and semiconductor chips is dealt with by the Agreement on Trade-Related Aspects of Intellectual Property Rights (TRIPs). Article 10 does require members to protect by copyright:

> "Compilations of data or other material, whether in machine readable or other form, which by reason of the selection or arrangement of their contents constitute intellectual creations..."

However, TRIPs does not address the question of any further *sui generis* rights to control unauthorised access.

(f) Beneficiaries of protection

The identities of the beneficiaries of the rights under the draft Database **5.27** Directive depend on the nature of the right. In the case of copyright, it is the author who is granted the right, that is, the natural (or, where permitted by national law, legal) person who "created" the database (Art 3(1)).

The identity of the beneficiary of the right to prevent unauthorised extraction **5.28** depends on whether the database is protected by copyright. If so, the beneficiary is the author (or the person to whom the author has granted the right) (Art 1(2)). If not, the beneficiary is the "maker." This term is not defined.

(g) Appraisal

The extent to which the proposed Directive as currently drafted would, if **5.29** adopted, restrict the availability of copyright protection for databases depends to a large extent on the way in which originality is interpreted by the courts. Even if this requirement is easy to satisfy, the extent of copyright protection is limited and so protection will depend to a large extent on the *sui generis* right to prevent unauthorised extraction. The fact that this right is not the subject of international agreement has given the Commission far greater flexibility to deal with the specific issues raised by electronic databases than it had to deal with the specific issues raised by computer programs. Thus, not only is the duration and content of the unfair extraction right limited but there is an overriding possibility of a compulsory licence in certain situations. The Commission may also have some control over international arrangements if those non-Community countries who desire protection for their nationals are expected to grant reciprocal protection. Unlike other new technologies discussed in this book, TRIPs does not deal with the right to prevent unauthorised extraction. This means that any move to national treatment would probably require further international agreement.

5.30   The amended proposal for a Database Directive was adopted in October 1993 and was drafted to require implementation by 1 January 1995. To date, the Directive remains a proposal and it is not clear if it will be adopted in its present form or, indeed, at all. Whatever the end result, the issues described above will have to be addressed at some point in time by Member State law.

3. Competition law issues

5.31   As in the case of hardware and software, the first and often one of the most difficult issues is how to define the relevant market, in particular, to determine dominance. Having looked at that question, this section will then examine one of the key issues in the IT industry: can a supplier refuse to make available spare parts and other assistance to deter a third party maintainer (TPM) from competing with the supplier in providing (frequently lucrative) after-sales service? The importance of this issue is demonstrated by the reaction to the recent decision of the US Supreme Court concerning Kodak's policies on the supply of spare parts for its photocopiers. Finally, this section will look at possible competition law concerns in some typical agreements for the supply of services within the IT industry.

(i) Market definition

5.32   Given that many firms are involved in both software and services—so-called SSOs—the best starting point may be to see how the Commission distinguishes between the supply of software products and the supply of services. In its merger decision in *IBM France/CGI* (Case IV.M336), the Commission noted that there was a "major conceptual distinction" between IT software and IT services. The distinction is based on the following definitions:

> "(a) the *IT services market* which includes consultancy services, operational support services and applications and delivery services is basically a

(b) the *IT software market* which includes the applications software (and also the systems software market which is not affected by the present concentration) is a product market in which the product (package) can be sold or licensed to the clients through independent distributors" (para 9).

There may be some overlap in these definitions where software is developed for a client but then packaged for wider marketing. In this case, the SSO's activity is presumably counted within both the services and the software markets.

5.33

Clearly, though, there are narrower segments within the broad IT services market which may be used for the definition of the relevant market. However, the Commission has not found it easy to isolate markets in the services sector. In *EDS/SD-Scicon* (Case IV.M112 [1993] 4 CMLR M77) the Commission admitted that

5.34

"Market definition within the services sector is particularly difficult. The boundaries between the various categories and sub-categories of such services are blurred. The ability to provide one service often leads to the ability to provide another. The status necessary to undertake contracts in the various categories are similar" (para 8).

This is welcome recognition by the Commission that, even where one firm has a large share of a particular niche market, there are few barriers to entry for potential competitors. In other words, however narrow the definition of the market, the existing players are constrained by other potential players.

5.35

In the *EDS/SD-Scicon* case, though, the Commission did identify certain "market segments" within the IT services market without concluding whether there should be considered to be relevant markets:

5.36

"1. Systems management/systems operation: the management, maintenance and operation of an existing system for a client.
2. Systems integration: this includes the integration of existing systems by means of the development and installation of custom software for clients. Some statistics include within this category the supply and installation of new systems (systems development).
3. Pure consulting: this frequently precedes the other activities and may take the form of advice on the best way to address a business problem, including some form of computerisation.
4. Processing services: this involves the 'contracting out' of certain data processing needs. A number of different industries use such services, particularly banking, insurance etc" (para 11).

One of the important questions in relation to services concerns the ability of suppliers to refuse to supply spare parts to TPMs. This unilateral action is likely to be caught (if at all) by Article 86. Naturally, then, the first question will be the extent of the relevant market against which dominance is to be judged. This has already been discussed (see para **3.41**). The conclusion is that

5.37

spare parts for the supplier's machines may be the relevant market if no third party supply exists. This is most likely where the supplier can rely on intellectual property rights to prevent third party manufacture.

(ii) Refusal to supply/license

5.38 In practice, one of the most important issues in EC competition law is the extent to which a supplier can control the provision of maintenance by third parties. One way is simply to tie the supply of maintenance to the sale of the original product (see para **3.90**). In the IT industry, it is often the case that a TPM needs access to spare parts or other facilities which can only be obtained from the original supplier. By controlling access to those facilities, the supplier can control the provision of maintenance.

5.39 These possibilities are well illustrated by the *Kodak* case recently decided by the US Supreme Court.[17] In the early 1980s, Kodak had supplied TPMs with the spare parts necessary to maintain its photocopiers. Then, in the mid-1980s, it changed its policy and refused to sell spare parts to TPMs. It only sold spare parts to customers if the maintenance was carried out either by Kodak or by the customer itself. So Kodak stopped TPMs by refusing to supply spare parts directly and by stopping access to spare parts indirectly through customers. A member of TPMs sued Kodak for infringing US anti-trust (or competition) law.

5.40 There were two allegations. Firstly, it was argued that Kodak had tied maintenance to the sale of spare parts by preventing customers from using TPMs to install spare parts purchased from Kodak. Tying is only contrary to section 1 of the Sherman Act 1890 if the supplier has market power in the tying product (in this case, the spare parts). Kodak argued that it could not have power in the market for spare parts because it did not have any power in the market for the photocopiers themselves. In the District Court, Kodak obtained summary judgment dismissing the TPM's action without the need for a trial on the facts. The Supreme Court reversed this decision. It held that a supplier could have power in the market for its own spare parts and this could only be decided on the facts of each case and not through the procedure for summary judgment. In particular, only an examination of the facts could determine whether Kodak was right in arguing that it could not derive abnormal profits from maintenance because it was constrained by competition in the primary market.

5.41 This is a key point for the IT industry and has been mentioned at various points already in this book. If a firm supplies all spare parts, say, because it relies on IPRs to stop third parties making substitutes, does this mean that it has market power? Customers may be locked in because it is cheaper to buy an expensive spare part than change the primary product. However, there is an argument that the supplier's actions on the spare parts market are constrained by competition for the primary product. In turn, the key question is whether

---

[17] *Eastman Kodak Co* v *Image Technical Services* 119 L Ed 2d 266 (1992), noted Stern (1992) EIPR 369.

customers take into account the price of spare parts in deciding from where to buy the primary product. As the Supreme Court put it:

> "For the service-market price to affect equipment demand, consumers must inform themselves of the total cost of the "package"—equipment, service and parts—at the time of purchase; that is, consumers must engage in accurate life cycle pricing" (at 288).

The Court doubted whether this was possible in all cases and so left the issue to be determined by a jury.

The second allegation in the *Kodak* case was that the refusal to supply spare **5.42** parts to TPMs was an "attempted monopolisation" of the maintenance market contrary to section 2 of the Sherman Act 1890. Again, the Supreme Court held that there was sufficient evidence for a trial over the issue whether Kodak had sufficient market power in the market for spare parts and maintenance for its own machines. The Supreme Court rejected the business justifications put forward by Kodak, namely, that its actions were necessary:

> "to promote interbrand equipment competition by allowing Kodak to stress the quality of its service; to improve asset management by reducing Kodak's inventory costs; and to prevent independent service organisations from free riding on Kodak's capital investment in equipment, parts and service" (at 294).

Commentators have criticised the *Kodak* decision.[18] In particular, it is **5.43** argued that there can be no power in the spare parts market if there is no power in the market for the machines themselves. The Supreme Court has now ruled that that conclusion cannot be reached without an enquiry into the facts.

How are these issues dealt with under EC law? Although the underlying law **5.44** is certainly different, the application of EC competition law may be even stricter than that laid down by the Supreme Court decision. So far as unique spare parts are concerned, in *Hugin/Liptons* (OJ 1978 L22/23; [1978] 1 CMLR D19), the Commission held that Hugin had contravened Article 86 in discontinuing supplies of spare parts of its cash registers to Liptons, a TPM. Hugin held 100% of the markets for its unique spare parts but only some 12% of the Community cash register market. The ECJ in fact overturned the Commission's decision on appeal but only on the ground that there was insufficient effect on trade between Member States (*Hugin v Commission* Case 22/78 [1979] ECR 1869; [1979] 3 CMLR 345). Further, the approach of the Commission, the CFI and the ECJ in the *Hilti* case[19] suggests that they may not fully take into account competition from the primary market, although, in fact, in this case, Hilti was held to be dominant in the primary market for nail guns.

---

[18] Katz & Arnold 10 The Computer Lawyer (July 1993) 9 who quote Charles Rule, a former Assistant Attorney–General in charge of the Antitrust Division at the Department of Justice, writing in the Wall Street Journal that the opinion is "truly bad news."

[19] Commission Decision OJ 1988 L65/19. Upheld on appeal *Hilti v Commission* Case T-30/89 [1991] ECR II-1439; [1992] 4 CMLR 16 (CFI) and Case C-53/92P [1994] ECR I-667; [1994] 4 CMLR 614 (ECJ). See para **3.40**.

5.45   If that is the position for the refusal to supply spare parts to TPMs, what about other facilities to which the TPM may need access in order properly to maintain either hardware or software? Firstly, a TPM may need access to technical information about the products, for example, circuit diagrams or source code. Can a TPM force the equipment supplier to provide it with such information? The first question is whether the TPM can obtain the information itself. There is nothing to stop a TPM taking apart a machine but the decompilation right in the Software Directive does not extend to information needed to maintain (see para **4.42**). Can the TPM rely on Article 86 in order to obtain this information which may be confidential? We have seen that the Commission has relied on Article 86 to force the disclosure of confidential information for interoperability and the Recitals to the Directive confirm that Article 86 can apply (see para **4.62** *et seq*). There are clear parallels between refusing to disclose interface information in order to control a separate product market and refusal to disclose information necessary to compete in a separate services market.

5.46   The position may be more difficult for diagnostic software the use of which involves copying. Whether a refusal to license the TPM to use such software is a breach of Article 86 or not depends on the application of the ECJ and CFI's rulings in the cases on the interface between Article 86 and intellectual property rights. We have seen that, in *Volvo* v *Veng* (Case 238/87 [1988] ECR 6211; [1989] 4 CMLR 122) (see para **3.51**), the ECJ held that relying on an intellectual property right is not itself contrary to Article 86 but may be so if there is additional abusive conduct. The ECJ's judgment in the *Magill* cases may provide more guidance on this issue (see para **2.150**).

5.47   One final issue on the question of the application of Article 86 to a refusal to license is whether there is any scope for such an argument in the case of the proposed right to prevent unauthorised extraction from a database (see para **5.23**). One argument in this case might be that the legislation establishing the right does itself provide for compulsory licences and, consequently, pre-empts the application of competition law. We have seen that competition law is not sufficient to determine whether a compulsory licence is required (see para **2.145**). There is a stronger argument that it should not apply for this purpose when the legislation itself has addressed the issue.

(iii) Mergers and joint ventures

5.48   A number of mergers and joint ventures are discussed in Chapter 6 (see para **6.46** *et seq*). Similar principles may apply to transactions involving the IT services industry outside of telecoms. The approach of the Commission to mergers is well demonstrated by its decision on the acquisition of SD-Scicon by EDS (Case IV.M112 [1993] 4 CMLR M77). The Commission mentioned the following factors in relation to the markets affected by the acquisition

"- the markets are fragmented,
  - the barriers to entry are low: in essence, the only requirement to enter the

market is technically qualified personnel,
- high degree of supply-side substitutability between the various sub-market categorisations,
- there is often demand-side substitutability between different suppliers" (para 17).

This indicates that typical mergers and joint ventures in the IT services sector should be looked at favourably by the Commission.

(iv) Bureau services/facilities management (FM)

Bureau service organisations were common in the days when only expensive **5.49** mainframes were available requiring a team of support staff but only performing basic accounting tasks. For many companies it was not economic to invest in the system. Instead, bureau services would invest in the hardware, software and staff and perform accounting activities on behalf of a number of other businesses. With the falling price of hardware and basic software as well as the scope for tailoring tasks for the individual customer, the demand for bureau services fell. More recently, there has been a trend towards out-sourcing some support activities to specialist firms who provide central processing and other services for their clients. These services are now more commonly called facilities management (FM). Outsourcing contracts can involve staggering amounts of money. It was reported that the value of the transaction when EDS took over Xerox's computer and telecoms network was US$ 3,200m.[20]

Clearly, there is nothing inherently objectionable in this kind of activity from **5.50** the point of view of competition law. However, restrictions can be placed in FM agreements which require consideration from the point of view of EC competition law. In particular, the client may wish to restrict the use by the FM provider of materials made available to it. EC competition generally would not catch an obligation to maintain the confidentiality of information disclosed pursuant to a legitimate transaction.[21] There could be concern if the obligation went further and prevented or had the effect of preventing the FM provider from acting in a similar capacity for other clients. Moreover, if the client owns software and restricts the use by the FM provider of that software, the restriction may be caught by EC competition law. Of course, EC law only applies if there is an appreciable effect on competition and on trade between Member States (see para **2.106** *et seq*).

(v) Consultancy

Many tasks in the IT industry are carried out by independent consultants, **5.51** particularly software and services organisation (SSOs). Licences to develop

---

[20] *Financial Times*, 15 June 1994.
[21] See, *e.g.*, the block exemption on know-how licences (OJ 1989 L61/1) Art 2(1)(1) and the Commission's Notice on sub-contracting agreements (OJ 1979 C1/2).

software have already been discussed (see para **4.77** *et seq*). What about the restriction on the future use of developed software? The Commission's Notice on Subcontracting indicates that there may be scope for restricting further use of technology provided to a third party contractor (OJ 1979 C1/2). However, the Notice only applies to a case where the principal makes available technology to the subcontractor. It does not extend to the results of research and development carried out by the contractor where those results can be exploited independently of the technology provided by the principal (Art 3).

5.52   One of the allegations against Microsoft investigated by the US Department of Justice and the European Commission was that Microsoft had unduly restricted the activities of firms to which it had made available information about its forthcoming operating systems software. In the settlement of the investigation, Microsoft undertook not to enter into non-disclosure agreements (NDAs), in particular those:

> "that would restrict in any manner any person subject to the NDA from developing software products that will run on competing Operating System Software products, provided that such development efforts do not entail the disclosure or use of any Microsoft proprietary information during the term of the NDA."

CONTENTS OF CHAPTER 6

Chapter 6
Telecoms

1. Introduction

A book on EC information technology law would be incomplete without a **6.1** discussion of EC telecommunications law. From the industry point of view, with the spread of digitisation and the growing use of networks, telecoms is now an important part of information technology and ever more important as we move towards US Vice President Al Gore's "information super-highways." From the legal point of view, there are fascinating issues raised by regulation and, in addition, particular problems are raised by the application of competition rules in the sector. The way in which those issues are resolved may be of use in predicting the application of competition rules in other sectors. Moreover, there are clear parallels between, on the one hand, the extent to which the States need to mould intellectual property rights (IPRs) to avoid stifling competition excessively and, on the other, circumscribing exclusive rights granted by the State for the operation of telecoms networks.

Until quite recently, public networks were not used extensively for digital **6.2** transmission. The recent application of technological advances to telecoms has allowed a growing use of telecoms networks for the transmission of data in digital form. This in turn has led to telecoms playing a vital role in many of the new applications of information technology, for example, videoconferencing.

The telecoms industry presents an excellent example of technology **6.3** outpacing regulation. Originally, most telecoms services were provided by State monopolies. As the continuing process of digitisation led to the convergence of technologies in the computer and telecoms arenas, so it became more and more apparent that the competitive computer industry was bringing technology to the consumer more quickly than the State monopolies. Indeed, the State monopolies were holding up the use of IT by failing to update the networks so as to allow fast and reliable digital traffic. This failure was one of the reasons for moves throughout the world towards limiting or removing the exclusive rights traditionally granted to the public network operators (PNOs).

Perhaps the most interesting aspect of the regulatory changes has been **6.4** government concern that regulatory changes did not jeopardise the availability of basic services to all at a reasonable cost. This "universal service" might be jeopardised in a telecoms free-for-all because the PNO would not be able to compete with other suppliers who do not bear the cost of universal service. This fear has led to attempts to balance the need to introduce competition with incentives to the industry to build and maintain national (or Community-wide) networks. The result has been increasingly complex regulation at a Community and national level.

6.5   The regulatory issues will only get more complicated with the relentless progress of digital convergence. This book does not cover television broadcasting but the increasing adoption of digital transmission by that industry will mean that IT law will encompass broadcasting as well. Now that cable television operators have built up a sufficient network in some countries, one of the key regulatory issues of the day is whether these operators should be allowed to carry voice telephony. Licences have been granted in the UK, for example.

6.6   These issues of digital convergence and regulation seem to have been at the heart of the recent unprecedented shake-up in the telecoms industry, particularly in the US. On the one hand, it appears that the PNOs feel the need to have access to the information as well as the means of supply of that information. On the other hand, the PNOs are concerned to ensure that they are not caught out by deregulation, in particular, allowing cable companies to carry voice telephony. In February 1994, Viacom, a US cable company, finally succeeded in its bid for Paramount by paying US\$ 10 billion. Nynex, one the seven US regional telephone monopolies (or Baby Bells), has a 25% stake in Viacom. In December 1993, it was announced that Bell Atlantic, was paying US\$ 33 billion for Tele-Communications Inc (TCI), the biggest cable television operator. When the deal was called off in March 1994, uncertainty on the regulatory front was blamed.

6.7   So telecoms play an increasingly important role in the IT industry. More importantly, perhaps, for the purposes of this book, many of the issues which have been discussed in previous chapters appear in the telecoms area as well. The difficulty for a book of this length is that these issues arise in the context of a vast and complex system of regulation. A full description of that system must be sought elsewhere.[1] This chapter is limited to an overview of the subject whilst picking out key issues.

2. Legislation

6.8   Historically, the Community's telecoms industry has been characterised by monopolies on the part of State-owned bodies. These telecoms administrations (TAs) would invariably be granted exclusive rights to operate the network and over other activities such as the sale of equipment. They would also generally be responsible for the necessary regulation. One reason for this control was to ensure universal service, that is, access for everyone to basic telephone services of a reasonable quality and at an affordable price. In fact, of course, the monopolies extended far beyond what was required to support universal service. It is no coincidence that telecoms regulation protected indigenous

---

[1] See, *e.g.* Denton Hall, *EC Telecommunications Law* (Wiley Chancery, 1993, looseleaf).

telecoms equipment producers from foreign competitors. There was a growing realisation particularly in the early 1980s that these monopolies were hindering both the efficient provision of services as well as the introduction of new services which had become possible as a result of technological advances. The UK began its own liberalisation programme in the 1980s with the privatisation of British Telecom and the grant of a licence to a second network operator, Mercury. Moves at the Community level date from about the same time but have been to some extent less radical not least because of the different state of network development from one Member State to the next. Significant progress was recently made with preliminary agreement to open up voice telephony to competition and the Commission has promised a Green Paper on infrastructure by the end of 1994.[2]

Now that public network operators in the Community include some which **6.9** are not owned by the State, they are commonly referred to as telecom operators (TOs).[3] If there is one industry which is worse than the computer industry for acronyms, it is the telecoms industry. Acronyms used in this chapter are included in the list of abbreviations at the start of this book.

(i) **Green Paper**

Some limited progress had been made before 1987[4] but current Community **6.10** policy is for the large part based on the Commission's 1987 Green Paper on the development of the common market for telecommunications services and equipment[5] which announced that it was time:

> "to initiate a common thinking process regarding the fundamental adjustment of the institutional and regulatory conditions which the telecommunications sector now faces. This world-wide transformation is due to the profound and technical change which is currently taking place: the progressive merger of telecommunications, data-processing, and, ultimately, audio-visual and television technology."

The Green Paper put forward ten "positions" or basic policies: **6.11**

(A) The Commission accepted the need for continued exclusive provision of and operation of the network itself in order to preserve network integrity. However, this did not mean that there should be exclusive access to the network. Indeed, one of the key elements of the Commission's programme is ensuring unfettered third party access to the network. The Commission recently pointed out that "It is now appropriate to seek agreement on the principle of infrastructure liberalisation in the telecommunications sector

---

[2] See Commission Communication on Europe's Way to the Information Society: An Action Plan COM(94)347 of 19 July 1994 at 3.

[3] See the definition in Art 1 of Dir 90/388 on competition in the markets for telecommunications services (OJ 1990 L192/10; [1991] 4 CMLR 932).

[4] *e.g.*, Council Dir 86/361 on the initial stage of the mutual recognition of type approval for telecommunications terminal equipment (OJ 1986 L217/21).

[5] COM(87)290 of 30 June 1987.

together with clear dates for its implementation."[6]

(B) Exclusive provision by a single national TO of a limited number of basic services—so-called "reserved services"—was acceptable in order to safeguard public service goals such as universal service. The only obvious candidate was voice telephony—the most basic of the services available on the public network (or PSTN). Since the overwhelming majority of TO revenue is derived from this service, it has since become clear that agreement would have to be reached to open up even this service to competition. Agreement has now been reached by the Council on a common position which will open up voice telephony to competition.[7]

(C) All other services should be opened up to competition immediately. These "competitive services" include value added services such as electronic messaging services.

(D) One of the Commission's main aims is to promote Community-wide networks. Support for Community networks has been boosted by amendments to the EC Treaty implemented by the TEU, in particular, a new Title XII on Trans-European Networks (TENs). Article 129b says

> "...the Community shall contribute to the establishment and development of trans-European networks in the areas of transport, telecommunications and energy infrastructures. Within the framework of a system of open and competitive markets, action by the Community shall aim at promoting the interconnection and inter-operability of national networks as well as access to such networks."

For example, the Commission recently proposed two Council decisions on development of the Integrated Services Digital Network (ISDN) as a trans-European network (OJ 1993 C259/4). One of the necessary prerequisites for a Community-wide network is the interoperability of the networks and equipment. The Green Paper proposed strict requirements on standards to achieve this aim.

(E) Standards are also important to "competitive services." It is not sufficient to permit third party access to the network. There must be control over the conditions laid down by the network provider to ensure a level playing field. If not, it would be open to the network provider, for example, to charge excessive prices in order to protect its own market. It is important that the level playing field extends across the Community in order to encourage pan-European services. The dual approach of liberalisation and harmonisation is the predominant theme of EC telecoms policy. The various elements required to ensure unfettered access are summarised in the phrase "open network provision" (or ONP).

(F) The Green Paper distinguished between services and equipment. Although there were arguments in favour of special rules for services, this

---

[6] See Commission Communication on Europe's Way to the Information Society: An Action Plan COM(94)347 of 19 July 1994 at 3.
[7] Amended proposal for a Directive on the application of open network provision (ONP) to voice telephony (OJ 1992 C263/20). Common position agreed on 30 June 1993.

was not the case for terminal equipment. The Commission advocated full competition in this sector save for the first telephone set which could be reserved to the TO for a limited period. Again, standards are essential to a Community-wide terminal equipment market. Some steps had already been taken before 1987, in particular, Directive 86/361[8] which required mutual recognition by Member States of conformity tests. More importantly, in line with the "new approach" to standards, Directive 91/263[9] requires Member States to allow the marketing of terminal equipment provided only that certain "essential requirements" are met. Like other "new approach" Directives, the Commission mandated the European standards bodies to prepare detailed standards compliance with which is presumed to satisfy the essential requirements. Unlike many "new approach" Directives, the Directive allows the Commission to make these European standards mandatory (Art 6). Clearly, laying down standards was a key part of the Commission's strategy to opening up a Community-wide market. In order to streamline the adoption procedure, the Commission led the drive to reorganise European standards bodies. This led to the establishment, in 1988, near Nice, of an institute devoted to setting standards in the telecoms field, the European Telecommunications Standards Institute (ETSI).

(G) One of principal bars to a free market was the fact that TOs were invariably both in the business as well as regulators. The Green Paper called for the separation of regulatory and operational or commercial activities. This is one of the key elements in the liberalisation directives adopted by the Commission on the basis of Article 90(3). The ECJ has confirmed that it is a breach of Article 90 in conjunction with Article 86 for a Member State to grant the exclusive right to approve equipment to the TO (*RTT* v *GB-Inno* Case C-18/88 [1991] ECR I-5941).

(H) The competition rules were seen as an important stick to ensure the proposed policy positions were not undermined. Thus, according to the Green Paper, there should be a continuous review of the commercial activities of TOs to ensure compliance with Articles 85 and 86. In 1991, the Commission finally published its guidelines on the application of competition rules to the telecoms sector (OJ 1991 C233/2; see Appendix A7). Article 90(2) may protect TOs from the application of the EC Treaty rules where that application would obstruct the performance of their public service obligations (see para **2.162** *et seq*). In the Guidelines, the Commission indicates that, as this is an exception to the application of these rules, it will be narrowly interpreted (para 21 et seq.). This issue was recently addressed by the Commission in its Green Paper on opening up the mobile telephony sector. It argues that exclusive rights over voice telephony should not extend to the mobile sector, particularly since

---

[8] Council Directive 86/361 on the initial stage of the mutual recognition of type approval for telecommunications terminal equipment (OJ 1986 L217/21).
[9] Council Directive of the approximation of the laws of the Member States concerning telecommunications terminal equipment, including the mutual recognition of their conformity (OJ 1991 L128/1).

liberalisation of that sector is likely to increase use of the fixed network rather than undermine the provision of universal service.[10]

(I) In the new world envisaged by the Green Paper, there would be far greater involvement of private firms in the provision of telecoms services and equipment. The Green Paper makes it clear that there will be similar review of their activities to ensure compliance with competition rules.

(J) Finally, the Commission confirmed its intention to play a full role on the international scene which was already highly developed. Moreover, the Commission insisted on vetting international arrangements affecting competition in the Community.

6.12 In 1988, the Council gave broad approval to the objectives in the Green Paper and invited the Commission to make the necessary proposals.[11]

6.13 There has been progress on the basis of the Green Paper policies but that progress has been patchy. It is clear from the Green Paper that there is a need for liberalisation, on the one hand, and harmonisation, on the other. Like the IT sector in general, harmonisation does not take place overnight not least when it requires agreement (even if only by qualified majority) amongst Member States with widely different levels of network and market development. On the other hand, the process of liberalisation has been helped by the Commission's power in Article 90(3) to adopt generally applicable directives to ensure the application of Treaty rules to undertakings granted exclusive rights by the State. It is to those liberalisation directives that we now turn.

(ii) Liberalisation

6.14 Article 90 confirms that Member States must comply with the Treaty in their dealings with public or privileged undertakings (Article 90(1)) and establishes a limited exception from the Treaty for undertakings entrusted with a service of general economic interest. The Commission has relied on Article 90(3) to adopt directives to further these aims. As a general rule, the Treaty only confers the power to legislate on the Council. The Commission's power to adopt directives under Article 90(3) is a rare exception to this rule.

(a) Terminal Equipment Directive[12]

6.15 In 1988, the Commission took its first step in carrying out its recommendations in the 1987 Green Paper for liberalisation of the telecoms industry. Although there were arguments that TOs should retain exclusive rights over the network as well as over some basic services, the Commission had recommended full liberalisation in the market for equipment to be connected to the network—"terminal equipment."

---

[10] Green Paper on a mobile and personal communications COM(94)145 of 27 April 1994 at 177.
[11] Council Resolution of 30 June 1988 on the development of the market for telecommunications services and equipment up to 1992 (OJ 1988 C257/1).
[12] Commission Dir 88/301 on competition in the markets in telecommunications terminal equipment (OJ 1988 L131/73; [1991] 4 CMLR 922).

The Directive set out the following four basic obligations: firstly, the **6.16** terminal equipment market must be opened up to competition. Thus, Article 2 of the Directive required Member States to withdraw any special or exclusive rights for "the importation, marketing, connection, bringing into service of telecommunications terminal equipment and/or maintenance of such equipment" (Art 1). By the same token, Member States have to ensure that any economic operator can carry out any of these activities. There are two qualifications to this freedom. On the one hand, Member States may stop the connection of equipment which does not satisfy the essential requirements laid down by Directive 86/361 (now replaced by Directive 91/263) (see para **6.31**); on the other hand, Member States can require economic operators to satisfy necessary technical qualifications.

Secondly, Article 4 of the Directive requires free access to network **6.17** termination points (NTPs). Moreover, the physical characteristics of NTPs must be published by the end of 1988. Member States are also required to publish technical specifications and type-approval procedures by certain specified dates (Art 5).

Thirdly, Article 6 of the Directive requires the separation of the commercial **6.18** operator from the standards setting and monitoring process. In other words, a separate national regulatory authority (NRA) must be established to ensure that the national TOs have no control over regulation of the industry.

Finally, Article 7 of the Directive obliges Member States to take the **6.19** necessary steps to ensure that customers can terminate existing leasing or maintenance contracts by no more than one year's notice.

Article 90 only allows the Commission to require respect for the underlying **6.20** Treaty rules. The Recitals to the Directive justify the Directive's provisions on the basis of Articles 3, 30, 37 and 86 in conjunction with Article 90. A number of Member States brought actions before the ECJ attacking the Commission's competence to adopt the Directive. In *France* v *Commission* (Case C-202/88 [1991] ECR I-1223; [1992] 5 CMLR 552), the ECJ endorsed the Commission's power to adopt general rules under Article 90(3) rather than having to rely on individual decisions. Furthermore, it held that Article 90 could be relied on to attack the exclusive rights themselves (see para **2.160**).

The ECJ then turned to the specific provisions of the Directive at issue in the **6.21** case. The obligation to remove exclusive rights and permit competition was justified on the basis of Article 30 because Community trade in terminal equipment could be affected. However, the Directive had not sufficiently defined "special rights" so this aspect of the Directive was struck down.

The obligation to split the operational and regulatory functions was **6.22** approved by the ECJ because:

"a system of undistorted competition, as laid down in the Treaty, can be guaranteed only if equality of opportunity is secured as between the various economic operators. To entrust an undertaking which markets terminal equipment with the task of drawing up the specifications for such equipment, monitoring their applications and granting type-approval in respect thereof is tantamount to conferring upon it the power to determine at will which terminal equipment may be connected to the public network, and thereby placing that undertaking at an obvious advantage over its competitors" (para 51).

6.23   Finally, the ECJ declared void Article 7 of the Directive on the right to terminate existing contracts. It held that the duty of supervision under Article 90 is only concerned with State measures. Since there was no evidence that the Member States had insisted on long-term contracts, the duration of these agreements was the responsibility of the TOs. The Commission could take action by individual decisions under Articles 85 and 86 but not by general directives under Article 90.

6.24   Overall, then, the ECJ's judgment was a strong endorsement of the Commission's powers under Article 90(3). The annulment of the Directive so far as it concerned special rights is unlikely to constrain future Commission action. The amendment of Article 7 is a greater constraint. It confirms a clear distinction between control of State involvement which can be carried out by quasi-legislative measures and control of the commercial activities of private or public undertakings which can only be effected by the Commission through individual decisions under Articles 85 and 86.

6.25   There have been a number of cases since the ECJ's judgment in *France* v *Commission* interpreting the Directive in the context of preliminary rulings referred by national courts, for example, *Ministère Public v Taillandier-Neny*[13] where it was held that Article 6 of the Directive precluded a national law banning the marketing of terminal equipment without a certificate of compliance with certain requirements if those requirements were not laid down by an independent entity.[14]

(b) Services Directive[15]

6.26   Like the Terminal Equipment Directive, the Services Directive is a liberalisation directive adopted on the basis of Article 90(3). This time the market at which the Commission's attention was directed was the services market (excluding telex, mobile radiotelephony, paging and satellite services). The basic obligations on Member States are, firstly, to open up the market for services by requiring Member States to withdraw any special or exclusive rights to provide such services and, secondly, to allow any economic operator to provide such services. Like the Terminal Equipment Directive, the Services Directive permits Member States to lay down essential requirements which those operators must fulfil through a licensing or declaration procedure.

6.27   One of the most important differences to the Terminal Equipment Directive is that the Services Directive embodies an application by the Commission of

---

[13] Case 92/91, Judgment of 27 October 1993.
[14] See also *Ministère Public* v *Rouffeteau & Badia* Case C-314/93, Judgment of 12 July 1994. Not yet reported.
[15] Commission Dir 90/388 on competition in the markets for telecommunications services (OJ 1990 L192/10; [1991] 4 CMLR 932).

Article 90(2). Article 2 of the Directive allows Member States to retain exclusive rights for the provision of voice telephony. The Council has now reached agreement on a common position to open up voice telephony to competition.[16] Furthermore, under Article 3 of the Directive, Member States which have granted exclusive rights to provide public data switched services may take steps over a limited period to protect that service, in particular, by prohibiting economic operators from engaging in simple resale of leased lines. Member States may also set down public service specifications for those providing such services.

Like the Terminal Equipment Directive, the Services Directive also **6.28** contains obligations to publish standards; to separate operational and regulatory functions; and to allow termination of long-term contracts. Like the Terminal Equipment Directive, the Services Directive was challenged before the ECJ. Its judgment in *Spain v Commission*[17] followed closely its approach in *France v Commission*. The Services Directive was upheld by the ECJ except for the insufficiently defined special rights and the contract termination provisions which were not Member State measures which could be controlled under Article 90.

The Commission has had to resort to Article 169 to initiate proceedings **6.29** against Member States for failing to implement the Services Directive ([1994] 4 CMLR 613).

(iii) **Harmonisation**

Article 90 only gives the Commission the power to require Member States to **6.30** comply with their existing obligations under the Treaty. It can be used to ensure compliance with free movement and competition rules; it cannot be used to harmonise national law in order to create a Community-wide level playing field. This requires harmonisation legislation.

(a) Terminal equipment standards

As we have seen, Directive 86/361 represented an initial stage towards **6.31** Community standards (see para **6.11**(F)). A second stage Directive was required for mutual recognition of essential requirements. This was the aim of Directive 91/263.[18] For this Directive fully to achieve its aim of freedom to sell the same terminal equipment throughout the Community, standards must be laid down. Unfortunately, ETSI has been swamped with work and priority seems to have been given to standards for interoperability of Community-wide networks at the expense of other standards.

---

[16] Amended proposal for a Directive on the application of open network provision (ONP) to voice telephony (OJ 1992 C263/20). Common position agreed on 30 June 1993.
[17] Cases C-271 & 281/90. Judgment of 17 November 1992.
[18] Council Directive of the approximation of the laws of the Member States concerning telecommunications terminal equipment, including the mutual recognition of their conformity (OJ 1991 L128/1).

(b) ONP Framework Directive[19]

6.32   This Directive established the framework for implementation of ONP. The Directive lays down basic principles as well as a three year work programme.

6.33   "Open network provision conditions" are defined as:

> "the conditions, harmonized according to the provisions of this Directive, which concern the open and efficient access to public telecommunications networks and, where applicable, public telecommunications services and the efficient use of those networks and services.
>
>   Without prejudice to their application on a case-by-case basis, the open network provision conditions may include harmonized conditions with regard to:
>
>   – technical interfaces, including the definition and implementation of network termination points, where required,
>
>   – usage conditions, including access to frequencies where required,
>
>   – tariff principles" (Art 1(10)).

6.34   In other words, ONP looks to the harmonisation of three areas: technical interfaces, usage conditions and tariff principles. In each case, the Directive states that the conditions must be objective, transparent and non-discriminatory (Art 3).

6.35   The framework Directive can only take effect in practice, firstly, by the adoption of the relevant European standards by ETSI and, secondly, through the adoption of individual directives such as the one on leased lines[20] and the forthcoming one on voice telephony.[21] There have also been recommendations on ONP, for example, for packet-switched data services (OJ 1992 L200/1) and ISDN (OJ 1992 L200/10).

6.36   Harmonising ONP conditions does not solve all problems. A good example of continuing issues which have to be resolved is the litigation at a national level over tariffs which should be paid by third parties for access to the network. The amount of the charge is closely tied to issues of competition and could have wider implications in other areas where a firm seeks access to a competitor's facilities. The issue is discussed in the section on competition law and pricing (see para **6.52** *et seq*).

(iv) Appraisal

6.37   The Commission has been at the forefront of wide-ranging regulatory change in the Community and there is now a vast and steadily increasing range of telecoms regulation at a Community level. However, many of the moves towards liberalising the market have probably been forced on Member States

---

[19] Council Dir 90/387 on the establishment of the internal market for telecommunications services through the implementation of open network provision (OJ 1990 L192/1).

[20] Council Directive 92/44 on the application of open network provision to leased lines (OJ 1992 L165/27).

[21] Amended proposal for a Directive on the application of open network provision (ONP) to voice telephony (OJ 1992 C263/20). Common position agreed on 30 June 1993.

by the technology and the market. For example, most Member States would have freed up the terminal equipment market even without the Commission's Terminal Equipment Directive. It is true that a number of Member States attacked the Directive before the ECJ but this was more to do with attempting to maintain the Council's exclusive power to legislate rather than because of objections to the content of the Directive.

Where Community input is desperately required is in creating a level **6.38** playing field throughout the Community. There are two principal aspects to this objective. Firstly, there is the need for Community-wide networks. Secondly, there is the need for free movement of equipment and services. On both these issues, the Community has not yet scored very highly. There is still no Europe-wide ISDN[22] or mobile network.[23] Perhaps the most important bar to progress has been the difficulty in adopting the standards required. There is no doubt also a reluctance on the part of the TOs to encourage moves towards the dismantlement of their long-standing monopolies.

Following a review by the Commission of telecoms policy, in 1993, the **6.39** Council laid down some short and long term goals (OJ 1993 C213/1). Short term goals included "rapid and effective implementation of existing Community legislation in the field of telecommunications services and ONP" as well as extension of these principles to the satellite and mobile sectors. Major long term goals included liberalisation of all public voice telephony whilst maintaining universal service and the working out of a future policy on network infrastructure. The Council subsequently adopted a resolution on universal service principles (OJ 1994 C48/1).

Community telecoms regulation is complemented by other Community **6.40** policies. Some of these policies are not covered in this book, for example, opening up the market for public procurement. Data protection rules are covered in the next chapter. We now turn to the competition rules which have played and will continue to play a pivotal role in ensuring that liberalisation and harmonisation do bring the benefits sought by the Commission.

3. Competition law issues

The Commission's 1991 Guidelines (OJ 1991 C233/2; [1991] 4 CMLR 946) **6.41** address many of the competition law issues which are raised in the telecoms field and are reproduced in Appendix A7. Many will agree with the Commission's comment that "There is a need for more certainty as to the application of competition rules" (para 6). The Guidelines go some way to addressing that problem.

The Guidelines deal first with the question of market definition (paras 25 et **6.42** seq.). They state the usual test but are not particularly helpful in how to apply

---

[22] Commission's Progress Report on the Coordinated Introduction of ISDN COM(94)81 of 25 March 1994.
[23] Green Paper on a mobile and personal communications COM(94)145 of 27 April 1994 at 201.

this test in the telecoms area. The Commission indicates some possible markets but adds that narrower markets may be appropriate. We can sympathise with the Commission's desire to maintain flexibility over the complex question of market definition. As the Commission has pointed out "The telecommunications market is developing fast and there is a high degree of uncertainty about how it will look in a few years' time..."[24]

In discussing the market for value added services, the Commission commented that "It is particularly difficult to give a precise picture of the existing structure of this emerging market because its principal feature is that it is in constant evolution."[25]

Despite these uncertainties, it has to be said that this part of the Guidelines does not go very far in eliminating uncertainties over the application of competition rules, particularly given the importance of market definition to both Article 85 and Article 86.

6.43   The Guidelines then go on to deal separately with the application of Article 85 and 86. So far as the former is concerned, the Guidelines distinguish between agreements involving the different types of entities, that is, TOs and other equipment and service providers. The Commission recognises that some agreements are essential to completing the internal market and competing in the global market. For example, moves towards setting up the Europe-wide digital mobile system, GSM, began with agreement between the national PNOs. On the other hand, the Commission notes that competition is essential to avoid "diseconomies" that may result from agreements which undermine the increased potential competition in a liberalised and harmonised Community telecoms market. For example, it records its intervention in the agreement between PNOs on conditions for the allocation of leased lines (para 46).

6.44   The Guidelines contain a detailed assessment of the application of Article 86 to behaviour of both TOs and other equipment and service providers. The basic principles apply outside the telecoms marketplace and are useful indicators of the Commission's approach to other fields, particularly other IT sectors.

6.45   There are a few issues which deserve fuller treatment than that accorded to them in the Guidelines, especially in the light of subsequent developments.

(i) Mergers and joint ventures

6.46   There have been a large number of mergers and joint ventures dealt with by the Commission under Article 85 and the Merger Regulation. A list is provided at the end of this chapter. There are some predominant themes.

6.47   Firstly, as we have seen, the Commission is very keen to encourage interconnection of the various national networks. To date, there is no such Community-wide network. Instead, customers are billed in the country where the call is made. In the Guidelines, the Commission recognises that agreement

---

[24] *BT/MCI* OJ 1994 L223/36, para 14.
[25] *BT/MCI* OJ 1994 L223/36, para 12.

between network operators may further the objective of Community-wide services through network interconnection (para 36). The objective may also be assisted by agreements between firms other than network operators. In *CMC/Talkline* (OJ 1994 C221/9), the Commission indicated that it would take a favourable approach to an agreement between mobile telephony service providers aimed at establishing a one-stop shopping and billing service to their customers by pooling airtime purchased in bulk by the parties from mobile network operators.

Where TOs are party to an arrangement, the main concern of the 6.48 Commission is to ensure that the TO does not use its rights over the network and reserved services to distort competition in the markets for competitive services. In particular, it will attempt to ensure that there is no risk of the TO subsidising a competitive service from revenue from services over which it has exclusive rights, for example, voice telephony. It will also seek to ensure that the TO does not discriminate against competing suppliers of the competitive service by hindering access to the network. The cases since the Guidelines show a variety of ways in which the Commission attempts to control these possible abuses of exclusive rights. In *STET/Italtel/AT&T/AT&T-NSI* (OJ 1992 C333/3), the parties entered into undertakings to the Commission that they would not cross-subsidise or discriminate. In *Infonet* (OJ 1992 C7/3), these concerns were dealt with through obligations on the parties in the relevant agreements and the Commission relied on undertakings to record relevant transactions and report annually to the Commission. In *BT/MCI* (OJ 1994 L223/36), though, the Commission relied on existing regulatory constraints to assuage its concerns although the Commission threatened to apply EC competition rules immediately should these regulatory constraints prove to be insufficient.

Finally, whether or not a TO is party to the arrangement, the Commission 6.49 will need to satisfy itself that the market is not unduly foreclosed by the parties; in other words, the Commission must judge the extent of market power created by the arrangement. There are a number of factors which are particularly relevant in the telecoms field. Firstly, it may well be the case that a joint venture is necessary in order to pool resources. For example, in the case of satellites, the Commission is aware that this may be necessary to compete effectively against the major US suppliers. In *Aérospatiale/Alcatel Espace* (OJ 1994 C47/6), the Commission took a favourable view towards an agreement for joint tendering. The same considerations were also relevant in the approval of the acquisition by Matra Marconi Space of British Aerospace Space Systems (Case IV.M437).

These cases concerning the satellite sector also show that the Commission 6.50 may take into account the countervailing market power of customers. In *Aérospatiale/Alcatel Espace*, it commented that "In general, the customers are very well informed of the state of the required technology and their precise requirements and in addition have very considerable purchasing power" (OJ 1994 C47/6 at 7).

These comments are equally applicable to cases where the arrangements concern other telecoms equipment or services to be supplied to the public network operators. In *Alcatel/Telettra*, for example, countervailing buying power was one reason why the Commission approved a merger despite the fact that the parties' combined shares of both the line transmission and microwave equipment markets exceeded 80% (OJ 1991 L122/48 para 37).

6.51 Lastly, reflecting the Commission's comments on the constant evolution of the market, there may well be arguments that high market shares are not sustainable or do not confer market power because of strong potential competition. In *Alcatel/Telettra*, the Commission took into account the fact that the two principal competitors were capable of increasing supply and that there would be no significant barrier from the demand side for strong competitors to enter the market. The Commission went on to say:

> "The technical costs of adaptation do not today in themselves constitute an appreciable barrier to entry for European-based competitors. There is no indication either for the time being that proprietary intellectual property rights could be exploited in such a way as to amount to a barrier to such competitors. Within the framework of standardization in ETSI the Commission has a strong interest in preventing such a barrier emerging" (para 42).

We return to the question of standards and ETSI at the end of this section (see para **6.59**).

(ii) Pricing

6.52 The 1987 Green Paper conceded that it may be appropriate for exclusive rights to be granted by Member States for the establishment and operation of the networks provided third party access was allowed. One of the most important issues in the new liberalised environment is the extent to which controls must be put in place to ensure that the PNOs have no more power from network operation than is required to fulfil their public service obligations such as universal service. The Guidelines highlight two particular fears. Firstly, there is the concern that the TOs will use profits from any reserved services to subsidise competitive services thereby gaining an unfair advantage. The Commission states that Article 86 will apply to this cross-subsidisation (paras 102 *et seq.*).

6.53 A more difficult problem arises from access charges. How much should the PNO be allowed to charge for access to the network given that the PNO should not be placed at a disadvantage due to the cost of complying with public service obligations but should not be placed at an advantage by charging more than its costs? The TO's argument would be that any payment must contribute to the cost of establishing and maintaining a universal network. Governments may well endorse this argument because, if the TO cannot make enough money to keep a universal service, there may well be calls for finance from the public purse. The argument of the third party would be that they should not be laden with the cost of an inefficient monopoly network owner.

The Commission points out in the Guidelines that ONP legislation is **6.54** complementary to competition rules (paras 15 *et seq.*). The question of access charges is a clear example of the way ONP and competition may work (or not work) together. Annex II to the ONP Framework Directive (see para **6.32**), sets down certain principles for harmonised tariff principles but adds that "the fixing of the actual tariff level will continue to be the province of national legislation and is not the subject of open network provision conditions." On the other hand "Any charge for access to network resources...must comply...with the competition rules of the Treaty and must also take into account the principle of fair sharing in the global cost of the resources used and the need for a reasonable level of return of investment."

The Guidelines supplement these principles by stating that Article 86 may **6.55** apply to usage restrictions. They add that "Conversely, it does not constitute an abuse provided it is shown, in each specific case, that the access charges correspond to costs which are entailed directly for the TOs for the access in question" (para 95).

Finally, the common position on ONP and voice telephony states that: **6.56**

> "...if interconnection agreements include specific compensation provisions for the telecommunications organisation in situations where different operating conditions e.g. price controls or universal service obligations, are imposed upon the respective parties, such compensation provisions shall be cost oriented, non-discriminatory and fully justified, and shall only be applied with the approval of the national regulatory authority in accordance with Community law."[26]

Predicting how these rules are to apply in practice may be assisted by analysis **6.57** of disputes over access charges at a national level. Such disputes are not uncommon. The issue was resolved in an interesting way in litigation in New Zealand.[27] In the absence of a specific test in the relevant legislation, the New Zealand High Court endorsed a test put forward by two US economists, Baumol and Sidak.[28] These economists argue that the third party should pay the opportunity cost suffered by the network owner in not supplying the service itself. The opportunity cost is measured by the profit which the network owner would have made if it had supplied the service now supplied by the third party. The argument is that, although this would give the network operator any monopoly profit which it would have made, the third party will have an incentive to be more efficient in order to undercut the network provider's price. This will reduce the network provider's opportunity cost which in turn will reduce the payment made by the third party. This virtuous circle will encourage efficiency on the part of the competitive supplier whilst ensuring that the network costs are covered.

---

[26] Common position of 30 June 1993.
[27] *Clear Communications* v *Telecom Corporation of New Zealand* [1992] 5 TCLR 166 (High Court), noted Tollemache (1994) ECLR 43 and [1993] 4 NZBLC 103,340 (Court of Appeal), noted Tollemache (1994) ECLR 236.
[28] See their work *Toward Competition in Local Telephony* (MIT Press).

6.58   The test put forward by Baumol and Sidak, the so-called Efficient Component Pricing Rule, was rejected by the New Zealand Court of Appeal. It held that it was wrong for the network provider to be paid a monopoly profit by a third party and was dubious about the benefits of the Rule in practice given difficulties and delays in calculating the opportunity cost which could be exploited by the network provider. Perhaps the most interesting aspect of the litigation is the fact that the courts may well be the final arbiter in these disputes. A further example is the 1994 challenge by Mercury of a decision by the UK's NRA, Oftel, on access charges. These pricing disputes raise complex arguments based on economic theory, both pure and applied. One wonders whether the courts are equipped to carry out this function. In the light of the appeal in the New Zealand litigation to the Privy Council, it looks like English courts are acquiring more experience than others.

(iii) Standards

6.59   One of the common themes throughout this book has been the interface between competition law and intellectual property rights (IPRs). This issue is also important in the telecoms field. One particular reason is the overwhelming importance of standards in creating a Community-wide market in which many service providers can compete. Standards are crucial to the interoperability of Community-wide networks as well as the freedom to sell the products which connect to them in the same form throughout the Community. The Commission has faced a number of difficulties in ensuring the smooth and speedy adoption of the hundreds of necessary standards. The process was streamlined with the creation of the European Telecommunications Standards Institute (ETSI) in 1988. One key problem which ETSI has had to face is the fact that standards can involve technology over which someone holds intellectual property protection. The solution to the problem is not straightforward. On the one hand, the existence of IPRs may encourage the development of new technologies including improved standards; on the other hand, if the IPR is enforced to prevent third party supply, the benefits of a standard will not be realised. Further, should the holder of the IPR be entitled to remuneration for the use of the protected technology in a standard?

6.60   This is one area in which the application of Article 86 may play a role. In the Guidelines, it is pointed out that "Infringements of Article 86 may be committed by the abusive exercise of industrial property rights in relation with standards, which are of crucial importance for telecommunications" (para 112).

     As we have seen (see para **3.49** *et seq*), this is a limited remedy requiring, in particular, the holder of the IPR to have a dominant position in the market. Such a dominant position does not flow automatically from the fact of the IPR. ETSI has attempted to address the issue with the adoption by the General Assembly in March 1993 of the "ETSI Policy and Undertaking." The objective of the Policy is to "reduce the risk" that the adoption of the optimal standard is thwarted by the existence of IPRs. The Policy "seeks a balance between the needs of standardisation for public use in the field of telecommunications and the rights of the owners of IPR" (s 2).

The 1993 Policy is only an interim one. It came into effect in April 1993 for a minimum period of 2 years with an evaluation of the Policy to be carried out no later than April 1997. The Policy requires its members to "use their best efforts to agree a definitive intellectual property rights Policy and Undertaking" (s 14).

The basic ETSI approach is to require members to sign an undertaking **6.61** which obliges them to notify ETSI of an IPR at an early stage of the standard setting procedure and to grant a licence for that IPR unless a refusal procedure is followed. At the end of the procedure, there is an obligation to give reasons but no obligation to grant a licence. The encouragement to license the IPR comes from the final part of the procedure—ETSI will send the reasoned refusal to the European Commission "for its consideration" (s 8.1). The encouragement to enter into the undertaking is that it is a condition of membership (s 3.1).

The Policy and Undertaking have sparked off a fierce debate over the extent **6.62** to which holders of IPRs should be encouraged, exhorted or even forced to license their IPRs.[29] The ECJ's judgment in the *Magill* cases may give some guidance on the extent to which EC competition law can be used to require IPR holders to license third parties to use technology incorportated into standards (see para **4.69** *et seq*).

---

[29] See, *e.g.*, Prins and Schiessl (1993) EIPR 263

List of Telecoms Mergers/Joint ventures

Mergers

Alcatel/Telettra Case IV.M042 of 12 April 1991 OJ 1991 L122/48.
Ericsson/Kolbe Case IV.M133 of 22 January 1992.
Eucom/Digital Case IV.M218 of 18 May 1992.
Northern Telecom/Matra Télécommunication Case IV.M249 of 10 August 1992.
Ericsson/Hewlett-Packard Case IV.M292 of 12 March 1993.
BT/MCI Case IV.M353 of 13 September 1993.
Alcatel/STC Case IV.M366 of 13 September 1993.
Matra Marconi Space/British Aerospace Space Systems Case IV.M437 of 23 August 1994.

Joint Ventures

Optical Fibres OJ 1986 L236/50.
GEC-ANT-Telettra-SAT OJ 1988 C180/3.
Alcatel Espace/ANT OJ 1990 L32/19; [1991] 4 CMLR 208.
Konsortium ECR 900 OJ 1990 L228/31.
Eirpage OJ 1991 L306/22; [1993] 4 CMLR 64.
Infonet OJ 1992 C7/3.
Encompass Europe OJ 1992 C233/2; [1992] 5 CMLR 557.
STET, Italtel AT&T and AT&T-NSI OJ 1992 C333/3.
Astra OJ 1993 L20/23.
Intrax OJ 1993 C117/3; [1993] 5 CMLR 190.
International Private Satellite Partners OJ 1993 C305/3.
Aérospatiale/Alcatel Espace OJ 1994 C47/6.
GEN OJ 1994 C55/3.
CMC-Talkline OJ 1994 C221/9.
BT/MCI OJ 1994 L223/36.

Chapter 7
Data Protection

1. Introduction

The subject of data protection merits its own chapter because it does not easily **7.1** fall within the industry classification adopted in this book. Indeed, the idea of data protection is by no means exclusively the preserve of information technology. The significance of collections of information on individuals was appreciated well before the invention of the computer. What changed with the advent of information technology was the exponential increase in possibilities for abuse of such collections of data both by the State and private enterprise. Every time a credit card is used, a phone call made or a flight booked data is created somewhere. Those who have access to the vast collections of data which result have unprecedented knowledge over the population's activities. This knowledge can be used for legitimate commercial means but can also be abused. In an article on a new Unisys airline information system, one IT commentator expressed a common concern by saying "What I wouldn't be too happy about is if by linking their various databases, they discovered more personal information about me."[1]

The concern is not limited to the private sector. The Government has control over particularly extensive collections of data. For example, plans were recently announced in the UK for a national computer to log the DNA profiles of anyone arrested for a criminal offence. The sample would be taken from mouth swabs.[2]

To some extent national laws have controlled certain types of abuse of **7.2** information. For example, some jurisdictions recognise a right to privacy. The extent of this control varies considerably from one country to the next.[3] Comprehensive regulation of data protection dates back to as recently as 1970 when the German State of Hessen adopted the world's first data protection statute. Since those early days the position in Europe has changed dramatically. In 1980, the OECD issued non-binding guidelines governing the protection of privacy and transborder flows of personal data. In 1985, the Council of Europe's Convention for the Protection of the Individual with Regard to the Automatic Processing of Data came into force. Currently, all but two of the EU Member States have adopted data protection legislation. The European Commission has now tabled proposals in the field which, if

---

[1] David Tebbutt, *Computer Weekly* 31 March 1994, 24.
[2] *Computer Weekly* 25 August 1994, 8.
[3] *e.g.*, English courts have consistently refused to recognise a right to privacy: *Kaye* v *Robertson* [1991] FSR 62.

adopted, will have an important impact on national law within Europe and beyond.

7.3   Another reason for a separate chapter on data protection is that the law in this field is based on rather different concerns to the other laws discussed in this book. The principal concern is with the right of individuals to have at least some control over the collection and use of information concerning them. On the other hand, one of the common themes in data protection at a European level echoes a common theme throughout EC information technology law. Encouraging legitimate transborder data flows whilst ensuring a reasonable level of protection in the countries involved means that there is always a concern with the law of other countries, particularly trading partners. By threatening to stop data flows to countries with inadequate protection, a country or trading bloc can attempt to force the introduction of data protection laws in other jurisdictions. The international reaction to the proposed EC law is one of its most interesting aspects.

7.4   Unlike the other areas covered in this book, data protection does not raise obvious competition law concerns. This chapter will be limited to an analysis of the proposed EC legislation, firstly, the proposal for a directive on data protection and, secondly, the proposal for a directive on data protection for public digital telecoms networks.

2. **Draft Data Protection Directive**[4]

(i) **Background**

7.5   As we have seen, most Member States have their own data protection legislation; the exceptions are Greece and Italy. As in the case of intellectual property, the fact that these laws are national can cause problems for the free flow of data across borders. A country which has introduced its own data protection legislation will be keen for others to do likewise to ensure a level playing field in order not to discourage inward investment. Moreover, when a country introduces legislation, it will probably want to ensure that the legislation is not avoided by the simple technique of transferring information on its citizens to a jurisdiction with no (or less strict) data protection law. For these reasons, international arrangements have turned out to be essential to protect the legitimate free flow of information on which international trade is dependent.

7.6   The OECD Guidelines and Council of Europe Convention were important in encouraging moves within Europe to introduce data protection legislation. They have not been wholly successful in ensuring the free flow of information across borders. Recognising that such flow of information is essential for the operation of an internal market in Europe, in 1990, the Commission proposed

---

[4] Amended proposal for a Council Directive on the protection of individuals with regard to the processing of personal data and on the free movement of such data (OJ 1992 C311/30). See Appendix A8.

an EC Directive (OJ 1990 C277/3). This first draft was criticised and, following amendments put forward by the European Parliament, the Commission issued a revised draft in 1992. The twin objectives of protecting the free flow of information within and outside the Community are reflected in the legal bases of the proposal, namely, Article 100a (internal market) and Article 113 (common commercial policy).

It should not be forgotten, though, that data protection rules are designed to   **7.7**
protect the rights of individuals over information concerning them. Although there were important economic reasons for a directive at a Community level, the Commission was keen to confirm its desire to achieve a high level of protection for individuals. The 1992 version of the draft Directive has watered down this protection but the draft is still clearly based on protection of individuals. The Recitals derive support from Article 8 of the European Convention for the Protection of Human Rights and Fundamental Freedoms which provides:

> "1. Everyone has the right to respect for his private and family life, his home and his correspondence.
> 2. There shall be no interference by a public authority with the exercise of this right except such as is in accordance with the law and is necessary in a democratic society in the interests of national security, public safety or the economic well-being of the country, for the protection of disorder or crime, for the protection of health or morals, or for the protection of the rights and freedoms of others."

The Recitals to the draft Data Protection Directive confirm that the Directive should "seek to ensure a high level of protection in the Community."

(ii) **Key terms and coverage**

The draft Directive deals with *personal data* (Art 2(a)), that is, data relating to   **7.8**
identifiable individuals, inelegantly referred to as *data subjects* (Art 2(a)). The obligations in the draft apply in the main to the natural or legal person who directs the way in which the data is processed, *the controller* (Art 2(d)). The controller may be the person who actually processes the information or, alternatively, the information may be processed by another on the controller's behalf, *the processor* (Art 2(e)). The draft defines processing very widely to include everything from collection and organisation through to use and dissemination (Art 2(b)).

As we have seen, data may be improperly used even when it is recorded   **7.9**
manually rather than digitally. Unlike the UK system,[5] the proposed Directive covers data processed "whether or not by automatic means" (Art 2(b)). Recognising that manual processing may not raise the same level of concern as automatic processing, some of the provisions of the proposal apply differently according to whether data is processed manually or automatically.

---

[5] Data Protection Act 1984, s 1(2).

For example, Member States are free to limit the need for notification to automatic processing (Art 20). In addition, the draft Directive only applies to manual processing if the data forms part of a *personal data file* (Art 3), that is, a structured set of data "which is accessible by specific criteria and whose object or effect is to facilitate the use or alignment of data to the data subject or subjects" (Art 2(c)). It will be by no means easy to apply this key definition.

7.10   The draft Directive applies both to the public and private sectors. Given that the underlying basis for data protection regulation may be different in the public and private sectors, it may be surprising that, in principle, the Directive applies in the same way to both sectors. In fact, many of the qualifications and exceptions in the draft will apply differently to the public and private sectors.

7.11   There are some important general exceptions to the obligations in the draft Directive. Thus, the Directive would not apply to data processing in the course of "an activity outside the scope of Community law" or a "purely private and personal activity" (Art 3(2)). In addition, Member States may exempt from the Directive data processing "solely for journalistic purposes by the press, the audio-visual media and journalists" (Art 9). Finally, many of the rights of data subjects are subject to a list of exceptions in Article 14 which includes, for example, national security and defence.

(iii) Data processing obligations

7.12   Chapter II, the main body of the draft Directive, sets out the obligations which make up data protection. These obligations are in general directed at the controller. Perhaps the most striking characteristic of these obligations is the extent to which qualifications to these obligations are left to Member State discretion. This resulted from the need to take account of subsidiarity principles in the revised proposal following the Maastricht Treaty on European Union (see para **2.39**). Article 5 confirms this position in providing that "Subject to this Chapter [II, Articles 5 to 21], Member States may more precisely determine the circumstances in which processing of personal data is lawful."

(a) Collection

7.13   The controller must ensure that personal data is collected for a "specified, explicit and legitimate purpose and used in a way compatible with those purposes" (Art 6(b)). Further, the data must be "adequate, relevant and not excessive in relation to the purposes for which they are processed" (Art 6(c)). These obligations are complemented by the obligation on the controller to give the data subject certain information when collecting information from that subject (Art 11(1)). This obligation to inform does not apply where it "would hinder or prevent the exercise of or the cooperation with the supervision and verification functions of a public authority or the maintenance of public order" (Art 11(2)). This is an example of a qualification which is directed at the public sector and would include, for example, police enquiries.

(b) Data quality

The controller must ensure that data is accurate, up to date and only kept in a   **7.14**
form in which the data subject is identifiable for as long as necessary (Art 6).
Article 6(a) adds that the personal data must be "processed fairly and
lawfully." This obligation seems readily capable of different interpretations
from one Member State to another.

(c) Processing

Articles 7 and 8 set out the important possible justifications for any processing   **7.15**
of personal data. Article 7 lays down six alternative grounds for processing
data. For example, such data may be processed if the data subject consents
(Art 7(a));[6] if necessary in order to protect the vital interests of the data subject
(Art 7(d)); or if necessary to comply with a Community or national legal
obligation (Art 7(c)). Although the grounds laid down in Article 7 are
exhaustive, they seem to be sufficiently widely defined to cover all legitimate
data processing. The final ground is interesting in allowing a balancing of
interests. It says that data can be processed if "necessary in pursuit of the
general interest or of the legitimate interests of the controller or of a third party
to whom the data are disclosed, except where such interests are overridden by
the interests of the data subjects" (Art 7(f)).

Ultimately, it will presumably be the courts which have to carry out this
difficult balancing operation.

Article 8 lays down special rules for sensitive data, that is: **7.16**

> "data revealing ethnic origin, political opinions, religious beliefs, philosophical
> or ethical persuasion or trade-union membership, and of data concerning health
> or sexual life" (Art 8(1)).

There are only three grounds for processing sensitive data (Art 8(2)). Such   **7.17**
data can be processed with the written consent of the data subject; or, in
certain circumstances, by "a foundation or non-profit making association of a
political, philosophical, religious or trade union character"; or, finally, if
"there is manifestly no infringement of privacy or fundamental freedoms." Not
only is this last ground capable of widely different interpretations but Member
States are also free to lay down exemptions "on grounds of important public
interest" (Art 8(3)). There are specific provisions for data on criminal
convictions (Art 8(4)).

Article 17 lays down obligations so far as security measures are concerned.   **7.18**
The obligations seem to be more onerous in the case of automatic processing
particularly in the case of a network and where remote access is possible.
Where the controller allows data to be processed on his behalf by a processor,
the controller has to ensure that the processor takes appropriate security
measures (Art 24).

---

[6] See also Art 2(g).

(d) Disclosure

7.19   Article 12 lays down the carefully circumscribed requirements to be fulfilled before the controller can disclose personal information concerning a data subject. The basic principle is that the controller must give the data subject certain information before disclosure such as the sort of data to be disclosed and to whom it will be disclosed. There is no need to inform if the data subject has consented to processing. There are a number of further exceptions, in particular, the exceptions to the right of access listed in Article 14 discussed below. In addition, Member States may allow for exemptions where "the provision of information to the data subject proves impossible or involves a disproportionate effort, or runs counter to the overriding legitimate interests of the controller or similar interests of a third party..." (Art 12(3)).

(e) Notification

7.20   Some of the Member State systems of data protection do not currently require everyone who processes data to register. For example, in Germany, there is a very limited obligation to notify a supervisory authority.[7] On the other hand, other Member States have a comprehensive registration system, for example, the UK. The Directive adopts the latter approach (Art 18), although Article 19 does require Member States to simplify or exempt from the need to notify "certain categories of processing operation which do not adversely affect the rights and freedoms of data subjects" (Art 19(1)). Moreover, Member States are free to limit notification for non-automatic processing (Art 20). Nonetheless, the wide-ranging obligation to notify is bound to be contentious in discussions within the Council. One commentator has remarked that "These regulations are a nightmare for German industry."[8]

(iv) Rights of data subjects

7.21   Perhaps the most important right which the draft Directive gives to the data subject is the right to a judicial remedy for breach of the Directive. The extent of this right is discussed below in a section on remedies (see para **7.28**). This section deals with certain specific rights granted to a data subject to allow control over the processing of personal data about him or herself.

(a) Right to know

7.22   Article 10 gives any person the right to know both of the existence of a processing operation and certain other related information such as the name and address of the controller. Although this right is not limited to data subjects, it is clearly aimed at allowing data subjects to find out about the processing of personal information about them. Indeed, Article 10 is included in the Section of the draft Directive headed "Information to be Given to the Data Subject."

---

[7] See Hoeren, *Information Management and Data Protection within the EC—The Amended EC Proposal for a Council Directive on Data Protection and its Impact on German Industry* [1993] IJL&IT 129 at 138.
[8] See Hoeren [1993] IJL&IT 129 at 138.

(b) Right of access

Perhaps the most important rights granted to the data subject are laid out in **7.23** Article 13. This Article 13 is entitled Right of Access but goes further than that. All data subjects are given the following key rights: firstly, the right to obtain confirmation of the existence of personal data on them; secondly, the right to refuse a third party demand that the first right be exercised; and, thirdly, the right to obtain rectification or erasure of inaccurate or incomplete data as well as notification of such steps.

Article 13(5) also deals with automated processing operations. It gives data **7.24** subjects the right to be informed of the reasoning applied in such an operation where the outcome is invoked against them. This right is complemented by Article 16 which grants "...the right to every person not to be subjected to an administrative or private decision adversely affecting him which is based solely on automatic processing defining a personality profile" (Art 16(1)).

Although limited, these rights seem to go beyond traditional notions of data **7.25** protection with a view to stopping computer-generated data processing which adversely affects the subjects of that processing.

The right of access laid down in Article 13 is subject to the exceptions listed **7.26** in Article 14 including national security and defence.

(c) Right to object

Article 15 provides quite simply that a data subject shall have "the right to **7.27** object at any time on legitimate grounds to the processing of data relating to him." Presumably legitimate grounds are those specified in the Directive together with any further grounds specified by Member States pursuant to the Directive.

(v) Remedies

Chapter III of the draft Directive lays down the remedies for breach of its **7.28** provisions. It has already been mentioned that Article 22 requires a remedy for any breach of the rights guaranteed by the Directive. In addition, there is a provision for compensation where a data subject suffers damage as a result of wrongful processing. Member States may set limits to this compensation where the controller has fulfilled the security requirements of Articles 17 and 24. Finally, Member States must impose "dissuasive penalties" for breach of national law implementing the Directive.

(vi) Transborder data flows

One of the principal reasons for the proposed Data Protection Directive is to **7.29** remove barriers to the legitimate free flow of information within the Community and beyond.

(a) Within the Community

7.30   Article 1(2) of the draft Directive states that Member States may not restrict or prohibit the free flow of personal data between Member States for reasons based on the matters dealt with by the Directive, in particular, the right to privacy. This is one aspect of the Directive which the Community institutions could relatively easily ensure is respected. The problem may be that a directive adopted along the lines of the current draft would allow significant differences between the laws of the various Member States, some requiring a high degree of data protection, others much lower. This would mean that, at least in the private sector, those with data could move their operations to the Member State where data protection rules were easiest to satisfy. Of course, this is the natural consequence and, indeed, objective of many of the moves to create an internal market in Europe. The peculiar factor in the case of data protection may be that any move to escape the control of a national law on the protection of citizens' personal data could be highly visible and, as a result, politically sensitive.

7.31   One further issue linked to this question is the extent of the jurisdiction of each Member State's national law. The basic principle is that national law which implements the Directive will catch the controller rather than the processing. Thus, Article 4(1)(a) provides that Member States shall apply their own law to controllers established in their territory or in their jurisdiction. It follows that a controller could establish itself in a different Member State to the data subject or the location of the processing. In these cases, individuals may not find it straightforward to rely on the rights proposed in the draft Directive.

7.32   Article 4 also deals with the situation where the controller is established outside the Community but processing takes place within the Community. In this case, the law of the Member State which will apply is that of the Member State where the "means" for processing are located. There is bound to be difficulty over the precise scope of this term.

(b) Outside the Community

7.33   One of the most interesting aspects of the proposal is the way in which the draft Directive deals with data flows to jurisdictions outside the Community. The basic approach in the Directive is to allow such flows of data provided the receiving jurisdiction has an adequate level of protection. Even if there is no such level of protection, transfer of data may be permitted by a Member State if the controller shows alternative protection, in particular, through contractual provisions. Even in the absence of such justification, there are a number of situations in which transfer can be permitted, in particular, if the data subject consents (Art 26(1)).

7.34   Assuming none of these exceptions apply, how is adequacy judged? Article 26(2) says adequacy is assessed in the light of all circumstances although it mentions specifically factors such as the nature of the data, the purpose and duration of the processing and the legislative and professional rules in the

receiving country. Naturally, opinions may differ over adequacy. In the first
instance, the Member State decides but it must notify the Commission. The
draft Directive says that the Commission may overrule the Member State. It
may be that the Council will want more control over this decision-making
process than the draft currently allows.

Will this be an important provision in practice? The fact that there is scant   **7.35**
regulation in the US suggests that it could be. If a Member State or the
Commission decided that the US did not provide an adequate level of
protection, the private sector would at a minimum have to ensure adequate
procedures to comply with the exceptions described above. On the other hand,
it is not unlikely that the US would consider improving its law on data
protection in order to ensure adequate protection according to the test
contained in the Directive. Here is another example of how legal issues arising
within the information technology industry require regulation which in turn
sparks off an international reaction.

(vii) **Supervisory authority**

As we have already seen, there are a number of different models of data   **7.36**
protection. One important difference between Member States is whether a
public supervisory authority is set up. This is another difference between the
UK and German systems. The proposed Directive opts for the UK system and
requires each Member State to "designate an independent public authority to
supervise the protection of personal data" (Art 30(1)). These national bodies
are to have powers to hear complaints, investigate, intervene and take action
in the courts. The supervisory authority also maintains the register on notified
processing operations (Art 21).

(viii) **Appraisal**

The Commission's first draft of the Data Protection Directive was criticised   **7.37**
because it went too far in harmonising all aspects of data protection. The
danger with the 1992 draft may be that it has gone so far the other way that its
objectives may be compromised. In particular, it is important that there is
public confidence in a national system of data protection. If private enterprise
can exploit widely different levels of protection in the Community, such
confidence may not last.

On the other hand, the adoption of the Directive could encourage   **7.38**
jurisdictions which have almost no data protection regulation to fall into line
with the principles of a Community Directive.

There is no doubt that the wide disparities amongst the existing systems of   **7.39**
data protection within the Member States have led to difficulties in agreeing
on the content of the Data Protection Directive. This has led to slippage on the
timetable included in the amended proposal which required Member States to
bring implement the Directive by the start of 1994 (Art 35(2)). However, it is

possible that the Council may be able to agree to a common position by the end of 1994 for implementation during 1996 or 1997. Some Member States are delaying amending their national laws in order to take into account the provisions agreed by the EU Council.[9]

3. Draft Telecoms Data Protection Directive[10]

(i) Background

7.40 The Data Protection Directive is a framework directive and may need supplementary measures in particular sectors. When it adopted its original draft Data Protection Directive in 1990, the Commission also proposed a specific directive on data protection and privacy for public digital telecommunications networks (OJ 1990 C277/12). Like the framework directive, the telecoms directive has now been amended to take into account the Parliament's suggested amendments, amendments to the draft framework directive as well as the principle of subsidiarity (see para **2.39**).

7.41 As the Commission points out in its Explanatory Memorandum:

> "With the rapidly increasing digitisation of the public telecommunications networks in the European Community it could become possible—without adequate data protection measures—to store and monitor systematically specific call-related data, such as origin of call."[11]

7.42 The Commission explains the purpose of the proposal as follows:

> "The proposed directive aims at the implementation of the general principles of protection of personal data and privacy with regard to the specific requirements of public digital telecommunications networks in order to prevent divergent developments in the Community which could endanger the common market for both telecommunications services and telecoms equipment" (at 11).

(ii) Obligations

7.43 The draft Directive lays down a number of obligations to be fulfilled by public network operators. For example, where calling-line identification is provided, the calling subscriber must be able to stop the transmission of the number (Art 8(1)). By the same token, the called subscriber must be able to limit calls received to those where calling line identification has been given (Art 8(3)). Both these facilities must be offered free of charge. The elimination of calling

---

[9] See, *e.g.*, the announcement by the UK's new Data Protection Registrar reported in *Computer Weekly* 8 September 1994, 6.

[10] Amended proposal for a European Parliament and Council Directive concerning the protection of personal data and privacy in the context of digital telecommunications networks, in particular the integrated services digital network (ISDN) and digital mobile networks (OJ 1994 C200/4). See Appendix A9.

[11] COM(94)128 of 13 June 1994, 3.

line identification may be overriden in exceptional cases, for example, to trace malicious calls (Art 9(1)).

A number of the obligations in the draft Directive apply both to the network operator as well as to other service providers. For example, access to billing data must be limited to the persons in charge of billing (Art 5). **7.44**

Compliance with some of the obligations in the draft Directive will require the involvement of Member State authorities. For example, subject to certain exceptions, listening or tapping devices require authorisation by the competent judiciary or administrative national authority (Art 12). **7.45**

(iii) Appraisal

The amended draft Directive does not contain some specific obligations of the earlier draft which had been criticised such as the ban on itemised billing statements which identify the last four digits of called numbers. It remains to be seen whether the amended proposal will command sufficient support to be adopted by the Council. **7.46**

Chapter 8
Conclusion and Common Themes

The challenge facing the Community is to ensure that EC rules are formulated 8.1
and applied in order to give sufficient incentive for innovation whilst ensuring
that society as a whole reaps the benefit. The first part of this challenge relates
to the need to mould any exclusive or special rights conferred by the law so that
firms have an incentive to innovate and bring that innovation to the market.
The second part of the challenge has more than one element. First, the
Community must ensure that any market power derived from exclusive rights
is not relied on to exclude competition in other markets. Second, it may be
necessary to control potential abuse of the technology such as the improper use
of the vast databases of personal data which information technology makes
possible.

Striking the balance between the need for incentive and control of market 8.2
power is important in many sectors. It is particularly important in the IT
industry because of new and changing technology. Thus, not only is legislation
required over new technologies which do not fit easily into existing intellectual
property regimes but exclusive rights may also be required to encourage the
massive private sector investment which will be required to build the promised
information superhighways.

Some may argue that one problem with exclusive rights is that they may 8.3
turn out to give more control than is acceptable. This book is littered with
examples of exclusive rights which raise the question whether subsequent
control over that exclusivity is needed. One example is the potential reliance
on intellectual property rights (IPRs) by the supplier of one product to control
the market for other products which interconnect with the first. The need for
interoperability is a common feature of all sectors of the IT industry and will be
ever more important as products become even more sophisticated and as
digitisation spreads still further.

One theme running throughout this book concerns the appropriate stage at 8.4
which to strike the balance between incentive and market power and the body
which should have authority to do so. Now that the law is finally dealing with
the particular issues raised by new technologies, naturally, the balance of
innovation and competition figure highly in the debate over how to mould any
exclusive right granted. Thus, arguments over the excessive scope of copyright
were at the heart of the debate over the Software Directive and, in particular,
the decompilation right.

One important factor in the debate is the need to ensure that rights in new 8.5
technologies arise in as many countries as possible. In some cases, this has been
achieved by complying with existing international arrangements even if they

were not developed with new technologies in mind. Again, an example of this approach is the drafting of the Software Directive to ensure that it complied with the Berne Convention on copyright. The benefit anticipated from following the requirements of the Convention is that all countries which are party to the Convention will grant protection to computer programs created by nationals of other member countries.

8.6   A different approach has been taken to the international position when the existing international arrangements do not cover the new technology. The most well known example is the 1984 US Semiconductor Chip Protection Act which only extended protection to countries with equivalent protection. The European Commission has adopted a similar approach to the right to prevent unauthorised extraction included in its proposed Database Directive. Some (but by no means all) of these issues should be resolved by the Agreement on Trade-Related Aspects of Intellectual Property Rights (TRIPs) signed in the context of the GATT Uruguay Round. TRIPs contains provisions on intellectual property protection for both computer programs and semiconductor chips.

8.7   Once an exclusive right has been established by legislation, attention then turns to the interpretation of that legislation by the courts. The interpretation of legislation will have a profound effect on the balance of intellectual property and competition. For example, there is doubt over the interpretation of the key concept of originality in the Software Directive. Will unique implementation of an interface be protected by copyright? If so, then the decompilation right may not be available to ensure free access to interface information. In the US, there have been a number of inconsistent court decisions over the extent of copyright protection for computer programs. The position is likely to be even more unsettled in the Community given different languages as well as differences between the traditional approaches of the Member States to the nature of IPRs. Ultimately, consistency will almost certainly require judgments of the ECJ which may take years.

8.8   Given that the balance of exclusivity and competition is so important in drafting and interpreting legislation, is it appropriate for competition law to play a role in dealing with reliance on IPRs? It can be argued that competition rules should play a role in limiting the exploitation of market power to the product over which the IPRs are held. In fact, economists question the need for widespread concern over the extension of the IPR monopoly to another market. There are even greater doubts whether competition law should be used as an instrument to limit the incentive provided by the IPR since this will invariably require a value jugment about whether IPRs should cover a particular type of technology. This is precisely the question that arises in the case of refusals to license an IPR. It can be argued that there is a role for a competition authority but only in advising on the impact on competition.

8.9   There are parallels between the application of competition law to IPRs, on the one hand, and to other types of exclusive rights, on the other. Thus, there are questions over the need for the grant of exclusivity over telecoms networks. There are also questions over the extension of any resulting market power to other markets. In the latter case, again, to the extent that efficiency is prejudiced, competition law should apply. But EC law is also being applied to circumscribe the extent of exclusive rights granted by the State. The main concern on this score is that exclusive rights granted to State monopolies will hold up the creation of trans-European networks and the provision of trans-European services. This is altogether a different issue to the application of competition law to IPRs.

The ECJ will rule shortly in the *Magill* cases on the application of **8.10** competition law to a refusal to license IPRs. It is likely that, even if the Commission's decision is overturned, the ECJ will leave open the possibility of forced IPR licences under EC competition rules. The key point for the IT industry is that there are strong arguments that control of technology does not in fact give any market power. For example, the fact that a firm is the sole supplier of a product which has no substitutes may well not mean market power in the IT industry, given the absence of barriers to entry for potential competition. The concern over market share seems most apparent in the case of markets for products which interoperate with another product. In other words, there is concern over control of architecture. The important point is that competition in the primary market may control the exploitation of market power in neighbouring or derivative markets.

It follows that the IT industry should be just as concerned that the **8.11** European Commission takes a realistic approach to market definition and market power as the industry seems to be with the application of EC competition law to refusals to license IPRs. The Commission's views on market power in the IT industry are slowly emerging from its decisions under the Merger Regulation but there is a real need for further guidance from the Commission on its approach so that companies do not waste resources on avoiding a law which should not be applicable anyway.

At this point in time, there is considerable uncertainty over the approach of **8.12** EC law to the IT industry on points of detail as well as of principle. A full awareness of the issues underlying the application of EC law in the various sectors of the IT industry is essential to the debate over the direction of EC law.

Select Bibliography on EC IT Law

General

Encyclopedia of Information Technology Law (Sweet & Maxwell, 1990, looseleaf)

Hardware

Dreier, *Protection of Semiconductor Integrated Circuits* (1988) IIC 427.

Hart, *Semiconductor topography: Protection in the UK contrasted with the US Semiconductor Chip Protection Act and the EEC Directive on topographies* (1988) CL&P 151.

Hart, *High Technology 'Reverse Engineering': The Dual Standard* (1987) EIPR 139.

Software

Czarnota & Hart, *Legal Protection of Computer Programs in Europe* (Butterworths, 1991).

Lehmann & Tapper, Eds, *A Handbook of European Software Law* (Clarendon Press, 1993, looseleaf).

Dreier, *The Council Directive of 14 May 1991 on the Legal Protection of Computer Programs* (1991) EIPR 319.

Reed, *Reverse Engineering Computer Programs without Infringing Copyright* (1991) EIPR 47.

Hart, *Interfaces, Interoperability and Maintenance* (1991) EIPR 111.

Karjala, *Recent United States and International Developments in Software Protection (Part 1)* (1994) EIPR 13 *(Part 2)* (1994) EIPR 58.

Weichselbaum, *The EEC Directive on the Legal Protection of Computer Programs and US Copyright Law: Should Copyright Law Permit Reverse Engineering of Computer Programs* (1990-1991) Fordham International Law Journal 1027.

Services

Hall, *New Thoughts on Databases: The Proposed EC Directive* (1992) ICCLR 275.

Thorne, *The Infringement of Database Compilations: A Case for Reform?* (1991) EIPR 331.

Metaxas, *Protection of Databases: Quietly Steering in the Wrong Direction?* (1990) EIPR 227.

Pattison, *The European Commission's Proposal on the Protection of Computer Databases* (1992) EIPR 113.

Telecoms

Denton Hall, *EC Telecommunications Law* (Chancery, 1993, looseleaf).

Ungerer and Costello, *Telecommunications in Europe* (EC Commission, 1990).

Overbury and Ravaioli, *The Application of EEC Law to Telecommunications* (1992) Fordham Corporate Law Institute 271.

Wainwright and Jessen, *Recent Developments in Community Law on Telecommunications* (1991) YEL 79.

Barrett, *EC Policy on Intellectual Property and Standardisation - The Impact on the Computer and Telecommunications Industries* (1993) CL&P 46.

Rhodes, *The Future of Telecommunications Services in Europe* (1994) CL&P 111.

Competition law

Vinje, *Compliance with Article 85 in Software Licensing* (1992) ECLR 165.

Forrester, *Software Licensing in the Light of Current EC Competition Law Considerations* (1992) ECLR 5.

Bay, *EC Competition Law and Software IPRs* (1993) CL&P 176.

Vajda, *The Application of Community Competition Law to the Distribution of Computer Products and Parts* (1992) 3 ECLR 110.

Klemens, *Selective Distribution of Personal Computers in the EEC: Is Article 85 IBM-Compatible?* (1985) Journal of Law and Commerce 505.

Darbyshire, *Computer Programs and Competition Policy: A Block Exemption for Software Licensing* (1994) EIPR 374.

Vinje, *Magill: Its Impact on the Information Technology Industry* (1992) EIPR 397 and (1993) EIPR 71.

Whish and Freeman, Eds, *Butterworths Competition Law* (looseleaf) Chapter 8 (Telecoms).

Data protection

Chalton, Gaskill and Sterling, Eds, *Encyclopedia of Data Protection* (Sweet & Maxwell, 1990, looseleaf) Part 7.

Chalton, *A Privacy Law for Europe: Back to the Data Protection Drawing Board* (1993) CL&P 4.

Hoeren, *Information Management and Data Protection within the EC - The Amended EC Proposal for a Council Directive on Data Protection and its Impact on German Industry* [1993] IJL&IT 129.

International

Cornish, *Computer Program Copyright and the Berne Convention* (1990) EIPR 129.

Schuz, *An Overview of the Berne Convention—generally and in relation to computer programs and semiconductor chips* (1993) CL&P 115.

Part 2

Appendices

CONTENTS OF APPENDICES

TEXT OF SELECTED ARTICLES OF THE EC TREATY

Article 30

A1.1 Quantitative restrictions on imports and all measures having equivalent effect shall, without prejudice to the following provisions, be prohibited between Member States.

Article 36

A1.2 The provisions of Articles 30 to 34 shall not preclude prohibitions or restrictions on imports, exports or goods in transit justified on grounds of public morality, public policy or public security; the protection of health and life of humans, animals or plants; the protection of national treasures possessing artistic, historic or archaeological value; or the protection of industrial and commercial property. Such prohibitions or restrictions shall not, however, constitute a means of arbitrary discrimination or a disguised restriction on trade between Member States.

Article 59

A1.3 Within the framework of the provisions set out below, restrictions on freedom to provide services within the Community shall be progressively abolished during the transitional period in respect of nationals of Member States who are established in a State of the Community other than that of the person for whom the services are intended.

The Council may, acting by a qualified majority on a proposal from the Commission, extend the provisions of this Chapter to nationals of a third country who provide services and who are established within the Community.

Article 85

A1.4 1. The following shall be prohibited as incompatible with the common market: all agreements between undertakings, decisions by associations of undertakings and concerted practices which may affect trade between Member States and which have as their object or effect the prevention, restriction or distortion of competition within the common market, and in particular those which:
   (a) directly or indirectly fix purchase or selling prices or any other trading conditions;
   (b) limit or control production, markets, technical development, or investment;
   (c) share markets or sources of supply;
   (d) apply dissimilar conditions to equivalent transactions with other trading parties, thereby placing them at a competitive disadvantage;
   (e) make the conclusion of contracts subject to acceptance by the other parties of supplementary obligations which, by their nature or according to commercial usage, have no connection with the subject of such contract.

2. Any agreements or decisions prohibited pursuant to this Article shall be automatically void.

3. The provisions of paragraph 1 may, however, be declared inapplicable in the case of:
   —any agreement or category of agreements between undertakings;
   —any decision or category of decisions by associations of undertakings;
   —any concerted practice or category of concerted practices;
   which contributes to improving the production or distribution of goods or to promoting technical or economic progress, while allowing consumers a fair share of the resulting benefit, and which does not:
   (a) impose on the undertakings concerned restrictions which are not indispensable to the attainment of these objectives;
   (b) afford such undertakings the pos-

sibility of eliminating competition in respect of a substantial part of the products in questions.

Article 86

A1.5 Any abuse by one or more undertakings of a dominant position within the common market or in a substantial part of it shall be prohibited as incompatible with the common market in so far as it may affect trade between Member States. Such abuse may, in particular, consist in:

(a) directly or indirectly imposing unfair purchase or selling prices or other unfair trading conditions;

(b) limiting production, markets or technical development to the prejudice of consumers;

(c) applying dissimilar conditions to equivalent transactions with other trading parties, thereby placing them at a competitive disadvantage;

(d) making the conclusion of contracts subject to acceptance by the other parties of supplementary obligations which, by their nature or according to commercial usage, have no connections with the subject of such contracts.

Article 90

A1.6 1. In the case of public undertakings and undertakings to which Member States grant special or exclusive rights, Member States shall neither enact nor maintain in force any measure contrary to the rules contained in this Treaty, in particular to those rules provided for in Article 6 and Articles 85 to 94.

2. Undertakings entrusted with the operation of services of general economic interest or having the character of a revenue-producing monopoly shall be subject to the rules contained in this Treaty, in particular to the rules on competition, in so far as the application of such rules does not obstruct the performance, in law or in fact, of the particular tasks assigned to them. The development of trade must not be affected to such an extent as would be contrary to the interests of the Community.

3. The Commission shall ensure the ap-

plication of the provisions of this Article and shall, where necessary, address appropriate directives or decisions to Member States.

Article 100

A1.7 The Council shall, acting unanimously on a proposal from the Commission and after consulting the European Parliament and the Economic and Social Committe, issue directives for the approximation of such law, regulations or administrative provisions of the Member States as directly affect the establishment or functioning of the common market.

Article 100a

A1.8 1. By way of derogation from Article 100 and save where otherwise provided in this Treaty, the following provisions shall apply for the achievement of the objectives set out in Article 7a. The Council shall, acting in accordance with the procedure referred to in Article 189b and after consulting the Economic and Social Committee, adopt the measures for the approximation of the provisions laid down by law, regulation or administrative action in Member States which have as their object the establishment and functioning of the internal market.

2. Paragraph 1 shall not apply to fiscal provisions, to those relating to the free movement of persons nor to those relating to the rights and interests of employed persons.

3. The Commission, in its proposals envisaged in paragraph 1 concerning health, safety, environmental protection and consumer protection, will take as a base a high level of protection.

4. If, after the adoption of a harmonisation measure by the Council acting by a qualified majority, a Member State deems it necessary to apply national provisions on grounds of major needs referred to in Article 36, or relating to protection of the environment or the working environment, it shall notify the Commission of these provisions.

The Commission shall confirm the provisions involved after having verified that they are not a means of arbitrary discrimination or a disguised restriction on trade between Member States.

By way of derogation from the procedure laid down in Articles 169 and 170, the Commission or any Member State may bring the matter directly before the Court of Justice if it considers that another Member State is making improper use of the powers provided for in this Article.

5. The harmonisation measures referred to above shall, in appropriate cases, include a safeguard clause authorising the Member States to take, for one or more of the non-economic reasons referred to in Article 36, provisional measures subject to a Community control procedure.

Article 235

If action by the Community should prove necessary to attain, in the course of the operation of the Common Market, one of the objectives of the Community and this Treaty has not provided the necessary powers, the Council shall, acting unanimously on a proposal from the Commission and after consulting the European Parliament, take the appropriate measures.

COUNCIL DIRECTIVE 87/54/EEC

of 16 December 1986

on the legal protection of topographies of semiconductor products*

THE COUNCIL OF THE
EUROPEAN COMMUNITIES,

A2.1

Having regard to the Treaty establishing the European Economic Community and in particular Article 100 thereof,

Having regard to the proposal from the Commission (OJ 1985 C360/14),

Having regard to the opinion of the European Parliament (OJ 1986 C255/249),

Having regard to the opinion of the Economic and Social Committee (OJ 1986 C189/5),

Whereas semiconductor products are playing an increasingly important role in a broad range of industries and semiconductor technology can accordingly be considered as being of fundamental importance for the community's industrial development;

Whereas the functions of semiconductor products depend in large part on the topographies of such products and whereas the development of such topographies requires the investment of considerable resources, human, technical and financial, while topographies of such products can be copied at a fraction of the cost needed to develop them independently;

Whereas topographies of semiconductor products are at present not clearly protected in all Member States by existing legislation and such protection, where it exists, has different attributes;

Whereas certain existing differences in the legal protection of semiconductor products offered by the laws of the Member States have direct and negative effects on the functioning of the Common Market as regards semiconductor products and such differences could well become greater as Member States introduce new legislation on this subject;

Whereas existing differences having such effects need to be removed and new ones having a negative effect on the Common Market prevented from arising;

Whereas, in relation to extension of protection to persons outside the community, member states should be free to act on their own behalf in so far as community decisions have not been taken within a limited period of time;

Whereas the Community's legal framework on the protection of topographies of semiconductor products can, in the first instance, be limited to certain basic principles by provisions specifying whom and what should be protected, the exclusive rights on which protected persons should be able to rely to authorize or prohibit certain acts, exceptions to these rights and for how long the protection should last;

Whereas other matters can for the time being be decided in accordance with national law, in particular, whether registration or deposit is required as a condition for protection and, subject to an exclusion of licences granted for the sole reason that a certain period of time has elapsed, whether and on what conditions non–voluntary licences may be granted in respect of protected topographies;

Whereas protection of topographies of semiconductor products in accordance with this directive should be without prejudice to the application of some other forms of protection;

Whereas further measures concerning the legal protection of topographies of semiconductor products in the Community can be considered at a later stage, if necessary, while the application of common basic principles by all member states in accordance with the provisions of this tioning of the on directive is an urgent necessity,

HAS ADOPTED THIS DIRECTIVE:

---

* OJ 1987 L24/36.

Chapter 1

Definitions

Article 1

A2.2   1.   For the purposes of this Directive:
(a) a 'semiconductor product' shall mean the final or an intermediate form of any product:
  (i)   consisting of a body of material which includes a layer of semiconducting material; and
  (ii) having one or more other layers composed of conducting, insulating or semiconducting material, the layers being arranged in accordance with a predetermined three-dimensional pattern; and
  (iii) intended to perform, exclusively or together with other functions, an electronic function;
(b) the 'topography' of a semiconductor product shall mean a series of related images, however fixed or encoded;
  (i)   representing the three-dimensional pattern of the layers of which a semiconductor product is composed; and
  (ii) in which series, each image has the pattern or part of the pattern of a surface of the semiconductor product at any stage of its manufacture;
(c) 'commercial exploitation' means the sale, rental, leasing or any other method of commercial distribution, or an offer for these purposes. However, for the purposes of Articles 3 (4), 4 (1), 7 (1), (3) and (4) 'commercial exploitation' shall not include exploitation under conditions of confidentiality to the extent that no further distribution to third parties occurs, except where exploitation of a topography takes place under conditions of confidentiality required by a measure taken in conformity with Article 223(1)(b) of the Treaty.
2.   The Council acting by qualified majority on a proposal from the Commission, may amend paragraph 1 (a) (i) and (ii) in order to adapt these provisions in the light of technical progress.

Chapter 2

Protection of topographies of semiconductor products

Article 2

1.   Member States shall protect the topo-   **A2.3**
graphies of semiconductor products by adopting legislative provisions conferring exclusive rights in accordance with the provisions of the directive.
2.   The topography of a semiconductor product shall be protected in so far as it satisfies the conditions that it is the result of its creator's own intellectual effort and is not commonplace in the semiconductor industry. Where the topography of a semiconductor product consists of elements that are commonplace in the semiconductor industry, it shall be protected only to the extent that the combination of such elements, taken as a whole, fulfils the abovementioned conditions.

Article 3

1.   Subject to paragraphs 2 to 5, the right   **A2.4**
to protection shall apply in favour of persons who are the creators of the topographies of semiconductor products.
2.   Member States may provide that,
(a) where a topography is created in the course of the creator's employment, the right to protection shall apply in favour of the creator's employer unless the terms of employment provide to the contrary;
(b) where a topography is created under a contract other than a contract of employment, the right to protection shall apply in favour of a party to the contract by whom the topography has been commissioned, unless the contract provides to the contrary.
3.   (a) as regards the persons referred to in paragraph 1, the right to protection shall apply in favour of natural persons who are nationals of a member state or who have their habitual residence on the territory of a member state.
  (b) where member states make provision in accordance with paragraph 2,

the right to protection shall apply in favour of:

(i) natural persons who are nationals of a member state or who have their habitual residence on the territory of a member state;

(ii) companies or other legal persons which have a real and effective industrial or commercial establishment on the territory of a Member State.

4. Where no right to protection exists in accordance with other provisions of this article, the right to protection shall also apply in favour of the persons referred to in paragraph 3 (b) (i) and (ii) who:

(a) first commercially exploit within a member state a topography which has not yet been exploited commercially anywhere in the world; and

(b) have been exclusively authorized to exploit commercially the topography throughout the community by the person entitled to dispose of it.

5. The right to protection shall also apply in favour of the successors in title of the persons mentioned in paragraphs 1 to 4.

6. Subject to paragraph 7, Member States may negotiate and conclude agreements or understandings with third states and multilateral conventions concerning the legal protection of topographies of semiconductor products whilst respecting community law and in particular the rules laid down in this directive.

7. Member States may enter into negotiations with third states with a view to extending the right to protection to persons who do not benefit from the right to protection according to the provisions of this directive. Member States who enter into such negotiations shall inform the Commission thereof.

When a Member State wishes to extend protection to persons who otherwise do not benefit from the right to protection according to the provisions of this directive or to conclude an agreement or understanding on the extension of protection with a non-Member State it shall notify the Commission. The Commision shall inform the other Member States thereof. The Member State shall hold the extension of protection or the conclusion of the agreement or understanding in abeyance for one month from the date on which it notifies the Commission. However, if within that period the Commission notifies the Member State concerned of its intention to submit a proposal to the Council for all Member States to extend protection in respect of the persons or non-Member State concerned, the Member State shall hold the extension of protection or the conclusion of the agreement or understanding in abeyance for a period of two months from the date of the notification by the Member State.

Where, before the end of this two-month period, the Commission submits such a proposal to the Council, the Member State shall hold the extension of protection or the conclusion of the agreement or understanding in abeyance for a further period of four months from the date on which the proposal was submitted.

In the absence of a Commission notification or proposal or a Council decision within the time limits prescribed above, the Member State may extend protection or conclude the agreement or understanding.

A proposal by the Commission to extend protection, whether or not it is made following a notification by a Member State in accordance with the preceding paragraphs shall be adopted by the Council acting by qualified majority.

A decision of the Council on the basis of a Commission proposal shall not prevent a Member State from extending protection to persons, in addition to those to benefit from protection in all Member States, who were included in the envisaged extension, agreement or understanding as notified, unless the Council acting by qualified majority has decided otherwise.

8. Commision proposals and Council

Decisions pursuant to paragraph 7 shall be published for information in the *Official Journal of the European Communities.*

Article 4

1. Member States may provide that the exclusive rights conferred in conformity with Article 2 shall not come into existence or shall no longer apply to the topography of a semiconductor product unless an application for registration in due form has been filed with a public authority within two years of its first commercial exploitation. Member States may require in addition to such registration that material identifying or exemplifying the topography or any combination thereof has been deposited with a public authority, as well as a statement as to the date of first commercial exploitation of the topography where it precedes the date of the application for registration.

2. Member States shall ensure that material deposited in conformity with paragraph 1 is not made available to the public where it is a trade secret. This provision shall be without prejudice to the disclosure of such material pursuant to an order of a court or other competent authority to persons involved in litigation concerning the validity or infringement of the exclusive rights referred to in Article 2.

3. Member States may require that transfers of rights in protected topographies be registered.

4. Member States may subject registration and deposit in accordance with paragraphs 1 and 3 to the payment of fees not exceeding their administrative costs.

5. Conditions prescribing the fulfilment of additional formalities for obtaining or maintaining protection shall not be admitted.

6. Member States which require registration shall provide for legal remedies in favour of a person having the right to protection in accordance with the provisions of this directive who can prove that another person has applied for or obtained the registration of a topography without his authorization.

Article 5

1. The exclusive rights referred to in article 2 shall include the rights to authorize or prohibit any of the following acts:
(a) reproduction of a topography in so far as it is protected under Article 2 (2);
(b) commercial exploitation or the importation for that purpose of a topography or of a semiconductor product manufactured by using the topography.

2. Notwithstanding paragraph 1, a member state may permit the reproduction of a topography privately for non commercial aims.

3. The exclusive rights referred to in paragraph 1 (a) shall not apply to reproduction for the purpose of analyzing, evaluating or teaching the concepts, processes, systems or techniques embodied in the topography or the topography itself.

4. The exclusive rights referred to in paragraph 1 shall not extend to any such act in relation to a topography meeting the requirements of article 2 (2) and created on the basis of an analysis and evaluation of another topography, carried out in conformity with paragraph 3.

5. The exclusive rights to authorize or prohibit the acts specified in paragraph 1 (b) shall not apply to any such act committed after the topography or the semiconductor product has been put on the market in a Member State by the person entitled to authorize its marketing or with his consent.

6. A person who, when he acquires a semiconductor product, does not know, or has no reasonable grounds to believe, that the product is protected by an exclusive right conferred by a member state in conformity with this directive shall not be prevented from commercially exploiting that product.

However, for acts committed after that person knows, or has reasonable grounds to believe, that the semiconductor product is so protected, member states shall ensure that on the demand of the rightholder a tribunal may require, in accordance with the provisions of the national law applicable, the payment of adequate remuneration.

7. The provisions of paragraph 6 shall apply to the successors in title of the person referred to in the first sentence of that paragraph.

Article 6

A2.7   Member States shall not subject the rights referred to in Article 2 to licences granted, for the sole reason that a certain period of time has elapsed, automatically, and by operation of law.

Article 7

A2.8   1. Member States shall provide that the exclusive rights referred to in Article 2 shall come into existence:

(a) where registration is the condition for the coming into existence of the exclusive rights in accordance with article 4, on the earlier of the following dates:

     (i) the date when the topography is first commercially exploited anywhere in the world;

     (ii) the date when an application or registration has been filed in due form; or

(b) when the topography is first commercially exploited anywhere in the world; or

(c) when the topography is first fixed or encoded.

2. Where the exclusive rights come into existence in accordance with paragraph 1 (a) or (b), the member states shall provide, for the period prior to those rights coming into existence, legal remedies in favour of a person having the right to protection in accordance with the provisions of this directive who can prove that another person has fraudulently reproduced or commercially exploited or imported for that purpose a topography. This paragraph shall be without prejudice to legal remedies made available to enforce the exclusive rights conferred in conformity with Article 2.

3. The exclusive rights shall come to an end 10 years from the end of the calendar year in which the topography is first commercially exploited anywhere in the world or, where registration is a condition for the coming into existence or continuing application of the exclusive rights, 10 years from the earlier of the following dates:

(a) the end of the calendar year in which the topography is first commercially exploited anywhere in the world;

(b) the end of the calendar year in which the application for registration has been filed in due form.

4. Where a topography has not been commercially exploited anywhere in the world within a period of 15 years from its first fixation or encoding, any exclusive rights in existence pursuant to paragraph 1 shall come to an end and no new exclusive rights shall come into existence unless an application for registration in due form has been filed within that period in those member states where registration is a condition for the coming into existence or continuing application of the exclusive rights.

Article 8

The protection granted to the topographies of semiconductor products in accordance with article 2 shall not extend to any concept, process, system, technique or encoded information embodied in the topography other than the topography te and concludeitself.   **A2.9**

Article 9

Where the legislation of member states provides that semiconductor products manufactured using protected topographies may carry any indication, the indication to be used shall be a capital T as follows: **A2.10**

$$T, \text{ `T', } [T], \textcircled{T}, T^* \text{ or } \boxed{T}.$$

Chapter 3

Continued application of other legal provisions

Article 10

1. The provisions of this Directive shall be without prejudice to legal provisions concerning patent and utility model rights.   **A2.11**

2. The provisions of this Directive shall be without prejudice:

(a) to rights conferred by the member states in fulfilment of their obligations under international agreements, including provisions extending such rights to nationals of, or residents in, the territory of the member state concerned;

(b) to the law of copyright in Member States, restricting the reproduction of drawing or other artistic representations of topographies by copying them in two dimensions.

3. Protection granted by national law to topographies of semiconductor products fixed or encoded before the entry into force of the national provisions enacting the Directive, but no later than date set out in Article 11 (1), shall not be affected by the provisions of this Directive.

Chapter 4

Final provisions

Article 11

1. Member States shall bring into force **A2.12** the laws, regulations or administrative provisions necessary to comply with this Directive by 7 November 1987.

2. Member States shall ensure that they communicate to the Commission the texts of the main provisions of national law which they adopt in the field covered by this Directive.

Article 12

This Directive is addressed to the Member **A2.13** States.

Done at Brussels, 16 December 1986.

COUNCIL DIRECTIVE 90/270/EEC

of 29 May 1990

on the minimum safety and health requirements for work with display screen equipment (fifth individual Directive within the meaning of Article 16 (1) of Directive 87/391/EEC)*

THE COUNCIL OF THE
EUROPEAN COMMUNITIES,

A3.1 Having regard to the Treaty establishing the European Economic Community, and in particular Article 118a thereof,

Having regard to the Commission proposal (OJ 1988 C113/7 and OJ 1989 C130/5) drawn up after consultation with the Advisory Committee on Safety, Hygiene and Health Protection at Work,

In cooperation with the European Parliament (OJ 1989 C12/92 and OJ 1990 C113)

Having regard to the opinion of the Economic and Social Committee (OJ 1988 C318/32),

Whereas Article 118a of the Treaty provides that the Council shall adopt, by means of Directives, minimum requirements designed to encourage improvements, especially in the working environment, to ensure a better level of protection of workers' safety and health;

Whereas, under the terms of that Article, those Directives shall avoid imposing administrative, financial and legal constraints, in a way which would hold back the creation and development of small and medium-sized undertakings;

Whereas the communication from the Commission on its programme concerning safety, hygiene and health at work (OJ 1988 C28/3) provides for the adoption of measures in respect of new technologies; whereas the Council has taken note thereof in its resolution of 21 December 1987 on safety, hygiene and health at work (OJ 1988 C28/1);

Whereas compliance with the minimum requirements for ensuring a better level of safety at workstations with display screens is essential for ensuring the safety and health of workers;

Whereas this Directive is an individual Directive within the meaning of Article 16 (1) of Council Directive 89/391/EEC of 12 June 1989 on the introduction of measures to encourage improvements in the safety and health of workers at work (OJ 1989 L183/1); whereas the provisions of the latter are therefore fully applicable to the use by workers of display screen equipment, without prejudice to more stringent and/or specific provisions contained in the present Directive;

Whereas employers are obliged to keep themselves informed of the latest advances in technology and scientific findings concerning workstation design so that they can make any changes necessary so as to be able to guarantee a better level of protection of workers' safety and health;

Whereas the ergonomic aspects are of particular importance for a workstation with display screen equipment;

Whereas this Directive is a practical contribution towards creating the social dimension of the internal market;

Whereas, pursuant to Decision 74/325/EEC (OJ 1974 L185/15), the Advisory Committee on Safety, Hygiene and Health Protection at Work shall be consulted by the Commission on the drawing-up of proposals in this field,

HAS ADOPTED THIS DIRECTIVE:

---

* OJ 1990 L156/14.

Section I

General Provisions

Article 1

Subject

A3.2 1. This Directive, which is the fifth individual Directive within the meaning of Article 16 (1) of Directive 89/391/EEC, lays down minimum safety and health requirements for work with display screen equipment as defined in Article 2.

2. The provisions of Directive 89/391/EEC are fully applicable to the whole field referred to in paragraph 1, without prejudice to more stringent and/or specific provisions contained in the present Directive.

3. This Directive shall not apply to:

(a) drivers' cabs or control cabs for vehicles or machinery;

(b) computer systems on board a means of transport;

(c) computer systems mainly intended for public use;

(d) 'portable' systems not in prolonged use at a workstation;

(e) calculators, cash registers and any equipment having a small data or measurement display required for direct use of the equipment;

(f) typewriters of traditional design, of the type known as 'typewriter with window'.

Article 2

Definitions

A3.3 For the purpose of this Directive, the following terms shall have the following meanings:

(a) *display screen equipment:* an alphanumeric or graphic display screen, regardless of the display process employed;

(b) *workstation:* an assembly comprising display screen equipment, which may be provided with a keyboard or input device and/or software determining the operator/machine interface, optional accessories, peripherals including the diskette drive, telephone, modem, printer, document holder, work chair and work desk or work surface, and the immediate work environment;

(c) *worker:* any worker as defined in Article 3 (a) of Directive 89/391/EEC who habitually uses display screen equipment as a significant part of his normal work.

Section II

Employers' Obligations

Article 3

Analysis of workstations

1. Employers shall be obliged to perform **A3.4** an analysis of workstations in order to evaluate the safety and health conditions to which they give rise for their workers, particularly as regards possible risks to eyesight, physical problems and problems of mental stress.

2. Employers shall take the appropriate measures to remedy the risks found, on the basis of the evaluation referred to in paragraph 1, taking account of the additional and/or combined effects of the risks so found.

Article 4

Workstations put into service for the first time

Employers must take the appropriate **A3.5** steps to ensure that workstations first put into service after 31 December 1992 meet the minimum requirements laid down in the Annex.

Article 5

Workstations already put into service

Employers must take the appropriate steps **A3.6** to ensure that workstations already put into service on or before 31 December 1992 are adapted to comply with the minimum requirements laid down in the Annex not later than four years after that date.

Article 6

Information for, and training of, workers

1. Without prejudice to Article 10 of **A3.7** Directive 89/391/EEC, workers shall receive information on all aspects of safety and health relating to their workstation, in particular information on such measures applicable to workstations as are implemented under Articles 3, 7 and 9.

In all cases, workers or their representatives shall be informed of any health and safety measure taken in compliance with this Directive.

2. Without prejudice to Article 12 of Directive 89/391/EEC, every worker shall also receive training in use of the workstation before commencing this type of work and whenever the organization of the workstation is substantially modified.

Article 7

Daily work routine

A3.8   The employer must plan the worker's activities in such a way that daily work on a display screen is periodically interrupted by breaks or changes of activity reducing the workload at the display screen.

Article 8

Worker consultation and participation

A3.9   Consulation and participation of workers and/or their representatives shall take place in accordance with Article 11 of Directive 89/391/EEC on the matters covered by this Directive, including its Annex.

Article 9

Protection of workers' eyes and eyesight

A3.10   1. Workers shall be entitled to an appropriate eye and eyesight test carried out by a person with the necessary capabilities:
—before commencing display screen work,
—at regular intervals thereafter, and
—if they experience visual difficulties which may be due to display screen work.

2. Workers shall be entitled to an ophthalmological examination if the results of the test referred to in paragraph 1 show that this is necessary.

3. If the results of the test referred to in paragraph 1 or of the examination referred to in paragraph 2 show that it is necessary and if normal corrective appliances cannot be used, workers must be provided with special corrective appliances appropriate for the work concerned.

4. Measures taken pursuant to this Article may in no circumstances involve workers in additional financial cost.

5. Protection of workers' eyes and eyesight may be provided as part of a national health system.

Section III

Miscellaneous provisions

Article 10

Adaptions to the Annex

The strictly technical adaptations to the Annex to take acount of technical progress, developments in international regulations and specifications and knowledge in the field of display screen equipment shall be adopted in accordance with the procedure laid down in article 17 of Directive 89/391/EEC.   **A3.11**

Article 11

Final provisions

1. Member States shall bring into force the laws, regulations and administrative provisions necessary to comply with this Directive by 31 December 1992.   **A3.12**
They shall forthwith inform the Commission thereof.

2. Member States shall communicate to the Commission the texts of the provisions of national law which they adopt, or have already adopted, in the field covered by this Directive.

3. Member States shall report to the Commission every four years on the practical implementation of the provisions of this Directive, indicating the points of view of employers and workers.
The Commission shall inform the European Parliament, the Council, the Economic and Social Committee and the Advisory Committee on Safety, Hygiene and Health Protection at Work.

4. The Commission shall submit a report on the implementation of this Directive at regular intervals to the European Parliament, the Council and the Economic and Social Committee, taking into account paragraphs 1, 2 and 3.

Article 12

This Directive is addressed to the Member States.   **A3.13**

Done at Brussels, 29 May 1990.

Annex

Minimum requirements

Articles 4 and 5

Preliminary remark

A3.14 The obligations laid down in this Annex shall apply in order to achieve the objectives of this Directive and to the extent that, firstly, the components concerned are present at the workstation, and secondly, the inherent requirements or characteristics of the task do not preclude it.

1. Equipment

(a) General comment

The use as such of the equipment must not be a source of risk for workers.

(b) Display screen

The characters on the screen shall be well-defined and clearly formed, of adequate size and with adequate spacing between the characters and lines.

The image on the screen should be stable, with no flickering or other forms of instability.

The brightness and/or the contrast between the characters and the background shall be easily adjustable by the operator, and also be easily adjustable to ambient conditions.

The screen must swivel and tilt easily and freely to suit the needs of the operator.

It shall be possible to use a separate base for the screen or an adjustable table.

The screen shall be free of reflective glare and reflections liable to cause discomfort to the user.

(c) Keyboard

The keyboard shall be tiltable and separate from the screen so as to allow the worker to find a comfortable working position avoiding fatigue in the arms or hands.

The space in front of the keyboard shall be sufficient to provide support for the hands and arms of the operator.

The keyboard shall have a matt surface to avoid reflective glare.

The arrangement of the keyboard and the characteristics of the keys shall be such as to facilitate the use of the keyboard.

The symbols on the keys shall be adequately contrasted and legible from the design working position.

(d) Work desk or work surface

The work desk or work surface shall have a sufficiently large, low-reflectance surface and allow a flexible arrangement of the screen, keyboard, documents and related equipment.

The document holder shall be stable and adjustable and shall be positioned so as to minimize the need for uncomfortable head and eye movements.

There shall be adequate space for workers to find a comfortable position.

(e) Work chair

The work chair shall be stable and allow the operator easy freedom of movement and a comfortable position.

The seat shall be adjustable in height.

The seat back shall be adjustable in both height and tilt.

A footrest shall be made available to any one who wishes for one.

2. Environment

(a) Space requirements

The workstation shall be dimen- **A3.15**
sioned and designed so as to provide sufficient space for the user to change position and vary movement.

185

(b) *Lighting*

Room lighting and/or spot lighting (work lamps) shall ensure satisfactory lighting conditions and an appropriate contrast between the screen and the background environment, taking into account the type of work and the user's vision requirements.

Possible disturbing glare and reflections on the screen or other equipment shall be prevented by coordinating workplace and workstation layout with the positioning and technical characteristics of the artificial light sources.

(c) *Reflections and glare*

Workstations shall be so designed that sources of light, such as windows and other openings, transparent or translucid walls, and brightly coloured fixtures or walls cause no direct glare and, as far as possible, no reflections on the screen.

Windows shall be fitted with a suitable system of adjustable covering to attentuate the daylight that falls on the workstation.

(d) *Noise*

Noise emitted by equipment belonging to workstation(s) shall be taken into account when a workstation is being equipped, in particular so as not to distract attention or disturb speech.

(e) *Heat*

Equipment belonging to workstation(s) shall not produce excess heat which could cause discomfort to workers.

(f) *Radiation*

All radiation with the exception of the visible part of the electromagnetic spectrum shall be reduced to negligible levels from the point of view of the protection of workers' safety and health.

(g) *Humidity*

An adequate level of humidity shall be established and maintained.

3. Operator/computer interface

In designing, selecting, commissioning **A3.16** and modifying software, and in designing tasks using display screen equipment, the employer shall take into account the following principles:

(a) software must be suitable for the task;
(b) software must be easy to use and, where appropriate, adaptable to the operator's level of knowledge or experience; no quantitative or qualitative checking facility may be used without the knowledge of the workers;
(c) systems must provide feedback to workers on their performance;
(d) systems must display information in a format and at a pace which are adapted to operators;
(e) the principles of software ergonomics must be applied, in particular to human data processing.

COUNCIL DIRECTIVE 91/250/EEC

of 14 May 1991

on the legal protection of computer programs*

A4.1 THE COUNCIL OF THE EUROPEAN COMMUNITIES,

Having regard to the Treaty establishing the European Economic Community and in particular Article 100a thereof,

Having regard to the proposal from the Commission (OJ 1989 C91/4 and OJ 1990 C320/22),

In cooperation with the European Parliament[1],

Having regard to the opinion of the Economic and Social Committee (OJ 1989 C329/4),

Whereas computer programs are at present not clearly protected in all Member States by existing legislation and such protection, where it exists, has different attributes;

Whereas the development of computer programs requires the investment of considerable human, technical and financial resources while computer programs can be copied at a fraction of the cost needed to develop them independently;

Whereas computer programs are playing an increasingly important role in a broad range of industries and computer program technology can accordingly be considered as being of fundamental importance for the Community's industrial development;

Whereas certain differences in the legal protection of computer programs offered by the laws of the Member States have direct and negative effects on the functioning of the common market as regards computer programs and such differences could well become greater as Member States introduce new legislation on this subject;

---

* OJ 1991 L122/42.
[1] OJ 1990 C231/78; and Decision of 17 April 1991, not yet published in the Official Journal).

Whereas existing differences having such effects need to be removed and new ones prevented from arising, while differences not adversely affecting the functioning of the common market to a substantial degree need not be removed or prevented from arising;

Whereas the Community's legal framework on the protection of computer programs can accordingly in the first instance be limited to establishing that Member States should accord protection to computer programs under copyright law as literary works and, further, to establishing who and what should be protected, the exclusive rights on which protected persons should be able to rely in order to authorize or prohibit certain acts and for how long the protection should apply;

Whereas, for the purpose of this Directive, the term 'computer program' shall include programs in any form, including those which are incorporated into hardware; whereas this term also includes preparatory design work leading to the development of a computer program provided that the nature of the preparatory work is such that a computer program can result from it at a later stage;

Whereas, in respect of the criteria to be applied in determining whether or not a computer program is an original work, no tests as to the qualitative or aesthetic merits of the program should be applied;

Whereas the Community is fully committed to the promotion of international standardization;

Whereas the function of a computer program is to communicate and work together with other components of a computer system and with users and, for this purpose, a logical and, where appropriate, physical interconnection and interaction is required to permit all elements of software and hardware to work with other software and hardware and with users in all the ways in which they are intended to function;

Whereas the parts of the program which provide for such interconnection and interaction between elements of software and hardware are generally known as 'interfaces';

Whereas this functional interconnection and interaction is generally known as 'interoperability'; whereas such interoperability can be defined as the ability to exchange information and mutually to use the information which has been exchanged;

Whereas, for the avoidance of doubt, it has to be made clear that only the expression of a computer program is protected and that ideas and principles which underlie any element of a program, including those which underlie its interfaces, are not protected by copyright under this Directive;

Whereas, in accordance with this principle of copyright, to the extent that logic, algorithms and programming languages comprise ideas and principles, those ideas and principles are not protected under this Directive;

Whereas, in accordance with the legislation and jurisprudence of the Member States and the international copyright conventions, the expression of those ideas and principles is to be protected by copyright;

A4.2   Whereas, for the purposes of this Directive, the term 'rental' means the making available for use, for a limited period of time and for profit-making purposes, of a computer program or a copy thereof; whereas this term does not include public lending, which, accordingly, remains outside the scope of this Directive;

Whereas the exclusive rights of the author to prevent the unauthorized reproduction of his work have to be subject to a limited exception in the case of a computer program to allow the reproduction technically necessary for the use of that program by the lawful acquirer;

Whereas this means that the acts of loading and running necessary for the use of a copy of a program which has been lawfully acquired, and the act of correction of its errors, may not be prohibited by contract; whereas, in the absence of specific contractual provisions, including when a copy of the program has been sold, any other act necessary for the use of the copy of a program may be performed in accordance with its intended purpose by a lawful acquirer of that copy;

Whereas a person having a right to use a computer program should not be prevented from performing acts necessary to observe, study or test the functioning of the program, provided that these acts do not infringe the copyright in the program;

Whereas the unauthorized reproduction, translation, adaptation or transformation of the form of the code in which a copy of a computer program has been made available constitutes an infringement of the exclusive rights of the author;

Whereas, nevertheless, circumstances   **A4.3** may exist when such a reproduction of the code and translation of its form within the meaning of Article 4 (a) and (b) are indispensable to obtain the necessary information to achieve the interoperability of an independently created program with other programs;

Whereas it has therefore to be considered that in these limited circumstances only, performance of the acts of reproduction and translation by or on behalf of a person having a right to use a copy of the program is legitimate and compatible with fair practice and must therefore be deemed not to require the authorization of the right-holder;

Whereas an objective of this exception is to make it possible to connect all components of a computer system, including those of different manufacturers, so that they can work together;

Whereas such an exception to the author's exclusive rights may not be used in a way which prejudices the legitimate interests of the rightholder or which conflicts with a normal exploitation of the program;

Whereas, in order to remain in accordance with the provisions of the Berne

Convention for the Protection of Literary and Artistic Works, the term of protection should be the life of the author and fifty years from the first of January of the year following the year of his death or, in the case of an anonymous or pseudonymous work, 50 years from the first of January of the year following the year in which the work is first published;

Whereas protection of computer programs under copyright laws should be without prejudice to the application, in appropriate cases, of other forms of protection; whereas, however, any contractual provisions contrary to Article 6 or to the exceptions provided for in Article 5 (2) and (3) should be null and void;

Whereas the provisions of this Directive are without prejudice to the application of the competition rules under Articles 85 and 86 of the Treaty if a dominant supplier refuses to make information available which is necessary for interoperability as defined in this Directive;

Whereas the provisions of this Directive should be without prejudice to specific requirements of Community law already enacted in respect of the publication of interfaces in the telecommunications sector or Council Decisions relating to standardization in the field of information technology and telecommunication;

Whereas this Directive does not affect derogations provided for under national legislation in accordance with the Berne Convention on points not covered by this Directive.

HAS ADOPTED THIS DIRECTIVE:

Article 1
Object of protection

A4.4 1.   In accordance with the provisions of this Directive, Member States shall protect computer programs, by copyright, as literary works within the meaning of the Berne Convention for the Protection of Literary and Artistic Works. For the purposes of this Directive, the term 'computer programs' shall include their preparatory design material.
2.   Protection in accordance with this

Directive shall apply to the expression in any form of a computer program. Ideas and principles which underlie any element of a computer program, including those which underlie its interfaces, are not protected by copyright under this Directive.
3.   A computer program shall be protected if it is original in the sense that it is the author's own intellectual creation. No other criteria shall be applied to determine its eligibility for protection.

Article 2
Authorship of computer programs

1.   The author of a computer program   **A4.5**
shall be the natural person or group of natural persons who has created the program or, where the legislation of the Member State permits, the legal person designated as the rightholder by that legislation. Where collective works are recognized by the legislation of a Member State, the person considered by the legislation of the Member State to have created the work shall be deemed to be its author.
2.   In respect of a computer program created by a group of natural persons jointly, the exclusive rights shall be owned jointly.
3.   Where a computer program is created by an employee in the execution of his duties or following the instructions given by his employer, the employer exclusively shall be entitled to exercise all economic rights in the program so created, unless otherwise provided by contract.

Article 3
Beneficiaries of protection

Protection shall be granted to all natural   **A4.6**
or legal persons eligible under national copyright legislation as applied to literary works.

Article 4
Restricted Acts

Subject to the provisions of Articles 5 and   **A4.7**
6, the exclusive rights of the rightholder within the meaning of Article 2, shall include the right to do or to authorize:
(a) the permanent or temporary reproduction of a computer program by

any means and in any form, in part or in whole. Insofar as loading, displaying, running, transmission or storage of the computer program necessitate such reproduction, such acts shall be subject to authorization by the rightholder;

(b) the translation, adaptation, arrangement and any other alteration of a computer program and the reproduction of the results thereof, without prejudice to the rights of the person who alters the program;

(c) any form of distribution to the public, including the rental, of the original computer program or of copies thereof. The first sale in the Community of a copy of a program by the rightholder or with his consent shall exhaust the distribution right within the Community of that copy, with the exception of the right to control further rental of the program or a copy thereof.

Article 5

Exceptions to the restricted acts

A4.8　1.　In the absence of specific contractual provisions, the acts referred to in Article 4 (a) and (b) shall not require authorization by the rightholder where they are necessary for the use of the computer program by the lawful acquirer in accordance with its intended purpose, including for error correction.

2.　The making of a back-up copy by a person having a right to use the computer program may not be prevented by contract insofar as it is necessary for that use.

3.　The person having a right to use a copy of a computer program shall be entitled, without the authorization of the rightholder, to observe, study or test the functioning of the program in order to determine the ideas and principles which underlie any element of the program if he does so while performing any of the acts of loading, displaying, running, transmitting or storing the program which he is entitled to do.

Article 6

Decompilation

1.　The authorization of the rightholder 　**A4.9** shall not be required where reproduction of the code and translation of its form within the meaning of Article 4 (a) and (b) are indispensable to obtain the information necessary to achieve the interoperability of an independently created computer program with other programs, provided that the following conditions are met:

(a) these acts are performed by the licensee or by other person having a right to use a copy of a program, or on their behalf by a person authorized to do so;

(b) the information necessary to achieve interoperability has not previously been readily available to the persons referred to in subparagraph (a); and

(c) these act are confined to the parts of the original program which are necessary to achieve interoperability.

2.　The provisions of paragraph 1 shall not permit the information obtained through its application:

(a) to be used for goals other than to achieve the interoperability of the independently created computer program;

(b) to be given to others, except when necessary for the interoperability of the independently created computer program; or

(c) to be used for the development, production or marketing of a computer program substantially similar in its expression, or for any other act which infringes copyright.

3.　In accordance with the provisions of the Berne Convention for the protection of Literary and Artistic Works, the provisions of this Article may not be interpreted in such a way as to allow its application to be used in a manner which unreasonably prejudices the right holder's legitimate interests or conflicts with a normal exploitation of the computer program.

Article 7

Special measures of protection

1.　Without prejudice to the provisions of 　**A4.10** Articles 4, 5 and 6, Member States shall provide, in accordance with their national legislation, appropriate remedies against a person committing any of the acts listed in subparagraphs (a), (b) and (c) below:

(a) any act of putting into circulation a copy of a computer program knowing, or having reason to believe, that it is an infringing copy;

(b) the possession, for commercial purposes, of a copy of a computer program knowing, or having reason to believe, that it is an infringing copy;

(c) any act of putting into circulation, or the possession for commercial purposes of, any means the sole intended purpose of which is to facilitate the unauthorized removal or circumvention of any technical device which may have been applied to protect a computer program.

2. Any infringing copy of a computer program shall be liable to seizure in accordance with the legislation of the Member State concerned.

3. Member States may provide for the seizure of any means referred to in paragraph 1 (c).

[Art 8]²

Article 9

Continued application of other legal provisions

A4.11 1. The provisions of this Directive shall be without prejudice to any other legal provisions such as those concerning patent rights, trade-marks, unfair competition, trade secrets, protection of semi-conductor products or the law of contract. Any contractual provisions contrary to Article 6 or to the exceptions provided for in Article 5 (2) and (3) shall be null and void.

2. The provisions of this Directive shall apply also to programs created before 1 January 1993 without prejudice to any acts concluded and rights acquired before that date.

Article 10

Final provisions

1. Member States shall bring into force   **A4.12** the laws, regulations and administrative provisions necessary to comply with this Directive before 1 January 1993.

When Member States adopt these measures, the latter shall contain a reference to this Directive or shall be accompanied by such reference on the occasion of their official publication. The methods of making such a reference shall be laid down by the Member States.

2. Member States shall communicate to the Commission the provisions of national law which they adopt in the field governed by this Directive.

Article 11

This Directive is addressed to the Member   **A4.13** States.

Done at Brussels, 14 May 1991.

---

² Art 8 repealed by Dir 93/98, Art 11.

Commission conclusions

decided on the occasion of the adoption of the Commission's proposal for a Council Directive on the legal protection of computer programs*

A5.1 In adopting a proposal for a Council Directive on the legal protection of computer programs the Commission approves the following policy guidelines. It affirms its conviction that computer programs, given the intellectual effort and the financial investment which may be necessary for their creation and the ease with which they can be copied, merit adequate legal protection. Following a worldwide trend, the Commission proposes copyright as a suitable legal basis for ensuring a balance between an effective level of protection and the interests of users. Divergencies between the copyright statutes of the Member States as to the availability and scope of the protection have caused the Commission to initiate the harmonization process in view of the objective of completing the internal market.

Software is an industrial tool which is essential to the Community's economic development. The grant of exclusive rights under copyright law will create incentives for software developers to invest their intellectual and financial resources and thereby to promote technical progress in the public interest. Technical progress and public welfare, however, are also ensured by a system of indistorted competition, one of the principal goals of the Treaty. Exclusive proprietary rights and free competition, while in principle designed to achieve the same objective by different means, may conflict where a copyright owner is in a position to exercise his statutory exclusive rights beyond their intended purpose. The exercise of exclusive copyrights will not prejudice the application of the competition rules and the imposition of effective remedies in appropriate cases. Further, the Community commitment to international standardization in the fields of information technology and telecommunications must not be compromised.

The relation between the Community's **A5.2** competition rules and copyright is governed by the European Court's distinction between the existence and the exercise of the intellectual property rights in question. Any arrangement or measure which goes beyond the existence of copyright can be subject to control under the competition rules. This means that for example any attempt to extend by contractual agreements or other arrangements the scope of protection to aspects of the programs for which protection under copyright is not available, or the prohibition of any act which is not reserved for the right owner may constitute an infringement of the competition rules.

Moreover, companies in a dominant position must not abuse that position within the meaning of Article 86 of the Treaty. For example, under certain circumstances the exercise of copyright as to the aspects of a program, which other companies need to use in order to write compatible programs, could amount to such an abuse. This could also be the case if a dominant company tries to use its exclusive rights in one product to gain an unfair advantage in relation to one or more products not covered by these rights.

Furthermore, the ability of a competing manufacturer to write an independent but compatible program often depends on his possibility to have access to the target program or to certain information relating to it. Access to information is not a matter of copyright law. Article 86 always applies where a dominant company abusively refuses access to such information or restricts unreasonably such access.

---

* OJ 1989 C91/16

192

Amended proposal for a Council Directive

on the legal protection of databases*

COM(93) 464 final—SYN 393

submitted by the Commission pursuant to Article 149 (3) of the EEC Treaty on 4 October 1993

THE COUNCIL OF THE EUROPEAN COMMUNITIES,

A6.1 Having regard to the Treaty establishing the European Economic Community, and in particular Articles 57(2), 66, 100a thereof,

Having regard to the proposal from Commission,

In cooperation with the European Parliament,

Having regard to the opinion of the Economic and Social Committee,

1. Whereas databases are at present not clearly protected in all Member States by existing legislation and such protection where it exists, has different attributes;

2. Whereas such differences in the legal protection offered by the legislation of the Member States have direct and negative effects on the establishment and functioning of the Internal Market as regards databases and in particular on the freedom of individuals and companies to provide on-line database goods and services on an equal legal basis throughout the Community; whereas such differences could well become more pronounced as Member States introduce new legislation on this subject, which is now taking on an increasingly international dimension;

3. Whereas existing differences having a distortive effect on the establishment and functioning of the internal market need to be removed and new ones prevented from arising, while differences not at the present time adversely affecting the establish-

ment and functioning of the internal market or the development of an information market within the Community need not be addressed in this Directive;

4. Whereas copyright protection for databases exists in varying forms in a number of Member States according to legislation or case-law and such unharmonized intellectual property rights, being territorial in nature, can have the effect of preventing the free movement of goods or services within the Community if differences in the scope, conditions, derogations or term of protection remain between the legislation of the Member States;

5. Whereas although copyright remains an appropriate form of exclusive right for the legal protection of databases and in particular an appropriate means to secure the remuneration of the author who has created a database, in addition to copyright protection, and in the absence as yet of a harmonized system of unfair competition legislation or of case-law in the Member States, other measures are required to prevent unfair extraction and re-utilization of the contents of a database;

6. Whereas database development requires the investment of considerable human, technical and financial resources while such databases can be copied at a fraction of the cost needed to develop them independently;

7. Whereas unauthorized access to a database and removal of its contents constitute acts which can have the gravest economic and technical con-

* OJ 1993 C308/1.

sequences;

8. Whereas databases are a vital tool in the development of an information market within the Community; whereas this tool will be of use to a large variety of other activities and industries;

9. Whereas the exponential growth, in the Community and worldwide, in the amount of information generated and processed annually in all sectors of commerce and industry requires investment in all the Member States in advanced information management systems;

A6.2 10. Whereas a correspondingly high rate of increase in publications of literary, artistic, musical and other works necessitates the creation of modern archiving, bibliographic and accessing techniques, to enable consumers to have at their disposal the most comprehensive collection of the Community's heritage;

11. Whereas there is at the present time a great imbalance in the level of investment in database creation both as between the Member States themselves, and between the Community and the world's largest database producing countries;

12. Whereas such an investment in modern information storage and retrieval systems will not take place within the Community unless a stable and uniform legal protection regime is introduced for the protection of the rights of authors of databases and the repression of acts of piracy and unfair competition;

13. Whereas this Directive protects collections, sometimes called compilations, of works or other materials whose arrangement, storage and access is performed by means which include electronic, electromagnetic or electro-optical processes or analogous processes;

14. Whereas the criteria by which such collections shall be eligible for protection by copyright should be that the author, in effecting the selection or the arrangement of the contents of the database, has made an intellectual creation;

15. Whereas no other criteria than originality in the sense of intellectual creation should be applied to determine the eligibility of the database for copyright protection, and in particular no aesthetic or qualitative criteria should be applied;

16. Whereas the term database should be understood to include collections of works, whether literary, artistic, musical or other, or of other material such as texts, sounds, images, numbers, facts, data or combinations of any of these;

17. Whereas the protection of a database should extend to the electronic materials without which the contents selected and arranged by the maker of the database cannot be used, such as, for example the system made to obtain information and present information to the user in electronic or non-electronic form, and the indexation and thesaurus used in the construction or operation of the database;

18. Whereas the term database should not be taken to extend to any computer programme used in the construction or operation of a database, which accordingly remain protected by Council Directive 91/250/ EEC(OJ 1991 L122/42);

19. Whereas the Directive should be taken as applying only to collections which are made by electronic means, but is without prejudice to the protection under copyright as collections, within the meaning of Article 2 (5) of the Berne Convention for the protection of literary and artistic works, (text of Paris Act of 1971) and under the legislation of the Member States, of collections made by other means;

20. Whereas works protected by copyright or by any other rights, which are incorporated into a database, remain the object of their author's exclusive rights and may not therefore be incoporated into or reproduced from the database without the permission of the author or his succesors in title; **A6.3**

21. Whereas the rights of the author of

such works incoporated into a database are not in any way affected by the existence of a separate right in the original selection or arrangement of these works in a database;

22. Whereas the moral rights of the natural person who has created the database should be owned and exercised according to the provisions of the legislation of the Member States consistent with the provisions of the Berne Convention, and remain therefore outside the scope of this Directive;

23. Whereas the author's exclusive rights should include the right to determine the way in which his work is exploited and by whom, and in particular to control the availability of his work to unauthorized persons;

24. Whereas nevertheless once the rightholder has chosen to make available a copy of the database to a user, whether by an on-line service or by other means of distribution, that lawful user must be able to access and use the database, for the purposes and in the way set out in the agreement with the rightholder, even if such access and use necessitate performance of otherwise restricted acts;

25. Whereas if the user and the rightholder have not concluded an agreement regulating the use which may be made of the database, the lawful user should be presumed to be able to perform any of the restricted acts which are necessary for access to and use of the database;

26. Whereas in respect of reproduction in the limited circumstances provided for in the Berne Convention, of the contents of the database by the lawful user, whether in electronic or non-electronic form, the same restrictions and exceptions should apply to the reproduction of such works from a database as would apply to the reproduction of the same works made available to the public by other forms of exploitation or distribution;

27. Whereas the increasing use of digital recording technology exposes the database maker to the risk that the contents of his database may be downloaded and re-arranged electronically without his authorization to produce a database of identical content but which does not infringe any copyright in the arrangement of his database;

28. Whereas in addition to protecting the copyright in the original selection or arrangement of the contents of a database this Directive seeks to safeguard the position of makers of databases against misappropriation of the results of the financial and professional investment incurred in obtaining and collecting data by providing that certain acts done in relation to the contents of a database are subject to restriction even when such contents are not themselves protected by copyright or other rights;

29. Whereas such protection of the contents of a database is to be achieved by a special right by which the maker of a database can prevent the unauthorized extraction or re-utilization of the contents of that database for commercial purposes; whereas this special right (hereafter called 'a right to prevent unfair extraction') is not to be considered in any way as an extension of copyright protection to mere facts or data;

30. Whereas the existence of a right to prevent the extraction and re-utilization for commercial purposes of works or materials from a given database should not give rise to the creation of any independent right in the works or materials themselves;   **A6.4**

31. Whereas in the interests of competition between suppliers of information products and services, the maker of a database which is commercially distributed whose database is the sole possible source of a given work or material, should make that work or material available under licence for use by others, providing that the works or materials so licensed are used in the independent creation of new works, and providing that no prior rights in

or obligations incurred in respect of those works or materials are infringed;

32. Whereas licences granted in such circumstances should be fair and non-discriminatory under conditions to be agreed with the rightholder;

33. Whereas such licences should not be requested for reasons of commercial expediency such as economy of time, effort or financial investment;

34. Whereas in the event that licences are refused or the parties cannot reach agreement on the terms to be concluded, a system of arbitration should be provided for by the Member States;

35. Whereas licences may not be refused in respect of the extraction and re-utilization of works or materials from a publicly available database created by a public body providing that such acts do not infringe the legislation or international obligations of Member States or the Community in respect of matters such as personal data protection, privacy, security or confidentiality;

36. Whereas the objective of the provisions of this Directive, which is to afford an appropriate and uniform level of protection of databases as a means to secure the remuneration of the author who has created the database, is different from the aims of the proposal for a Council Directive concerning the protection of individuals in relation to the processing of personal data (OJ 1990 C277/3) which are to guarantee free circulation of personal data on the basis of a harmonized standard of rules designed to protect the fundamental rights, notably the right to privacy which is recognized in Article 8 of the European Convention for the protection of human rights and fundamental freedoms; whereas the provisions of this Directive are without prejudice to the data legislation;

37. Whereas notwithstanding the right to prevent unfair extraction from a database, it should still be possible for the lawful user to quote from or otherwise use, for commercial and private purposes, the contents of the database which he is authorized to use, providing that this exception is subject to narrow limitations and is not used in a way which would conflict with the author's normal exploitation of his work or which would unreasonably prejudice his legitimate interests;

Whereas the right to prevent unfair extraction from a database may only be extended to databases whose authors or makers are nationals or habitual residents of third countries and to those produced by companies or firms not established in a Member State within the meaning of the Treaty if such third countries offer comparable protection to databases produced by nationals of the Member States or habitual residents of the Community;

38. (a) Whereas distributors of databases should make appropriate provision in their contracts as regards the unauthorized re-utilization of the contents of the database by the lawful user where such re-utilization is for strictly private purposes or for the purposes of teaching or research, provided such re-utilization is not carried out for commercial purposes and does not prejudice the exclusive rights of the maker of the database to exploit that database;

39. Whereas, in addition to remedies provided under the legislation of the Member States for infringements of copyright or other rights, Member States should provide for appropriate remedies against unfair extraction from a database;

40. Whereas in addition to the protection given under this Directive to the database by copyright, and to its content against unfair extraction, other legal provisions existing in the laws of the Member States relevant to the supply of database goods and service should continue to apply,

HAS ADOPTED THIS DIRECTIVE:

Chapter I

Definitions

Article 1

Definitions

For the purposes of this Directive:

A6.5
1. 'database' means a collection of data, works or other materials arranged, stored and accessed by electronic means, and the materials necessary for the operation of the database such as its thesaurus, index or system for obtaining or presenting information; it shall not apply to any computer program used in the making or operation of the database;
2. 'owner of the rights in a database' means:
    (a) the author of a database; or
    (b) the natural or legal person to whom the author has lawfully granted the right to prevent unauthorized extraction of material from a database; or
    (c) where the database is not eligible for protection by copyright the maker of the database.

Chapter II

Copyright

Article 2

Object of protection

A6.6
1. In accordance with the provisions of this Directive, Member States shall protect databases by copyright as collections within the meaning of Article 2 (5) of the Berne Convention for the protection of literary and artistic works (text of the Paris Act of 1971).
2. The definition of database in point 1 of Article 1 is without prejudice to the protection by copyright of collections of works or materials arranged, stored or accessed by non-electronic means, which accordingly remain protected to the extent provided for by Article 2 (5) of the Berne Convention.
3. A database shall be protected by copyright if it is originaly in the sense that it is a collection of works or materials

which, by reason of their selection or their arrangement, constitutes the author's own intellectual creation. No other criteria shall be applied to determine the eligibility of a database for this protection.
4. The copyright protection of a database given by this Directive shall not extend to the works or materials contained therein, irrespective of whether or not they are themselves protected by copyright; the protection of a database shall be without prejudice to any rights subsisting in those works or materials themselves.

Article 3

Authorship

1. The author of a database shall be the natural person or group of natural persons who created the database, or where the legislation of the Member States permits, the legal person designated as the rightholder by that legislation. **A6.7**
2. Where collective works are recognized by the legislation of a Member State, the person considered by that legislation to have created the database shall be deemed to be its author.
3. In respect of a database created by a group of natural persons jointly, the exclusive rights shall be owned jointly.
4. Where a database is created an employee in the execution of his duties or following the instructions given by his employer, the employer exclusively shall be entitled to exercise all economic rights in the database so created, unless otherwise provided by contract.

Article 4

Entitlement to protection under copyright

Protection under copyright shall be granted to all owners of rights, whether natural or legal persons who fulfil the requirements laid down in national legislation or international agreements on copyright applicable to literary works. **A6.8**

Article 5

Incorporation of works or materials into a database

1. The incorporation into a database of any works or materials shall remain sub- **A6.9**

ject to the authorization of the owner of any copyright or other rights acquired or obligations incurred therein.

2. The incorporation into a database of bibliographical references, abstracts (with the exception of substantial descriptions or summaries of the content or the form of existing works) or brief quotations, shall not require the authorization of the owners of rights in those works, provided the name of the author and the source of the quotation are clearly indicated in accordance with Article 10 (3) of the Berne Convention.

Article 6

Restricted acts

A6.10 The owner of the rights in a database shall have, in respect of:

—the selection or arrangement of the contents of the database, and

—the electronic material referred to in point 1 of Article 1 used in creation or operation of the database,

the exclusive right within the meaning of Article 2 (1) to do or to authorize:

(a) the temporary or permanent repro-
duction of the database by any means and in any form, in whole or in part;

(b) the translation, adaptation, arrangement and any other alteration of the database;

(c) the reproduction of the results of any of the acts listed in (a) or (b);

(d) any form of distribution to the public, including the rental, of the database or of copies thereof. The first sale in the Community of a copy of the database by the rightholder or with his consent shall exhaust the distribution right within the Community of that copy, with the exception of the right to control further rental of the database or a copy thereof;

(e) any communication, display or performance of the database to the public.

Article 7

Exceptions to the restricted acts: copyright in the selection or arrangement

A6.11 1. The lawful user of a database may perform any of the acts listed in Article 5

which is necessary in order to use that database in the manner determined by contractual arrangements with the rightholder.

2. In the absence of any contractual arrangements between the rightholder and the user of a database in respect of its use, the performance by the lawful ac-
quirer of a database of any of the acts listed in Article 5 which is necessary in order to gain access to the contents of the database and use thereof shall not require the authorization of the rightholder.

3. The exceptions referred to in para-
graphs 1 and 2 relate to the subject matter listed in Article 5 and are without prejudice to any rights subsisting in the works or materials contained in the database.

Article 8

Exceptions to the restricted acts in relation to the copyright in the contents

1. Member States shall apply the same   **A6.12**
exceptions to any copyright or other rights of the author of a work contained in a database as those which apply in the legislation of the Member States to that work, in respect of brief quotations, and illustrations for the purposes of teaching, provided that such utilization is compatible with fair practice, in accordance with Article 10 (3) of the Berne Convention.

2. Where the legislation of the Member States or contractual arrangements concluded with the author or a work con-
tained in a database permit the user of that database to carry out acts which are permitted as derogations to any exclusive rights of the author of the work, performance of such acts shall not be taken to infringe the rights of the author of the database laid down in Article 6.

3. The provisions of paragraphs 1 and 2 above shall also apply in respect of owners of neighbouring rights attaching to materials contained in a database.

Article 9

Terms of protection

1. The duration of the period of copy-   **A6.13**
right protection of the database shall be the same as that provided for literary works.

2. (a) A substantial change to the selection or arrangement of the contents of a database shall give rise to the creation of a new database, which shall be protected from that moment for the period recognized in paragraph 1 of this Article. Such protection shall not prejudice existing rights in respect of the original database.

(b) For the purposes of the term of protection provided for in this Article 'substantial change' means: additions, deletions or alterations, which involve substantial modification to the selection or arrangement of the contents of a database, resulting in a new edition of that database.

3. (a) Insubstantial changes to the selection or arrangement of the contents of a database shall not entail a fresh period of copyright protection of that database.

(b) For the purpose of the term of protection provided for in this Article, 'insubstantial change' means: additions, deletions or alterations to the selection or arrangement of the contents of a database which are necessary for the database to continue to function in the way it was intended by its maker to function.

Chapter III

Sui Generis right

Article 10

Object of protection: right to prevent unauthorized extraction from a database

A6.14 1. For the purposes of this Directive 'right to prevent authorized extraction' means the right of the owner of the rights in a database to prevent acts of extraction and re-utilization of part or all of the material from that database.

2. Member States shall provide for a right for the owner of the rights in a database to prevent the unauthorized extraction or re-utilization, from that database, of its contents, in whole or in substantial part, for commercial purposes.

This right to prevent unauthorized extraction of the contents of a database shall apply irrespective of the eligibility of that database for protection under copyright. It shall not apply to the contents of a database where these are works already protected by copyright or neighbouring rights.

Article 11

Acts performed in relation to the contents of a database — unauthorized extraction of the contents

1. Notwithstanding the right provided **A6.15** for in Article 10 (2) to prevent the unauthorized extraction and re-utilization of the contents of a database, if the works or materials contained in a database which is made publicly available cannot be independently created, collected or obtained from any other source, the right to extract and re-utilize, in whole or substantial part, works or materials from that database for commercial purposes that are not for reasons such as economy of time, effort or financial investment, shall be licensed on fair and non-discriminatory terms. A declaration shall be submitted clearly setting out the justification of the commercial purposes pursued and requiring the issue of a licence.

2. The right to extract and re-utilize the contents of a database shall also be licensed on fair and non-discriminatory terms if the database is made publicly available by:

(a) public authorities or public corporations or bodies which are either established or authorized to assemble of to disclose information pursuant to legislation, or are under a general duty to do so;

(b) firms or entities enjoying a monopoly status by virtue of an exclusive concession by a public body.

3. For the purposes of this Article, databases shall not be deemed to have been made publicly available unless they may be freely interrogated.

4. Member States shall provide appropriate measures for arbitration between the parties in respect of such licences.

5. The lawful user of a database may, without authorization of the database

199

maker, extract and re-utilize insubstantial parts of works or materials from a database for commercial purposes provided that acknowledgement is made of the source.

6. The lawful user of a database may, without authorization of the database maker, and without acknowledgement of the source, extract and re-utilize insubstantial parts of works or materials from that database for personal private use only.

7. For the purposes of this Article, 'commercial purposes' means any use, which is not:

(a) private, personal; and

(b) for non-profit making purposes.

8. (a) For the purposes of paragaphs 4 and 5 of this Article, 'insubstantial parts' means part of a database made available to the public whose reproduction, evaluated quantitatively and qualitatively in relation to the database from which they are copied, can be considered not to prejudice the exclusive rights of the owner of that database to exploit the database.

(b) In both instances, it shall likewise be incumbent on the lawful user to demonstrate that the extraction and re-utilization of insubstantial parts do not prejudice the exclusive rights of the owner of that database to exploit the database, and that such practices are not carried out any more than is necessary to achieve the desired objective.

9. The provisions of this Article shall apply only to the extent that such extraction and re-utilization does not conflict with any other prior rights or obligations, including the legislation or international obligations of the Member States or of the community in respect of matters such as personal data protection, privacy, security or confidentiality.

Article 12

Term of protection

A6.16 1. The right to prevent unauthorized extraction shall run from the date of creation of the database for 15 years, starting on 1 January of the year following:

(a) the date when the database was first made available to the public; or

(b) any substantial change to the database.

2. (a) Any substantial change to the contents of a database shall give rise to a fresh period of protection by the right to prevent unauthorized extraction.

(b) For the purpose of the term of protection provided for in this Article 'substantial change' means the successive accumulation of insubstantial additions, deletions or alterations in respect of the contents of a database resulting in substantial modification to all or part of a database.

3. (a) Insubstantial changes to the contents of a database shall not entail a fresh period of protection of that database by the right to prevent unauthorized extraction.

(b) For the purpose of the term of protection provided for in this Article 'insubstantial change' means insubstantial additions, deletions or alterations which, taken together, do not substantially modify the contents of a database.

Article 13

Beneficiaries of protection under right to prevent unauthorized extraction from a database

1. Protection granted pursuant to the   **A6.17** Directive to the contents of a database against unauthorized extraction or re-utilization shall apply to databases whose makers are nationals of a Member State or who have their habitual residence on the territory of the Community.

2. Where databases are created under the provisions of Article 3 (4), paragraph 1 above shall also apply to companies and firms formed in accordance with the legislation of a Member State and having their registered office, central administration or principal place of business within the Community. Should the company or firm

formed in accordance with the legislation of a Member State have only its registered office in the territory of the Community, its operations must possess an effective and continuous link with the economy of one of the Member States.

3. Agreements extending the right to prevent unauthorized extraction to databases produced in third countries and falling outside the provisions of paragraphs 1 and 2 shall be concluded by the Council acting on a proposal from the Commission. The term of any protection extended to databases by virtue of this procedure shall not exceed that available pursuant to Article 12 (1).

Chapter IV

Common Provisions

Article 14

Remedies

A6.18   Member States shall provide appropriate remedies in respect of infringements of the rights provided for in this Directive.

Article 15

Continued application of other legal provisions

A6.19   1. The provisions of this Directive shall be without prejudice to copyright or any other right subsisting in the works or materials incorporated into a database as well as to other legal provisions such as patent rights, trade marks, design rights, unfair competition, trade secrets, confidentiality, data protection and privacy, and the law of contract applicable to the database itself or to its contents.

2. Protection pursuant to the provisions of this Directive as regards copyright and

the right to prevent unauthorized extraction and re-utilization of the contents of the database shall also be available in respect of databases created prior to the date of publication of the Directive which on that date fulfilled the requirements laid down therein as regards the protection of databases. Such protection shall be without prejudice to any contracts concluded and rights acquired before that date.

Article 16

Final provisions

1. Member States shall bring into force   **A6.20** the laws, regulations and administrative provisions necessary to comply with this Directive before 1 January 1995.

When Member States adopt these provisions, these shall contain a reference to this Directive or shall be accompanied by such reference at the time of their official publication. The procedure for such reference shall be adopted by Member States.

2. Member States shall communicate to the Commission the provisions of national law which they adopt in the field covered by this Directive.

3. Not later than at the end of the fifth year of implementaion of this Directive and every two years thereafter the Commission shall submit to the European Parliament, the Council and the Economic and Social Committee a report on the application of this Directive and, where necessary, shall submit proposals for its adjustment in line with developments in the area of databases.

Article 17

This Directive is addressed to the Member   **A6.21** States.

GUIDELINES ON THE APPLICATION OF EEC COMPETITION RULES IN THE TELECOMMUNICATIONS SECTOR*

Preface

A7.1 These guidelines aim at clarifying the application of Community competition rules to the market participants in the telecommunications sector. They must be viewed in the context of the special conditions of the telecommunications sector, and the overall Community telecommunications policy will be taken into account in their application. In particular, account will have to be taken of the actions the Commission will be in a position to propose for the telecommunications industry as a whole, actions deriving from the assessment of the state of play and issues at stake for this industry, as has already been the case for the European electronics and information technology industry in the communication of the Commission of 3 April 1991.[1]

A major political aim, as emphasized by the Commission, the Council, and the European Parliament, must be the development of efficient Europe-wide networks and services, at the lowest cost and of the highest quality, to provide the European user in the single market of 1992 with a basic infrastructure for efficient operation.

The Commission has made it clear in the past that in this context it is considered that liberalization and harmonization in the sector must go hand in hand.

Given the competition context in the telecommunications sector, the telecommunications operators should be allowed, and encouraged, to establish the necessary cooperation mechanisms, in order to create—or ensure—Community-wide full interconnectivity between public networks, and where required between services to enable European users to benefit from a wider range of better and cheaper telecommunications services.

This can and has to be done in compliance with, and respect of, EEC competition rules in order to avoid the diseconomies which otherwise could result. For the same reasons, operators and other firms that may be in a dominant market position should be made aware of the prohibition of abuse of such positions.

The guidelines should be read in the light of this objective. They set out to clarify, *inter alia*, which forms of cooperation amount to undesirable collusion, and in this sense they list what is *not* acceptable. They should therefore be seen as one aspect of an overall Community policy towards telecommunications, and notably of policies and actions to encourage and stimulate those forms of cooperation which promote the development and availability of advanced communications for Europe.

The full application of competition rules forms a major part of the Community's overall approach to telecommunications. These guidelines should help market participants to shape their strategies and arrangements for Europe-wide networks and services from the outset in a manner which allows them to be fully in line with these rules. In the event of significant changes in the conditions which prevailed when the guidelines were drawn up, the Commission may find it appropriate to adapt the guidelines to the evolution of the situation in the telecommunications sector.

I. Summary

1. The Commission of the European **A7.2** Communities in its Green Paper on the development of the common market for telecommunications services and equipment (COM(87)290) dated 30 June 1987 proposed a number of Community positions. Amongst these, positions (H) and

---

*OJ 1991 C233/2.

[1] The European electronics and information technology industry: state of play, issues at stake and proposals for action, SEC(91) 565, 3 April 1991.

(I) are as follows:

'(H) strict continuous review of operational (commercial) activities of telecommunications administrations according to Articles 85, 86 and 90 of the EEC Treaty. This applies in particular to practices of cross-subsidization of activities in the competitive services sector and of activities in manufacturing;

(J) strict continuous review of all private providers in the newly opened sectors according to Articles 85 and 86, in order to avoid the abuse of dominant positions;'.

2. These positions were restated in the Commission's document of 9 February 1988 'Implementing the Green Paper on the development of the common market for telecommunications services and equipment/state of discussions and proposals by the Commission' (COM(88)48). Among the areas where the development of concrete policy actions is now possible, the Commission indicated the following:

'Ensuring fair conditions of competition:

Ensuring an open competitive market makes continuous review of the telecommunications sector necessary.

The Commission intends to issue guidelines regarding the application of competition rules to the telecommunications sector and on the way that the review should be carried out.'

This is the objective of this communication.

The telecommunications sector in many cases requires cooperation agreements, *inter alia*, between telecommunications organizations (TOs) in order to ensure network and services interconnectivity, one-stop shopping and one-stop billing which are necessary to provide for Europe-wide services and to offer optimum service to users. These objectives can be achieved, *inter alia*, by TOs cooperating—for example, in those areas where exclusive or special rights for provision may continue in accordance with Community law, including competition law, as well as in areas where optimum service will require certain features of cooperation. On the other hand the overriding

objective to develop the conditions for the market to provide European users with a greater variety of telecommunications services, of better quality and at lower cost requires the introduction and safeguarding of a strong competitive structure. Competition plays a central role for the Community, especially in view of the completion of the single market for 1992. This role has already been emphasized in the Green Paper.

The single market will represent a new dimension for telecoms operators and users. Competition will give them the opportunity to make full use of technological development and to accelerate it, and encouraging them to restructure and reach the necessary economies of scale to become competitive not only on the Community market, but worldwide.

With this in mind, these guidelines recall the main principles which the Commission, according to its mandate under the Treaty's competition rules, has applied and will apply in the sector without prejudging the outcome of any specific case which will have to be considered on the facts.

The objective is, *inter alia*, to contribute to more certainty of conditions for investment in the sector and the development of Europe-wide services.

The mechanisms for creating certainty for individual cases (apart from complaints and ex-officio investigations) are provided for by the notification and negative clearance procedures provided under Regulation No 17, which give a formal procedure for clearing cooperation agreements in this area whenever a formal clearance is requested. This is set out in further detail in this communication.

II. Introduction

3. The fundamental technological de- **A7.3** velopment worldwide in the telecommunications sector[2] has caused considerable changes in the competition

---

[2] Telecommunications embraces any transmission, emission or reception of signs, signals, writing, images and sounds or intelligence of any nature by wire, radio, optical and other electromagnetic systems (Art 2 of WATTC Regulation of 9 December 1988).

conditions. The traditional monopolistic administrations cannot alone take up the challenge of the technological revolution. New economic forces have appeared on the telecoms scene which are capable of offering users the numerous enhanced services generated by the new technologies. This has given rise to and stimulated a wide deregulation process propagated in the Community with various degrees of intensity.

This move is progressively changing the face of the European market structure. New private suppliers have penetrated the market with more and more transnational value-added services and equipment. The telecommunications administrations, although keeping a central role as public services providers, have acquired a business-like way of thinking. They have started competing dynamically with private operators in services and equipment. Wide restructuring, through mergers and joint ventures, is taking place in order to compete more effectively on the deregulated market through economies of scale and rationalization. All these events have a multiplier effect on technological progress.

4. In the light of this, the central role of competition for the Community appears clear, especially in view of the completion of the single market for 1992. This role has already been emphasized in the Green Paper.

5. In the application of competition rules the Commission endeavours to avoid the adopting of State measures or undertakings erecting or maintaining artificial barriers incompatible with the single market. But it also favours all forms of cooperation which foster innovation and economic progress, as contemplated by competition law. Pursuing effective competition in telecoms is not a matter of political choice. The choice of a free market and a competition-oriented economy was already envisaged in the EEC Treaty, and the competition rules of the Treaty are directly applicable within the Community. The abovementioned fundamental changes make necessary the full application of competition law.

6. There is a need for more certainty as to the aplication of competition rules. The

telecommunication administrations together with keeping their duties of public interest, are now confronted with the application of these rules practically without transition from a long tradition of legal protection. Their scope and actual implications are often not easily perceivable. As the technology is fast-moving and huge investments are necessary, in order to benefit from the new possibilities on the market-place, all the operators, public or private, have to take quick decisions, taking into account the competition regulatory framework.

7. This need for more certainty regarding the application of competition rules is already met by assessments made in several individual cases. However, assessments of individual cases so far have enabled a response to only some of the numerous competition questions which arise in telecommunications. Future cases will further develop the Commission's practice in this sector.

Purpose of these guidelines

8. These guidelines are intended to advise public telecommunications operators, other telecommunications service and equipment suppliers and users, the legal profession and the interested members of the public about the general legal and economic principles which have been and are being followed by the Commission in the application of competition rules to undertakings in the telecommunications sector, based on experience gained in individual cases in compliance with the rulings of the Court of Justice of the European Communities.

9. The Commission will apply these principles also to future individual cases in a flexible way, and taking the particular context of each case into account. These guidelines do not cover all the general principles governing the application of competition rules, but only those which are of specific relevance to telecommunication issues. The general principles of competition rules not specifically connected with telecommunications but entirely applicable to these can be found, *inter alia*, in the regulatory acts, the Court judgments and the Commission decisions deal-

A7.4

ing with the individual cases, the Commission's yearly reports on competition policy, press releases and other public information originating from the Commission.

10. These guidelines do not create enforceable rights. Moreover, they do not prejudice the application of EEC competition rules by the Court of Justice of the European Communities and by national authorities (as these rules may be directly applied in each Member State, by the national authorities, administrative or judicial).

11. A change in the economic and legal situation will not automatically bring about a simultaneous amendment to the guidelines. The Commission, however, reserves the possibility to make such an amendment when it considers that these guidelines no longer satisfy their purpose, because of fundamental and/or repeated changes in legal precedents, methods of applying competition rules, and the regulatory, economic and technical context.

12. These guidelines essentially concern the direct application of competition rules to undertakings, i.e. Articles 85 and 86 of the EEC Treaty. They do not concern those applicable to the Member States, in particular Articles 5 and 90 (1) and (3). Principles ruling the application of Article 90 in telecommunications are expressed in Commission Directives adopted under Article 90 (3) for the implementation of the Green Paper.[3]

Relationship between competition rules applicable to undertakings and those applicable to Member States

A7.5 13. The Court of Justice of the European Communities[4] has ruled that while it is true that Articles 85 and 86 of the Treaty concern the conduct of undertakings and not the laws or regulations of the Member States, by virtue of Article 5 (2) of the EEC Treaty, Member States must not adopt or maintain in force any measure which could deprive those provisions of their effectiveness. The Court has stated that such would be the case, in particular, if a Member State were to require or favour prohibited cartels or reinforce the effects thereof or to encourage abuses by dominant undertakings.

If those measures are adopted or maintained in force *vis-à-vis* public undertakings or undertakings to which a Member State grants special or exclusive rights, Article 90 might also apply.

14. When the conduct of a public undertaking or an undertaking to which a Member State grants special or exclusive rights arises entirely as a result of the exercise of the undertaking's autonomous behaviour, it can only be caught by Articles 85 and 86.

When this behaviour is imposed by a mandatory State measure (regulative or administrative), leaving no discretionary choice to the undertakings concerned, Article 90 may apply to the State involved in association with Articles 85 and 86. In this case Articles 85 and 86 apply to the undertakings' behaviour taking into account the constraints to which the undertakings are submitted by the mandatory State measure.

Ultimately, when the behaviour arises from the free choice of the undertakings involved, but the State has taken a measure which encourages the behaviour or strengthens its effects, Articles 85 and/ or 86 apply to the undertakings' behaviour and Article 90 may apply to the State measure. This could be the case, *inter alia*, when the State has approved and/or legally endorsed the result of the undertakings' behaviour (for instance tariffs).

These guidelines and the Article 90 Directives complement each other to a

[3] Commission Dir 88/301/EEC of 16 May 1988 on competition in the markets in telecommunications terminal equipment (OJ L131/73). Commission Dir 90/388/EEC of 28 June 1990 on competition in the markets for telecommunications services (OJ 1990 L192/10).
Judgment of 10. 1. 1985 in Case 229/83, *Leclerc/gasoline* [1985] ECR 17; Judgment of 11. 7. 1985 in Case 299/83, *Leclerc/books* [1985] ECR 2517; Judgment of 30. 4. 1986 in

Cases from 209 to 213/84, *Ministère public* v *Asjes* [1986] ECR 1425; Judgment of 1. 10. 1987 in Case 311/85, *Vereniging van Vlaamse Reisbureaus* v *Sociale Dienst van de Plaatselijke en Gewestelijke Overheidsdiensten* [1987] ECR 3801.

certain extent in that they cover the principles governing the application of the competition rules: Articles 85 and 86 on the one hand, Article 90 on the other.

Application of competition rules and other Community law, including open network provision (ONP) rules

A7.6   15.   Articles 85 and 86 and Regulations implementing those Articles in application of Article 87 of the EEC Treaty constitute law in force and enforceable throughout the Community. Conflicts should not arise with other Community rules because Community law forms a coherent regulatory framework. Other Community rules, and in particular those specifically governing the telecommunications sector, cannot be considered as provisions implementing Articles 85 and 86 in this sector. However it is obvious that Community acts adopted in the telecommunications sector are to be interpreted in a way consistent with competition rules, so to ensure the best possible implementation of all aspects of the Community telecommunications policy.

16.   This applies, *inter alia*, to the relationship between competition rules applicable to undertakings and the ONP rules. According to the Council Resolution of 30 June 1988 on the development of the common market for telecommunications services and equipment up to 1992 (OJ 1988 C257/1), ONP comprises the 'rapid definition, by Council Directives, of technical conditions, usage conditions, and tariff principles for open network provision, starting with harmonized conditions for the use of leased lines'. The details of the ONP procedures have been fixed by Directive 90/387/EEC (OJ 1990 L192/1) on the establishment of the internal market for telecommunications services through the implementation of open network provision, adopted by Council on 28 June 1990 under Article 100a of the EEC Treaty.

17.   ONP has a fundamental role in providing European-wide access to Community-wide interconnected public networks. When ONP harmonization is im-

plemented, a network user will be offered harmonized access conditions throughout the EEC, whichever country they address. Harmonized access will be ensured in compliance with the competition rules as mentioned above, as the ONP rules specifically provide.

ONP rules cannot be considered as competition rules which apply to States and/or to undertakings' behaviour. ONP and competition rules therefore constitute two different but coherent sets of rules. Hence, the competition rules have full application, even when all ONP rules have been adopted.

18.   Competition rules are and will be applied in a coherent manner with Community trade rules in force. However, competition rules apply in a non-discriminatory manner to EEC undertakings and to non-EEC ones which have access to the EEC market.

III. Common Principles of Application of Articles 85 and 86

Equal application of Articles 85 and 86

19.   Articles 85 and 86 apply directly and   **A7.7** throughout the Community to all undertakings, whether public or private, on equal terms and to the same extent, apart from the exception provided in Article 90 (2).[5]

The Commission and national administrative and judicial authorities are competent to apply these rules under the conditions set out in Council Regulation No 17.[6]

20.   Therefore, Articles 85 and 86 apply

---

[5] Article 90 (2) states: 'Undertakings entrusted with the operation of services of general economic interest or having the character of a revenue-producing monopoly shall be subject to the rules contained in this Treaty, in particular to the rules on competition, in so far as the application of such rules does not obstruct the performance, in law or in fact, of the particular tasks assigned to them. The development of trade must not be affected to such an extent as would be contrary to the interests of the Community'.

[6] OJ 1962 13 204/62 (Special Edition 1959–62, 87).

both to private enterprises and public telecommunications operators embracing telecommunications administrations and recognized private operating agencies, hereinafter called 'telecommunications organizations' (TOs).

TOs are undertakings within the meaning of Articles 85 and 86 to the extent that they exert an economic activity, for the manufacturing and/or sale of telecommunications equipment and/or for the provision of telecommunications services, regardless of other facts such as, for example, whether their nature is economic or not and whether they are legally distinct entities or form part of the State organization.[7] Associations of TOs are associations of undertakings within the meaning of Article 85, even though TOs participate as undertakings in organizations in which governmental authorities are also represented.

Articles 85 and 86 apply also to undertakings located outside the EEC when restrictive agreements are implemented or intended to be implemented or abuses are committed by those undertakings within the common market to the extent that trade between Member States is affected.[8]

Competition restrictions justified under Article 90 (2) or by essential requirements

A7.8   21.   The exception provided in Article 90 (2) may apply both the State measures and to practices by undertakings. The Services Directive 90/388/EEC, in particular in Article 3, makes provision for a Member State to impose specified restrictions in the licences which it can grant for the provision of certain telecommunications services. These restrictions may be imposed under Article 90 (2) or in order to ensure the compliance with State essential requirements specified in the Directive.

22.   As far as Article 90 (2) is concerned, the benefit of the exception provided by this provision may still be invoked for a TO's behaviour when it brings about competition restrictions which its Member State did not impose in application of the Services Directive. However, the fact should be taken into account that in this case the State whose function is to protect the public and the general economic interest, did not deem it necessary to impose the said restrictions. This makes particularly hard the burden of proving that the Article 90 (2) exception still applies to an undertakings's behaviour involving these restrictions.

23.   The Commission infers from the case law of the Court of Justice[9] that it has exclusive competence, under the control of the Court, to decide that the exception of Article 90 (2) applies. The national authorities including judicial authorities can assess that this exception does not apply, when they find that the competition rules clearly do not obstruct the performance of the task of general economic interest assigned to undertakings. When those authorities cannot make a clear assessment in this sense they should suspend their decision in order to enable the Commission to find that the conditions for the application of that provision are fulfilled.

24.   As to measures aiming at the compliance with 'essential requirements' within the meaning of the Services Directive, under Article 1 of the latter,[10] they can only be taken by Member States and not by undertakings.

The relevant market

25.   In order to assess the effects of an   **A7.9** agreement on competition for the purposes of Article 85 and whether there is a dominant position on the market for the purposes of Article 86, it is necessary to define the relevant market(s), product or

---

[7] See Judgment of the Court 16. 6. 1987 in Case 118/85, *Commission* v *Italy* — Transparency of Financial Relations between Member States and Public Undertakings [1987] ECR 2599.

[8] See Judgment of the Court of 27. 9. 1988 in Joined Cases 89, 104, 114, 116, 117, 125, 126, 127, 129/85, *Ålström & others* v *Commission* (*'Woodpulp'*), [1988] ECR 5193.

[9] Case 10/71, *Mueller-Hein* [1971] ECR 723; Judgment of 11. 4. 1989 in Case 66/86, *Ahmed Saeed* [1989] ECR 803.

[10] '... the non-economic reasons in the general interest which may cause a Member State to restrict access to the public telecommunications network or public telecommunications services.'

service market(s) and geographic market(s), within the domain of telecommunications. In a context of fast-moving technology the relevant market definition is dynamic and variable.

(a) The product market

6. A product market comprises the totality of the products which, with respect to their characteristics, are particularly suitable for satisfying constant needs and are only to a limited extent interchangeable with other products in terms of price, usage and consumer preference. An examination limited to the objective characteristics only of the relevant products cannot be sufficient: the competitive conditions and the structure of supply and demand on the market must also be taken into consideration.[11]

The Commission can precisely define these markets only within the framework of individual cases.

27. For the guidelines' purpose it can only be indicated that distinct service markets could exist at least for terrestrial network provision, voice communication, data communication and satellites. With regard to the equipment market, the following areas could all be taken into account for the purposes of market definition: public switches, private switches, transmission systems and more particularly, in the field of terminals, telephone sets, modems, telex terminals, data transmission terminals and mobile telephones. The above indications are without prejudice to the definition of further narrower distinct markets. As to other services — such as value-added ones — as well as terminal and network equipment, it cannot be specified here whether there is a market for each of them or for an aggregate of them, or for both, depending upon the interchangeability existing in different geographic markets. This is mainly determined by the supply and the requirements in those markets.

28. Since the various national public networks compete for the installation of the telecommunication hubs of large users, market definition may accordingly

vary. Indeed, large telecommunications users, whether or not they are service providers, locate their premises depending, *inter alia*, upon the features of the telecommunications services supplied by each TO. Therefore, they compare national public networks and other services provided by the TOs in terms of characteristics and prices.

29. As to satellite provision, the question is whether or not it is substantially interchangeable with terrestrial network provision:

(a) communication by satellite can be of various kinds: fixed service (point to point communication), multipoint (point to multipoint and multipoint to multipoint), one-way or two-way;

(b) satellites' main characteristics are: coverage of a wide geographic area not limited by national borders, insensitivity of costs to distance, flexibility and ease of networks deployment, in particular in the very small aperture terminals (VSAT) systems;

(c) satellites' uses can be broken down into the following categories: public switched voice and data transmission, business value-added services and broadcasting;

(d) a satellite provision presents a broad interchangeability with the terrestrial transmission link for the basic voice and data transmission on long distance. Conversely, because of its characteristics it is not substantially interchangeable but rather complementary to terrestrial transmission links for several specific voice and data transmission uses. These uses are: services to peripheral or less-developed regions, links between non-contiguous countries, reconfiguration of capacity and provision of routing for traffic restoration. Moreover, satellites are not currently substantially interchangeable for direct broadcasting and multipoint private networks for value-added business services. Therefore, for all those uses satelites should constitute distinct product markets. Within satellites, there may be distinct markets.

30. In mobile communications distinct services seem to exist such as cellular tele-   **A7.10**

---

[11] Case 322/81, *Michelin* v *Commission*, 9 November 1983 [1983] ECR 3529, Ground 37.

phone, paging, telepoint, cordless voice and cordless data communication. Technical development permits providing each of these systems with more and more enhanced features. A consequence of this is that the differences between all these systems are progressively blurring and their interchangeability increasing. Therefore, it cannot be excluded that in future for certain uses several of those systems be embraced by a single product market. By the same token, it is likely that, for certain uses, mobile systems will be comprised in a single market with certain services offered on the public switched network.

(b) The geographic market

31.   A geographic market is an area:
—where undertakings enter into competition with each other, and
—where the objective conditions of competition applying to the product or service in question are similar for all traders.[12]

32.   Without prejudice to the definition of the geographic market in individual cases, each national territory within the EEC seems still to be a distinct geographic market as regards those relevant services or products, where:
—the customer's needs cannot be satisfied by using a non-domestic service,
—there are different regulatory conditions of access to services, in particular special or exclusive rights which are apt to isolate national territories,
—as to equipment and network, there are no Community-common standards, whether mandatory or voluntary, whose absence could also isolate the national markets. The absence of voluntary Community-wide standards shows different national customers' requirements.

However, it is expected that the geographic market will progressively extend to the EEC territory at the pace of the progressive realization of a single EEC market.

---

[12] Judgment of 14. 2. 1978 in Case 27/76, *United Brands* v *Commission* [1978] ECR 207, Ground 44. In the telecommunications sector: Judgment of 5. 10. 1988 in Case 247/86, *Alsatel-Novasam* [1988] ECR 5987.

33.   It has also to be ascertained whether each national market or a part thereof is a substantial part of the common market. This is the case where the services of the product involved represent a substantial percentage of volume within the EEC. This applies to all services and products involved.

34.   As to satellite uplinks, for cross-border communication by satellite the uplink could be provided from any of several countries. In this case, the geographic market is wider than the national territory and may cover the whole EEC.

As to space segment capacity, the extension of the geographic market will depend on the power of the satellite and its ability to compete with other satellites for transmission to a given area, in other words on its range. This can be assessed only case by case.

35.   As to services in general as well as terminal and network equipment, the Commission assesses the market power of the undertakings concerned and the result for EEC competition of the undertakings' conduct, taking into account their interrelated activities and interaction between the EEC and world markets. This is even more necessary to the extent that the EEC market is progressively being opened. This could have a considerable effect on the structure of the markets in the EEC, on the overall competitivity of the undertakings operating in those markets, and in the long run, on their capacity to remain independent operators.

IV. *Application of Article 85*

36.   The Commission recalls that a major   **A7.11** policy target of the Council Resolution of 30 June 1988 on the development of the common market for telecommunications service and equipment up to 1992 was that of:

'. . . . . stimulating European cooperation at all levels, as far as compatible with Community competition rules, and particularly in the field of research and development, in order to secure a strong European presence on the telecommunications markets and to ensure the full participation of all Member States'.

In many cases Europe-wide services can be achieved by TOs' cooperation — for example, by ensuring interconnectivity and interoperability

   (i) in those areas where exclusive or special rights for provision may continue in accordance with Community law and in particular with the Services Directive 90/388/EEC; and

   (ii) in areas where optimum service will require certain features of cooperation, such as so-called 'one-stop shopping' arrangements, i.e. the possibility of acquiring Europe-wide services at a single sales point.

The Council is giving guidance, by Directives, Decisions, recommendations and resolutions on those areas where Europe-wide services are most urgently needed: such as by Recommendation 86/659/EEC on the coordinated introduction of the integrated services digital network (ISDN) in the European Community (OJ 1986 L382/36) and by Recommendation 87/371/EEC on the coordinated introduction of public pan-European cellular digital land-based mobile communications in the Community (OJ 1987 L196/8).

The Commission welcomes and fully supports the necessity of cooperation particularly in order to promote the development of trans-European services and strengthen the competitivity of the EEC industry throughout the Community and in the world markets. However, this cooperation can only attain that objective if it complies with Community competition rules. Regulation No 17 provides well-defined clearing procedures for such cooperation agreements. The procedures foreseen by Regulation No 17 are:

   (i) the application for negative clearance, by which the Commission certifies that the agreements are not caught by Article 85, because they do not restrict competition and/or do not affect trade between Member States; and

   (ii) the notification of agreements caught by Article 85 in order to obtain an exemption under Article 85 (3). Although if a particular agreement is caught by Article 85,

an exemption can be granted by the Commission under Article 85 (3), this is only so when the agreement brings about economic benefits — assessed on the basis of the criteria in the said paragraph 3 — which outweigh its restrictions on competition. In any event competition may not be eliminated for a substantial part of the products in question. Notification is not an obligation; but if, for reasons of legal certainty, the parties decide to request an exemption pursuant to Article 4 of Regulation No 17 the agreements may not be exempted until they have been notified to the Commission.

37. Cooperation agreements may be covered by one of the Commission block exemption Regulations or Notices.[13] In the first case the agreement is automatically exempted under Article 85 (3). In the latter case, in the Commission's view, the agreement does not appreciably restrict competition and trade between Member States and therefore does not justify a Commission action. In either case, the agreement does not need to be notified; but it may be notified in case of doubt. If the Commission receives a multitude of notifications of similar cooperation agreements in the telecommunications sector, it may consider whether a specific block exemption regulation for such agreements would be appropriate.

38. The categories of agreements[14] which seem to be typical in telecommunications and may be caught by Article 85 are listed below. This list provides examples only and is, therefore, not exhaustive. The Commission is thereby indicating possible competition restrictions which could be caught by Article 85 and cases where there may be the possibility of an exemption.

39. These agreements may affect trade between Member States for the following reasons:

---

[13] Reported in 'Competition Law in the European Communities' Volume I (situation at 31. 12. 1989) published by the Commission.

[14] For simplification's sake this term stands also for 'decisions by associations' and 'concerned practices' within the meaning of Art 85.

(i) services other than services reserved to TOs equipment and spatial segment facilities are traded throughout the EEC; agreements on these services and equipment are therefore likely to affect trade. Although at present cross-frontier trade is limited, there is potentially no reason to suppose that suppliers of such facilities will in future confine themselves to their national market;

(ii) as to reserved network services, one can consider that they also are traded throughout the Community. These services could be provided by an operator located in one Member State to customers located in other Member States, which decide to move their telecommunications hub into the first one because it is economically or qualitatively advantageous. Moreover, agreements on these matters are likely to affect EEC trade at least to the extent they influence the conditions under which the other services and equipment are supplied throughout the EEC.

40. Finally, to the extent that the TOs hold dominant positions in facilities, services and equipment markets, their behaviour leading to — and including the conclusion of — the agreements in question could also give rise to a violation of Article 86, if agreements have or are likely to have as their effect hindering the maintenance of the degree of competition still existing in the market or the growth of that competition, or causing the TOs to reap trading benefits which they would not have reaped if there had been normal and sufficiently effective competition.

A. Horizontal agreements concerning the provision of terrestrial facilities and reserved services

41. Agreements concerning terrestrial facilities (public switched network or leased circuits) or services (e.g. voice telephony for the general public) can currently only be concluded between TOs because of this legal regime providing for exclusive or special rights. The fact that the Services Directive recognizes the possibility for a Member State to reserve this provision to certain operators does not exempt those operators from complying with the competition rules in providing these facilities or services. These agreements may restrict competition within a Member State only where such exclusive rights are granted to more than one provider.

42. These agreements may restrict the competition between TOs for retaining or attracting large telecommunications users for their telecommunications centres. Such 'hub competition' is substantially based upon favourable rates and other conditions, as well as the quality of the services. Member States are not allowed to prevent such competition since the Directive allows only the granting of exclusive and special rights by each Member State in its own territory.

43. Finally, these agreements may restrict competition in non-reserved services from third party undertakings, which are supported by the facilities in question, for example if they impose discriminatory or inequitable trading conditions on certain users.

44. *(aa) Price agreements*

All TOs' agreements on prices, discounting or collection charges for international services, are apt to restrict the hub competition to an appreciable extent. Coordination on or prohibition of discounting could cause particularly serious restrictions. In situations of public knowledge such as exists in respect of the tariff level, discounting could remain the only possibility of effective price competition.

45. In several cases the Court of Justice and the Commission have considered price agreements among the most serious infringements of Article 85.[15] While harmonization of tariff structures may be a major element for the provision of Com-

---

[15] *PVC*, Commission Decision 89/190/EEC, OJ 1989 L74/1; Case 123/85, *B.NIC* v *Clair* [1985] ECR 391; Case 8/72, *Cementhandelaren* v *Commission* (1972) ECR 977; *Polypropylene*, Commission Decision 86/398/EEC (OJ 1986 L230/1) on appeal, Case 179/86.

munity-wide services, this goal should be pursued as far as compatible with Community competition rules and should include definition of efficient pricing principles throughout the Community. Price competition is a crucial, if not the principal, element of customer choice and is apt to stimulate technical progress. Without prejudice to any application for individual exemption that may be made, the justification of any price agreement in terms of Article 85 (3) would be the subject of very rigorous examination by the Commission.
46. Conversely, where the agreements concern only the setting up of common tariff structures or principles, the Commission may consider whether this would not constitute one of the economic benefits under Article 85 (3) which outweigh the competition restriction. Indeed, this could provide the necessary transparency on tariff calculations and facilitate users' decisions about traffic flow or the location of headquarters or premises. Such agreements could also contribute to achieving one of the Green Paper's economic objectives — more cost-orientated tariffs.

In this connection, following the intervention of the Commission, the CEPT has decided to abolish recommendation PGT/10 on the general principles for the lease of international telecommunications circuits and the establishment of private international networks. This recommendation recommended, *inter alia*, the imposition of a 30% surcharge or an access charge where third-part traffic was carried on an international telecommunications leased circuit, or if such a circuit was interconnected to the public telecommunications network. It also recommended the application of uniform tariff coefficients in order to determine the relative price level of international telecommunications leased circuits. Thanks to the CEPT's cooperation with the Commission leading to the abolition of the recommendation, competition between telecoms operators for the supply of international leased circuits is re-established, to the benefit of users, especially suppliers of non-reserved services. The Commission had found that the recommendation amounted to a price agreement between undertakings under Article 85 of the Treaty which substantially restricted competition within the European Community.[16]

47. (ab) Agreements on other conditions for the provision of facilities

These agreements may limit hub competition between the partners. Moreover, they may limit the access of users to the network, and thus restrict third undertakings' competition as to non-reserved services. This applies especially to the use of leased circuits. The abolished CEPT recommendation PGT/10 on tariffs had also recommended restrictions on conditions of sale which the Commission objected to. These restrictions were mainly:

—making the use of leased circuits between the customer and third parties subject to the condition that the communication concern exclusively the activity for which the circuit has been granted,
—a ban on subleasing,
—authorization of private networks only for customers tied to each other by economic links and which carry out the same activity,
—prior consultation between the TOs for any approval of a private network and of any modification of the use of the network, and for any interconnection of private networks.

For the purpose of an exemption under Article 85 (3), the granting of special conditions for a particular facility in order to promote its development could be taken into account among other elements. This could foster technologies which reduce the cost of services and contribute to increasing competitiveness of European industry structures. Naturally, the other Article 85 (3) requirements should also be met.

48. (ac) Agreements on the choice of telecommunication routes.

These may have the following restrictive effects:
(i) to the extent that they coordinate the TOs' choice of the routes to be set up in international serivices, they may

A7.13

---

16 See Commission press release IP(90) 188 of 6 March 1990.

limit competition between TOs as suppliers to users' communications hubs, in terms of investments and production, with a possible effect on tariffs. It should be determined whether this restriction of their business autonomy is sufficiently appreciable to be caught by Article 85. In any event, an argument for an exemption under Article 85 (3) could be more easily sustained if common routes designation were necessary to enable interconnections and, therefore, the use of a Europe-wide network;

(ii) to the extent that they reserve the choice of routes already set up to the TOs, and this choice concerns one determined facility, they could limit the use of other facilities and thus services provision possibly to the detriment of technological progress. By contrast, the choice of routes does not seem restrictive in principle to the extent that it constitutes a technical requirement.

49. *(ad)   Agreements on the imposition of technical and quality standards on the services provided on the public network*

Standardization brings substantial economic benefits which can be relevant under Article 85 (3). It facilitates *inter alia* the provision of pan-European telecommunications services. As set out in the framework of the Community's approach to standardization, products and services complying with standards may be used Community-wide. In the context of this approach, European standards institutions have developed in this field (ETSI and CEN-Cenelec). National markets in the EC would be opened up and form a Community market. Service and equipment markets would be enlarged, hence favouring economies of scale. Cheaper products and services are thus available to users. Standardization may also offer an alternative to specifications controlled by undertakings dominant in the network architecture and in non-reserved services. Standardization agreements may, therefore, lessen the risk of abuses by these undertakings which could block the access

to the markets for non-reserved services and for equipment. However, certain standardization agreements can have restrictive effects on competition: hindering innovation, freezing a particular stage of technical development, blocking the network access of some users/service providers. This restriction could be appreciable, for example when deciding to what extent intelligence will in future be located in the network or continue to be permitted in customers' equipment. The imposition of specifications other than those provided for by Community law could have restrictive effects on competition. Agreements having these effects are, therefore, caught by Article 85.

The balance between economic benefits and competition restrictions is complex. In principle, an exemption could be granted if an agreement brings more openness and facilitates access to the market, and these benefits outweigh the restrictions caused by it.

50.   Standards jointly developed and/or published in accordance with the ONP procedures carry with them the presumption that the cooperating TOs which comply with those standards fulfil the requirement of open and efficient access (see the ONP Directive mentioned in paragraph 16). This presumption can be rebutted, *inter alia*, if the agreement contains restrictions which are not foreseen by Community law and are not indispensable for the standardization sought.

51.   One important Article 85 (3) requirement is that users must also be allowed a fair share of the resulting benefit. This is more likely to happen when users are directly involved in the standardization process in order to contribute to deciding what products or services will meet their needs. Also, the involvement of manufacturers or service providers other than TOs seems a positive element for Article 85 (3) purposes. However, this involvement must be open and widely representative in order to avoid competition restrictions to the detriment of excluded   manufacturers   or   service providers. Licensing other manufacturers may be deemed necessary, for the purpose of granting an exemption to these agreements under Article 85 (3).

52. *(ae)   Agreements foreseeing special treatment for TOs' terminal equipment or other companies' equipment for the interconnection or interoperation of terminal equipment with reserved services and facilities*

53. *(af)   Agreements on the exchange of information*

A7.14   A general exchange of information could indeed be necessary for the good functioning of international telecommunications services, and for cooperation aimed at ensuring interconnectivity or one-stop shopping and billing. It should not be extended to competition-sensitive information, such as certain tariff information which constitutes business secrets, discounting, customers and commercial strategy, including that concerning new products. The exchange of this information would affect the autonomy of each TO's commercial policy and it is not necessary to attain the said objectives.

B.   Agreements concerning the provision of non-reserved services and terminal equipment

54.   Unlike facilities markets, where only the TOs are the providers, in the services markets the actual or potential competitors are numerous and include, besides the TOs, international private companies, computer companies, publishers and others. Agreements on services and terminal equipment could therefore be concluded between TOs, between Tos and private companies, and between private companies.

55.   The liberalizing process has led mostly to strategic agreements between (i) TOs, and (ii) TOs and other companies. These agreements usually take the form of joint ventures.

56. *(ba)   Agreements between TOs*

The scope of these agreements, in general, is the provision by each partner of a value-added service including the management of the service. Those agreements are mostly based on the 'one-stop shopping' principle, i.e. each partner offers to the customer the entire package of services

which he needs. These managed services are called managed data network services (MDNS). An MDNS essentially consists of a broad package of services including facilities, value-added services and management. The agreements may also concern such basic service as satellite uplink.

57.   These agreements could restrict competition in the MDNS market and also in the markets for a service or a group of services included in the MDNS:

(i) between the participating TOs themselves; and

(ii) *vis-à-vis* other actual or potential third-party providers.

58. *(i)   Restrictions of competition between TOs*

Cooperation between TOs could limit the number of potential individual MDNS offered by each participating TO.   **A7.15**

The agreements may affect competition at least in certain aspects which are contemplated as specific examples of prohibited practices under Article 85 (1) (a) to (c), in the event that:

—they fix or recommend, or at least lead (through the exchange of price information) to coordination of prices charged by each participant to customers,

—they provide for joint specification of MDNS products, quotas, joint delivery, specification of customers' systems; all this would amount to controlling production, markets, technical development and investments,

—they contemplate joint purchase of MDNS hardware and/or software, which would amount to sharing markets or sources of supply.

59. *(ii)   Restrictive effects on third party undertakings*

Third parties' market entry could be precluded or hampered if the participating TOs:

—refuse to provide facilities to third party suppliers of services,

—apply usage restrictions only to third parties and not to themselves (e.g. a private provider is precluded from placing multiple customers on a leased line facility to obtain lower unit costs),

—favour their MDNS offerings over those of private suppliers with respect to access, availability, quality and prices of leased circuits, maintenance and other services,

—apply especially low rates to their MDNS offerings, cross-subsidizing them with higher rates for monopoly services.

Examples of this could be the restrictions imposed by the TOs on private network operators as to the qualifications of the users, the nature of the messages to be exchanged over the network or the use of international private leased circuits.

60. Finally, as the participating TOs hold, individually or collectively, a dominant position for the creation and the exploitation of the network in each national market, any restrictive behaviour described in paragraph 59 could amount to an abuse of a dominant position under Article 86 (see V *infra*).

61. On the other hand, agreements between TOs may bring economic benefits which could be taken into account for the possible granting of an exemption under Article 85 (3). *Inter alia*, the possible benefits could be as follows:

—a European-wide service and 'one-stop shopping' could favour business in Europe. Large multinational undertakings are provided with a European communication service using only a single point of contact,

—the cooperation could lead to a certain amount of European-wide standardization even before further EEC legislation on this matter is adopted,

—the cooperation could bring cost reduction and consequently cheaper offerings to the advantage of consumers,

—a general improvement of public infrastructure could arise from a joint service provision.

62. Only by notification of the cases in question, in accordance with the appropriate procedures under Regulation No 17, will the Commission be able, where requested, to ascertain, on the merits, whether these benefits outweigh the competition restrictions. But in any event, restrictions on access for third parties seem likely to be considered as not indispensable and to lead

to the elimination of competition for a substantial part of the products and services concerned within the meaning of Article 85 (3), thus excluding the possibility of an exemption. Moreover, if an MDNS agreement strengthens appreciably a dominant position which a participating TO holds in the market for a service included in the MDNS, this is also likely to lead to a rejection of the exemption.

63. The Commission has outlined the   **A7.16** conditions for exempting such forms of cooperation in a case concerning a proposed joint venture between 22 TOs for the provision of a Europe-wide MDNS, later abandoned for commercial reasons,[17] The Commission considered that the MDNS project presented the risks of restriction of competition between the operators themselves and private service suppliers but it accepted that the project also offered economic benefits to telecommunications users such as access to Europe-wide services through a single operator. Such cooperation could also have accelerated European standardization, reduced costs and increased the quality of the services. The Commission had informed the participants that approval of the project would have to be subject to guarantees designed to prevent undue restriction of competition in the telecommunications services markets, such as discrimination against private servics suppliers and cross-subsidization. Such guarantees would be essential conditions for the granting of an exemption under the competition rules to cooperation agreements involving TOs. The requirement for an appropriate guarantee of non-discrimination and non-cross-subsidization will be specified in individual cases according to the examples of discrimination indicated in Section V below concerning the application of Article 86.

64. *(bb) Agreements between TOs and other service providers*

Cooperation between TOs and other operators is increasing in telecommunications services. It frequently takes the form of a joint venture. The Commission recog-

---

[17] Commission press release IP(89) 948 of 14. 12. 1989.

nizes that it may have beneficial effects. However, this cooperation may also adversely affect competition and the opening up of services markets. Beneficial and harmful effects must therefore be carefully weighed.

65. Such agreements may restrict competition for the provision of telecommunications services:

(i) between the partners; and

(ii) from third parties.

66. (i) Competition between the partners may be restricted when these are actual or potential competitors for the relevant telecommunications service. This is generally the case, even when only the other partners and not the TOs are already providing the service. Indeed, TOs may have the required financial capacity, technical and commercial skills to enter the market for non-reserved services and could reasonably bear the technical and financial risk of doing it. This is also generally the case as far as private operators are concerned, when they do not yet provide the service in the geographical market covered by the cooperation, but do provide this service elsewhere. They may therefore be potential competitors in this geographic market.

67. (ii) The cooperation may restrict competition from third parties because:

—there is an appreciable risk that the participant TO, i.e. the dominant network provider, will give more favourable network access to its cooperation partners than to other service providers in competition with the partners,

—potential competitors may refrain from entering the market because of this objective risk or, in any event, because of the presence on the market-place of a cooperation involving the monopolist for the network provision. This is especially the case when market entry barriers are high: the market structure allows only few suppliers and the size and the market power of the partners are considerable.

68. On the other hand, the cooperation may bring economic benefits which outweigh its harmful effect and therefore justify the granting of an exemption under Article 85 (3). The economic benefits can consist, *inter alia*, of the rationalization of

the production and distribution of telecommunication services, in improvements in existing services or development of new services, or transfer of technology which improves the efficiency and the competitiveness of the European industrial structures.

69. In the absence of such economic benefits a complementarity between partners, i.e. between the provision of a reserved activity and that of a service under competition, is not a benefit as such. Considering it as a benefit would be equal to justifying an involvement through restrictive agreements of TOs in any non-reservd provision. This would be to hinder a competitive structure in this market.

In certain cases, the cooperation could consolidate or extend the dominant position of the TOs concerned to a non-reserved services market, in violation of Article 86.

70. The imposition or the proposal of cooperation with the service provider as a condition for the provision of the network may be deemed abusive (see paragraph 98 (vi)).

71. *(bc) Agreements between service providers other than TOs*

The Commission will apply the same principle indicated in (ba) and (bb) above also to agreements between private service providers, *inter alia*, agreements providing quotas, price fixing, market and/or customer allocation. In principle, they are unlikely to qualify for an exemption. The Commission will be particularly vigilant in order to avoid cooperation on services leading to a strengthening of dominant positions of the partners or restricting competition from third parties. There is a danger of this occurring for example when an undertaking is dominant with regard to the network architecture and its proprietary standard is adopted to support the service contemplated by the cooperation. This architecture enabling interconnection between computer systems of the partners could attract some partners to the dominant partner. The dominant position for the network architecture will be strengthened and Article 86 may apply.

72. In any exemption of agreements

between TOs and other services and/or equipment providers, or between these providers, the Commission will require from the partners appropriate guarantees of non-cross-subsidization and non-discrimination. The risk of cross-subsidization and discrimination is higher when the TOs or the other partners provide both services and equipment, whether within or outside the Community.

C. Agreements on research and development (R&D)

73. As in other high technology based sectors, R&D in telecommunications is essential for keeping pace with technological progress and being competitive on the market-place to the benefit of users. R&D requires more and more important financial, technical and human resources which only few undertakings can generate individually. Cooperation is therefore crucial for attaining the above objectives.

74. The Commission has adopted a Regulation for the block exemption under Article 85 (3) of R&D agreements in all sectors, including telecommunications.[18]

75. Agreements which are not covered by this Regulation (or the other Commission block exemption Regulations) could still obtain an individual exemption from the Commission if Article 85 (3) requirements are met individually. However, not in all cases do the economic benefits of an R&D agreement outweigh its competition restrictions. In telecommunications, one major asset, enabling access to new markets, is the launch of new products or services. Competition is based not only on price, but also on technology. R&D agreements could constitute the means for powerful undertakings with high market shares to avoid or limit competition from more innovative rivals. The risk of excessive restrictions of competition increases when the cooperation is extended from R&D to manufacturing and even more to distribution.

76. The importance which the Commission attaches to R&D and innovation is demonstrated by the fact that it has launched several programmes for this pur-

pose. The joint companies' activities which may result from these programmes are not automatically cleared or exempted as such in all aspects from the application of the competition rules. However, most of those joint activities may be covered by the Commission's block exemption Regulations. If not, the joint activities in question may be exempted, where required, in accordance with the appropriate criteria and procedures.

77. In the Commission's experience joint distribution linked to joint R&D which is not covered by the Regulation on R&D does not play the crucial role in the exploitation of the results of R&D. Nevertheless, in individual cases, provided that a competitive environment is maintained, the Commission is prepared to consider full-range cooperation even between large firms. This should lead to improving the structure of European industry and thus enable it to meet strong competition in the world market place.

V. *Application of Article 86*

78. Article 86 applies when: **A7.18**
   (i) the undertaking concerned holds an individual or a joint dominant position;
   (ii) it commits an abuse of that dominant position; and
   (iii) the abuse may affect trade between Member States.

Dominant position

79. In each national market the TOs hold individually or collectively a dominant position for the creation and the exploitation of the network, since they are protected by exclusive or special rights granted by the State. Moreover, the TOs hold a dominant position for some telecommunications services, in so far as they hold exclusive or special rights with respect to those services.[19]

80. The TOs may also hold dominant

---

[18] Regulation (EEC) No 418/85, OJ 1985 L53/5.

[19] Commission Decision 82/861/EEC in the *British Telecommunications* case, point 26, OJ 1982 L360/36, confirmed in the Judgment of 20. 3. 1985 in Case 41/83, *Italian Republic* v *Commission* [1985] ECR 873, generally known as '*British Telecom*'.

positions on the markets for certain equipment or services, even though they no longer hold any exclusive rights on those markets. After the elimination of these rights, they may have kept very important market shares in this sector. When the market share in itself does not suffice to give the TOs a dominant position, it could do it in combination with the other factors such as the monopoly for the network or other related services and a powerful and wide distribution network. As to the equipment, for example terminal equipment, even if the TOs are not involved in the equipment manufacturing or in the services provision, they may hold a dominant position in the market as distributors.

81. Also, firms other than TOs may hold individual or collective dominant positions in markets where there are no exclusive rights. This may be the case especially for certain non-reserved services because of either the market shares alone of those undertakings, or because of a combination of several factors. Among these factors, in addition to the market shares, two of particular importance are the technological advance and the holding of the information concerning access protocols or interfaces necessary to ensure interoperability of software and hardware. When this information is covered by intellectual property rights this is a furthr factor of dominance.

82. Finally, the TOs hold, individually or collectively, dominant positions in the demand for some telecommunication equipment, works or software services. Being dominant for the network and other services provisions they may account for a purchaser's share high enough to give them dominance as to the demand, i.e. making suppliers dependent on them. Dependence could exist when the supplier cannot sell to other customers a substantial part of its production or change a production. In certain national markets, for example in large switching equipment, big purchasers such as the TOs face big suppliers. In this situation, it should be weighed up case by case whether the supplier or the customer position will prevail on the other to such an extent as to be considered dominant under Article 86.

With the liberalization of services and the expansion of new forces on the services markets, dominant positions of undertakings other than the TOs may arise for the purchasing of equipment.

Abuse

83. Commission's activity may concern **A7.19** mainly the following broad areas of abuses:

A. *TOs' abuses:* in particular, they may take advantage of their monopoly or at least dominant position to acquire a foothold or to extend their power in non-reserved neighbouring markets, to the detriment of competitors and customers.

B. *Abuses by undertakings other than TOs:* these may take advantage of the fundamental information they hold, whether or not covered by intellectual property rights, with the object and/or effect of restricting competition.

C. *Abuses of a dominant purchasing position:* for the time being this concerns mainly the TOs, especially to the extent that they hold a dominant position for reserved activities in the national market. However, it may also increasingly concern other undertakings which have entered the market.

A. *TOs' Abuses*

84. The Commission has recognized in **A7.20** the Green Paper the central role of the TOs, which justifies the maintenance of certain monopolies to enable them to perform their public task. This public task consists of the provision and exploitation of a universal network or, where appropriate, universal service, i.e. one having general coverage and available to all users (including service providers and the TOs themselves) upon request on reasonable and non-discriminatory conditions.

This fundamental obligation could justify the benefit of the exception provided in Article 90 (2) under certain circumstances, as laid down in the Services Directive.

85. In most cases, however, the competition rules, far from obstructing the fulfilment of this obligation, contribute to ensuring it. In particular, Article 86 can apply to behaviour of dominant undertakings resulting in a refusal to supply, dis-

crimination, restrictive tying clauses, unfair prices or other inequitable conditions.

If one of these types of behaviour occurs in the provision of one of the monopoly services, the fundamental obligation indicated above is not performed. This could be the case when a TO tries to take advantage of its monopoly for certain services (for instance: network provision) in order to limit the competition they have to face in respect of non-reserved services, which in turn are supported by those monopoly services.

It is not necessary for the purpose of the application of Article 86 that competition be restricted as to a service which is supported by the monopoly provision in question. It would suffice that the behaviour results in an appreciable restriction of competition in whatever way. This means that an abuse may occur when the company affected by the behaviour is not a service provider but an end user who could himself be disadvantaged in competition in the course of his own business.

86. The Court of Justice has set out this fundamental principle of competition in telecommunications in one of its judgments.[20] An abuse within the meaning of Article 86 is committed where, without any objective necessity, an undertaking holding a dominant position on a particular market reserves to itself or to an undertaking belonging to the same group an ancillary activity which might be carried out by another undertaking as part of its activities on a neighbouring but separate market, with the possibility of eliminating all competition from such undertaking.

The Commission believes that this principle applies, not only when a dominant undertaking monopolizes other markets, but also when by anti-competitive means it extends its activity to other markets.

Hampering the provision of non-reserved services could limit production, markets and above all the technical progress which is a key factor of telecommunications. The Commission has already

shown these adverse effects of usage restrictions on monopoly provision in its decision in the 'British Telecom' case.[21] In this Decision it was found that the restrictions imposed by British Telecom on telex and telephone networks usage, namely on the transmission of international messages on behalf of third parties:

(i) limited the activity of economic operators to the detriment of technological progress;

(ii) discriminated against these operators, thereby placing them at a competitive disadvantage *vis-à-vis* TOs not bound by these restrictions; and

(iii) made the conclusion of the contracts for the supply of telex circuits subject to acceptance by the other parties of supplementary obligations which had no connection with such contracts. These were considered abuses of a dominant position identified respectively in Article 86 (b), (c) and (d).

This could be done:

(a) as above, by refusing or restricting the usage of the service provided under monopoly so as to limit the provision of non-reserved services by third parties; or

(b) by predatory behaviour, as a result of cross-subsidization.

87. The separation of the TOs' regulatory power from their business activity is a crucial matter in the context of the application of Article 86. This separation is provided in the Article 90 Directives on terminals and on services mentioned in Note 3 above.

(a) Usage restrictions

88. Usage restrictions on provisions of reserved services are likely to correspond to the specific examples of abuses indicated in Article 86. In particular:

—they may limit the provision of telecommunications services in free competition, the investments and the technical progress, to the prejudice of telecommunications consumers (Article 86 (b)),

---

[20] Case 311/84, *Centre Belge de'études de marché Télémarketing (CBEM) SA* v *Compagnie Luxembourgoise de télédiffusion SA and Information Publicité Benelux SA*, 3 October 1985 [1985] ECR 3261, Grounds 26 and 27.

[21] See Note 19.

—to the extent that these usage restrictions are not applied to all users, including the TOs themselves as users, they may result in discrimination against certain users, placing them at a competitive disadvantage (Article 86 (c)),

—they may make the usage of the reserved services subject to the acceptance of obligations which have no connection with this usage (Article 86 (d)).

89.   The usage restrictions in question mainly concern public networks (public switched telephone network (PSTN) or public switched data networks (PSDN)) and especially leased circuits. They may also concern other provisions such as satellite uplink, and mobile communication networks. The most frequent types of behaviour are as follows:

(i) *Prohibition imposed by TOs on third parties*

(a) to connect private leased circuits by means of concentrator, multiplexer or other equipment to the public switched network; and/or

(b) to use private leased circuits for providing services, to the extent that these services are not reserved, but under competition.

A7.21   90.   To the extent that the user is granted a licence by State regulatory authorities under national law in compliance with EEC law, these prohibitions limit the user's freedom of access to the leased circuits, the provision of which is a public service. Moreover, it discriminates between users, depending upon the usage (Article 86 (c)). This is one of the most serious restrictions and could substantially hinder the development of international telecommunications services (Article 86 (b)).

91.   When the usage restriction limits the provision of non-reserved service in competition with that provided by the TO itself the abuse is even more serious and the principles of the abovementioned '*Télémarketing*' judgment (Note 20 *supra*) apply.

92.   In individual cases, the Commission will assess whether the service provided on the leased circuit is reserved or not, on the basis of the Community regulatory acts interpreted in the technical and economic context of each case. Even though a service could be considered reserved accord-

ing to the law, the fact that a TO actually prohibits the usage of the leased circuit only to some users and not to others could constitute a discrimination under Article 86 (c).

93.   The Commission has taken action in respect of the Belgian *Régis des télégraphes et téléphones* after receiving a complaint concerning an alleged abuse of dominant position from a private supplier of value-added telecommunications services relating to the conditions under which telecommunications circuits were being leased. Following discussions with the Commission, the RTT authorized the private supplier concerned to use the leased telecommunications circuits subject to no restrictions other than that they should not be used for the simple transport of data.

Moreover, pending the possible adoption of new rules in Belgium, and without prejudice to any such rules, the RTT undertook that all its existing and potential clients for leased telecommunications circuits to which third parties may have access shall be governed by the same conditions as those which were agreed with the private sector supplier mentioned above.[22]

(ii) *Refusal by TOs to provide reserved services (in particular the network and leased circuits) to third parties*

94.   Refusal to supply has been considered an abuse by the Commission and the Court of Justice.[23] This behaviour would make it impossible or at least appreciably difficult for third parties to provide non-reserved services. This, in turn, would lead to a limitation of services and of technical development (Article 86 (b)) and, if applied only to some users, result in discrimination (Article 86 (c)).   **A7.22**

(iii) *Imposition of extra charges or other special conditions for certain usages of reserved services*

95.   An example would be the imposition of access charges to leased circuits when they are connected to the public switched network or other special prices and

---

[22] Commission Press release IP(90) 67 of 29. 1. 1990.

[23] Cases 6 and 7/73 *Commercial Solvents* v *Commission* [1974] ECR 223; *United Brands* v *Commission* (Note 12, above).

charges for service provision to third parties. Such access charges may discriminate between users of the same service (leased circuits provision) depending upon the usage and result in imposing unfair trading conditions. This will limit the usage of leased circuits and finally non-reserved service provision. Conversely, it does not constitute an abuse provided that it is shown, in each specific case, that the access charges correspond to costs which are entailed directly for the TOs for the access in question. In this case, access charges can be imposed only on an equal basis to all users, including TOs themselves.

96.   Apart from these possible additional costs which should be covered by an extra charge, the interconnection of a leased circuit to the public switched network is already remunerated by the price related to the use of this network. Certainly, a leased circuit can represent a subjective value for a user depending on the profitability of the enhanced service to be provided on that leased circuit. However, this cannot be a criterion on which a dominant undertaking, and above all a public service provider, can base the price of this public service.

97.   The Commission appreciates that the substantial difference between leased circuits and the public switched network causes a problem of obtaining the necessary revenues to cover the costs of the switched network. However, the remedy chosen must not be contrary to law, i.e. the EEC Treaty, as discriminatory pricing between customers would be.

(iv) *Discriminatory price or quality of the service provided*

98.   This behaviour may relate, *inter alia*, to tariffs or to restrictions or delays in connection to the public switched network or leased circuits provision, in installation, maintenance and repair, in effecting interconnection of systems or in providing information concerning network planning, signalling protocols, technical standards and all other information necessary for an appropriate interconnection and interoperation with the reserved service and which may affect the interworking of competitive services or terminal equipment offerings.

(v) *Tying the provision of the reserved service to the supply by the TOs or others of terminal equipment to be interconnected or interoperated, in particular through imposition, pressure, offer of special prices or other trading conditions for the reserved service linked to the equipment.*

(vi) *Tying the provision of the reserved service to the agreement of the user to enter into cooperation with the reserved service provider himself as to the non-reserved service to be carried on the network*

(vii) *Reserving to itself for the purpose of non-reserved service provision or to other service providers information obtained in the exercise of a reserved service in particular information concerning users of a reserved services providers more favourable conditions for the supply of this information*

This latter information could be important for the provision of services under competition to the extent that it permits the targeting of customers of those services and the definition of business strategy. The behaviour indicated above could result in a discrimination against undertakings to which the use of this information is denied in violation of Article 86 (c). The information in question can only be disclosed with the agreement of the users concerned and in accordance with relevant data protection legislation (see the proposal for a Council Directive concerning the protection of personal data and privacy in the context of public digital telecommunications networks, in particular the integrated services digital network (ISDN) and public digital mobile networks).[24]

(viii) *Imposition of unneeded reserved services by supplying reserved and/or non-reserved services when the former reserved services are reasonably separable from the others*

99.   The practices under (v) (vi) (vii) and (viii) result in applying conditions which have no connection with the reserved service, contravening Article 86 (d).

---

[24] Commission document COM (90) 314 of 13. 9. 1990.

100. Most of these practices were in fact identified in the Services Directive as restrictions on the provision of services within the meaning of Article 59 and Article 86 of the Treaty brought about by State measures. They are therefore covered by the broader concept of 'restrictions' which under Article 6 of the Directive have to be removed by Member States.

101. The Commission believes that the Directives on terminals and on services also clarify some principles of application of Articles 85 and 86 in the sector.

The Services Directive does not apply to important sectors such as mobile communications and satellites; however, competition rules apply fully to these sectors. Moreover, as to the services covered by the Directive it will depend very much on the degree of precision of the licences given by the regulatory body whether the TOs still have a discretionary margin for imposing conditions which should be scrutinized under competition rules. Not all the conditions can be regulated in licences: consequently, there could be room for discretionary action. The application of competition rules to companies will therefore depend very much on a case-by-case examination of the licences. Nothing more than a class licence can be required for terminals.

(b) Cross-subsidization

A7.24   102. Cross-subsidization means that an undertaking allocates all or part of the costs of its activity in one product or geographic market to its activity in another product or geographic market. Under certain circumstances, cross-subsidization in telecommunications could distort competition, i.e. lead to beating other competitors with offers which are made possible not by efficiency and performance but by artificial means such as subsidies. Avoiding cross-subsidization leading to unfair competition is crucial for the development of service provision and equipment supply.

103. Cross-subsidization does not lead to predatory pricing and does not restrict competition when it is the costs of reserved activities which are subsidized by the revenue generated by other reserved activities since there is no competition possible as to these activities. This form of subsidization is even necessary, as it enables the TOs holders of exclusive rights to perform their obligation to provide a public service universally and on the same conditions to everybody. For instance, telephone provision in unprofitable rural areas is subsidized through revenues from telephone provision in profitable urban areas or long-distance calls. The same could be said of subsidizing the provision of reserved services through revenues generated by activities under competition. The application of the general principle of cost-orientation should be the ultimate goal, in order, *inter alia*, to ensure that prices are not inequitable as between users.

104. Subsidizing activities under competition, whether concerning services or equipment, by allocating their costs to monopoly activities, however, is likely to distort competition in violation of Article 86. It could amount to an abuse by an undertaking holding a dominant position within the Community. Moreover, users of activities under monopoly have to bear unrelated costs for the provision of these activities. Cross-subsidization can also exist between monopoly provision and equipment manufacturing and sale. Cross-subsidization can be carried out through:
— funding the operation of the activities in question with capital remunerated substantially below the market rate;
— providing for those activities premises, equipment, experts and/or services with a remuneration substantially lower than the market price.

105. As to funding through monopoly revenues or making available monopoly material and intellectual means for the starting up of new activities under competition, this constitutes an investment whose costs should be allocated to the new activity. Offering the new product or service should normally include a reasonable remuneration of such investment in the long run. If it does not, the Commission will assess the case on the basis of the remuneration plans of the undertaking concerned and of the economic context.

106. Transparency in the TOs' accounting should enable the Commission to ascertain whether there is cross-subsidization in the cases in which this question arises. The ONP Directive provides in this respect for the definition of harmonized tariff principles which should lessen the number of these cases.

This transparency can be provided by an accounting system which ensures the fully proportionate distribution of all costs between reserved and non-reserved activities. Proper allocation of costs is more easily ensured in cases of structural separation, i.e. creating distinct entities for running each of these two categories of activities.

An appropriate accounting system approach should permit the identification and allocation of all costs between the activities which they support. In this system all products and services should bear proportionally all the relevant costs, including costs of research and development, facilities and overheads. It should enable the production of recorded figures which can be verified by accountants.

107. As indicated above (paragraph 59), in cases of cooperation agreements involving TOs a guarantee of no cross-subsidization is one of the conditions required by the Commission for exemption under Article 85 (3). In order to monitor properly compliance with that guarantee, the Commission now envisages requesting the parties to ensure an appropriate accounting system as described above, the accounts being regularly submitted to the Commission. Where the accounting method is chosen, the Commission will reserve the possibility of submitting the accounts of independent audit, especially if any doubt arises as to the capability of the system to ensure the necessary transparency or to detect any cross-subsidization. If the guarantee cannot be properly monitored, the Commission may withdraw the exemption.

108. In all other cases, the Commission does not envisage requiring such transparency of the TOs. However, if in a specific case there are substantial elements converging in indicating the existence of an abusive cross-subsidization and/or predatory pricing, the Commission could establish a presumption of such cross-subsidization and predatory pricing. An appropriate separate accounting system could be important in order to counter this presumption.

109. Cross-subsidization of a reserved activity by a non-reserved one does not in principle restrict competition. However, the application of the exception provided in Article 90 (2) to this non-reserved activity could not as a rule be justified by the fact that the financial viability of the TO in question rests on the non-reserved activity. Its financial viability and the performance of its task of general economic interest can only be ensured by the State where appropriate by the granting of an exclusive or special right and by imposing restrictions on activities competing with the reserved ones.

110. Also cross-subsidization by a public or private operator outside the EEC may be deemed abusive in terms of Article 86 if that operator holds a dominant position for equipment or non-reserved services within the EEC. The existence of this dominant position, which allows the holder to behave to an appreciable extent independently of its competitors and customers and ultimately of consumers, will be assessed in the light of all elements in the EEC and outside.

B. Abuses by undertakings other than the TOs

111. Further to the liberalization of services, undertakings other than the TOs may increasingly extend their power to acquire dominant positions in non-reserved markets. They may already hold such a position in some services markets which had not been reserved. When they take advantage of their dominant position to restrict competition and to extend their power, Article 86 may also apply to them. The abuses in which they might indulge are broadly similar to most of those previously described in relation to the TOs.

112. Infringements of Article 86 may be committed by the abusive exercise of industrial property rights in relation with standards, which are of crucial importance for telecommunications. Standards may be either the results of international

223

standardization, or *de facto* standards and the property of undertakings.

113. Producers of equipment or suppliers of services are dependent on proprietary standards to ensure the interconnectivity of their computer resources. An undertaking which owns a dominant network architecture may abuse its dominant position by refusing to provide the necessary information for the interconnection of other architecture resources to its architecture products. Other possible abuses — similar to those indicated as to the TOs — are, *inter alia*, delays in providing the information, discrimination in the quality of the information, discriminatory pricing or other trading conditions, and making the information provision subject to the acceptance by the producer, supplier or user of unfair trading conditions.

114. On 1 August 1984, the Commission accepted a unilateral undertaking from IBM to provide other manufacturers with the technical interface information needed to permit competitive products to be used with IBM's then most powerful range of computers, the System/370. The Commission thereupon suspended the proceedings under Article 86 which it had initiated against IBM in December 1980. The IBM Undertaking[25] also contains a commitment relating to SNA formats and protocols.

115. The question how to reconcile copyrights on standards with the competition requirements is particularly difficult. In any event, copyright cannot be used unduly to restrict competition.

C. Abuses of dominant purchasing position

116. Article 86 also applies to behaviour of undertakings holding a dominant purchasing position. The examples of abuses indicated in that Article may therefore also concern that behaviour.

117. The Council Directive 90/531/EEC (OJ 1990 L297/1) based on Articles 57 (2), 66, 100a and 113 of the EEC Treaty on the procurement procedures of entities

operating in *inter alia* the telecommunications sector regulates essentially:

(i) procurement procedures in order to ensure on a reciprocal basis non-discrimination on the basis of nationality; and

(ii) for products or services for use in reserved markets, not in competitive markets. That Directive, which is addressed to States, does not exclude the application of Article 86 to the purchasing of products within the scope of the Directive. The Commission will decide case by case how to ensure that these different sets of rules are applied in a coherent manner.

118. Furthermore, both in reserved and competitive markets, practices other than those covered by the Directive may be established in violation of Article 86. One example is taking advantage of a dominant purchasing position for imposing excessively favourable prices or other trading conditions, in comparison with other purchasers and suppliers (Article 86 (a)). This could result in discrimination under Article 86 (c). Also obtaining, whether or not through imposition, an exclusive distributorship for the purchased product by the dominant purchaser may constitute an abusive extension of its economic power to other markets (see '*Télémarketing*' Court judgment (Note 20 *supra*)).

119. Another abusive practice could be that of making the purchase subject to licensing by the supplier of standards for the product to be purchased or for other products, to the purchaser itself, or to other suppliers (Article 86 (d)).

120. Moreover, even in competitive markets, discriminatory procedures on the basis of nationality may exist, because national pressures and traditional links of a non-economic nature do not always disappear quickly after the liberalization of the markets. In this case, a systematic exclusion or considerably unfavourable treatment of a supplier, without economic necessity, could be examined under Article 86, especially (b) (limitation of outlets) and (c) (discrimination). In assessing the case, the Commission will substantially examine whether the same criteria for awarding the contract have been fol-

---

[25] Reproduced in full in EC Bulletin 10-1984 (point 3.4.1). As to its continued application, see Commission press release No IP(88) 814 of 15 December 1988.

lowed by the dominant undertaking for all suppliers. The Commission will normally take into account criteria similar to those indicated in Article 27 (1) of the Directive.[26] The purchases in question being outside the scope of the Directive, the Commission will not require that transparent purchasing procedures be pursued.

D. Effect on trade between Member States

121.   The same principle outlined regarding Article 85 applies here. Moreover, in certain circumstances, such as the case of the elimination of a competitor by an undertaking holding a dominant position, although trade between Member States is not directly affected, for the purposes of Article 86 it is sufficient to show that there will be repercussions on the competitive structure of the common market.

VI. *Application of Articles 85 and 86 in the field of satellites*

A7.27   122.   The development of this sector is addressed globally by the Commission in the 'Green Paper on a common approach in the field of satellite communications in the European Community' of 20 November 1990 (Doc. COM(90) 490 final). Due to the increasing importance of satellites and the particular uncertainty among undertakings as to the application of competition rules to individual cases in this sector, it is appropriate to address the sector in a distinct section in these guidlines.
123.   State regulations on satellites are not covered by the Commission Directives under Article 90 of the EEC Treaty re-

---

[26] (See Note 23) Art 27 (1) (a) and (b). The criteria on which the contracting entities shall base the award of the contracts shall be: (a) the most economically advantageous tender involving various criteria such as delivery date, period for completion, running costs, cost-effectiveness, quality, aesthetic and functional characteristics, technical merit, after-sales services and technical assistance, commitments with regard to spare parts, security of supplies and price; or (b) the lowest price only.

spectively on terminals and services mentioned above except in the Directive on terminals which contemplates receive-only satellite stations not connected to a public network. The Commission's position on the reguatory framework compatible with the Treaty competition rules is stated in the Commission Green Paper on satellites mentioned above.
124.   In any even the Treaty competition rules fully apply to the satellites domain, *inter alia*, Articles 85 and 86 to undertakings. Below is indicated how the principles set out above, in particular in Sections IV and V, apply to satellites.
125.   Agreements between European TOs in particular within international conventions may play an important role in providing European satellites systems and a harmonious development of satellite services throughout the Community. These benefits are taken into consideration under competition rules, provided that the agreements do not contain restrictions which are not indispensable for the attainment of these objectives.
126.   Agreements between TOs concerning the operation of satellite systems in the broadest sense may be caught by Article 85. As to space segment capacity, the TOs are each other's competitors, whether actual or potential. In pooling together totally or partially their supplies of space segment capacity they may restrict competition between themselves. Moreover, they are likely to restrict competition *vis-à-vis* third parties to the extent that their agreements contain provisions with this object or effect: for instance provisions limiting their supplies in quality and/or quantity, or restricting their business autonomy by imposing directly or indirectly a coordination between these third parties and the parties to the agreements. It should be examined whether such agreements could qualify for an exemption under Article 85 (3) provided that they are notified. However, restrictions on third parties' ability to compete are likely to preclude such an exemption. It should also be examined whether such agreements strengthen any individual or collective dominant position of the parties, which also would exclude the granting of an exemption. This could be the case in

particular if the agreement provides that the parties are exclusive distributors of the space segment capacity provided by the agreement.

127. Such agreements between TOs could also restrict competition as to the uplink with respect to which TOs are competitors. In certain cases the customer for satellite communication has the choice between providers in several countries, and his choice will be substantially determined by the quality, price and other sales conditions of each provider. This choice will be even ampler since uplink is being progressively liberalized and to the extent that the application of EEC rules to State legislations will open up the uplink markets. Community-wide agreements providing directly or indirectly for coordination as to the parties' uplink provision are therefore caught by Article 85.

128. Agreements between TOs and private operators on space segment capacity may be also caught by Article 85, as that provision applies, *inter alia*, to cooperation, and in particular joint venture agreements. These agreements could be exempted if they bring specific benefits such as technology transfer, improvement of the quality of the service or enabling better marketing, especially for a new capacity, outweighing the restrictions. In any event, imposing on customers the bundled uplink and space segment capacity provision is likely to exclude an exemption since it limits competition in uplink provision to the detriment of the customer's choice, and in the current market situation will almost certainly strengthen the TOs' dominant position in violation of Article 86. An exemption is unlikely to be granted also when the agreement has the effect of reducing substantially the supply in an oligopolistic market, and even more clearly when an effect of the agreement is to prevent the only potential competitor of a dominant provider in a given market from offering its services independently. This could amount to a violation of Article 86. Direct or indirect imposition of any kind of agreement by a TO, for instance by making the uplink subject to the conclusion of an agreement with a third party, would constitute an infringement of Article 86.

VII. Restructuring in telecommunications

129. Deregulation, the objective of a single market for 1992 and the fundamental changes in the telecommunications technology have caused wide strategic restructuring in Europe and throughout the world as well. They have mostly taken the form of mergers and joint ventures. **A7.28**

(a) Mergers

130. In assessing telecom mergers in the framework of Council Regulation (EEC) No 4064/89 on the control of concentrations between undertakings (OJ 1989 L395/1; Corrigendum OJ 1990 L257/13) the Commission will take into account, *inter alia*, the following elements. **A7.29**

131. Restructuring moves are in general beneficial to the European telecommunications industry. They may enable the companies to rationalize and to reach the critical mass necessary to obtain the economies of scale needed to make the important investments in research and development. These are necessary to develop new technologies and to remain competitive in the world market.

However, in certain cases they may also lead to the anti-competitive creation or strengthening of dominant positions.

132. The economic benefits resulting from critical mass must be demonstrated. The concentration operation could result in a mere aggregation of market shares, unaccompanied by restructuring measures or plans. This operation may create or strengthen Community or national dominant positions in a way which impedes competition.

133. When concentration operations have this sole effect, they can hardly be justified by the objective of increasing the competitivity of Community industry in the world market. This objective, strongly pursued by the Commission, rather requires competition in EEC domestic markets in order that the EEC undertakings acquire the competitive structure and attitude needed to operate in the world market.

134. In assessing concentration cases in telecommunications, the Commission will

be particularly vigilant to avoid the strengthening of dominant positions through integration. If dominant service providers are allowed to integrate into the equipment market by way of mergers, access to this market by other equipment suppliers may be seriously hindered. A dominant service provider is likely to give preferential treatment to its own equipment subsidiary.

Moreover, the possibility of disclosure by the service provider to its subsidiary of sensitive information obtained from competing equipment manufacturers can put the latter at a competitive disadvantage.

The Commission will examine case by case whether vertical integration has such effects or rather is likely to reinforce the competitive structure in the Community.

135. The Commission has enforced principles on restructuring in a case concerning the GEC and Siemens joint bid for Plessey.[27]

136. Article 85 (1) applies to the acquisition by an undertaking of a minority shareholding in a competitor where, *inter alia*, the arrangements involve the creation of a structure of cooperation between the investor and the other undertakings, which will influence these undertakings' competitive conduct.[28]

(b) Joint ventures

137. A joint venture can be of a cooperative or a concentrative nature. It is of a cooperative nature when it has as its object or effect the coordination of the competitive behaviour of undertakings which remain independent. The principles governing cooperative joint ventures are to be set out in Commission guidelines to that effect. Concentrative joint ventures fall under Regulation (EEC) No 4064/89 (OJ 1990 C203/10).

138. In some of the latest joint venture cases the Commission granted an exemp-

---

[27] Commission Decision rejecting Plessey's complaint against the GEC-Siemens bid (Case IV/33.018 *GEC-Siemens/Plessey*), OJ 1990 C239/2.

[28] *British American Tobacco Company Ltd and RJ Reynolds Industries Inc* v *Commission* (Joined Cases 142 and 156/84) of 17. 11. 1987 [1987] ECR 4487.

tion under Article 85 (3) on grounds which are particularly relevant to telecommunications. Precisely in a decision concerning telecommunications, the *Optical Fibres* case (Decision 86/405/EEC, OJ 1986 L236/30), the Commission considered that the joint venture enabled European companies to produce a high technology product, promoted technical progress, and facilitated technology transfer. Therefore, the joint venture permits European companies to withstand competition from non-Community producers, especially in the USA and Japan, in an area of fast-moving technology characterized by international markets. The Commission confirmed this approach in the *Canon-Olivetti* case (Decision 88/88/EEC, OJ 1988 L52/51).

VIII. Impact of the International Conventions on the application of EEC Competitions Rules to telecommunications

139. International conventions (such as **A7.30** the Convention of International Telecommunication Union (ITU) or Conventions on Satellites) play a fundamental role in ensuring worlwide cooperation for the provision of international services. However, application of such international conventions on telecommunications by EEC Member States must not affect compliance with the EEC law, in particular with competition rules.

140. Article 234 of the EEC Treaty regulates this matter.[29] The relevant obligations provided in the various conventions or related Acts do not pre-date the

---

[29] 'The rights and obligations arising from agreements concluded before the entry into force of this Treaty between one or more Member States on the one hand and one or more third countries on the other, shall not be affected by the provisions of this Treaty. To the extent that such agreements are not compatible with this Treaty, the Member State or States concerned shall take all appropriate steps to eliminate the incompatibilities established. Member States shall, where necessary, assist each other to this end and shall, where appropriate, adopt a common attitude...'

entry into force of the Treaty. As to the ITU and World Administrative Telegraph and Telephone Conference (WATTC), whenever a revision or a new adoption of the ITU Convention or of the WATTC Regulations occurs, the ITU or WATTC members recover their freedom of action. The Satellites Conventions were adopted much later.

Moreover, as to all conventions, the application of EEC rules does not seem to affect the fulfilment of obligations of Member States *vis-à-vis* third countries. Article 234 does not protect obligations between EEC Member States entered into in international treaties. The purpose of Article 234 is to protect the right of third countries only and it is not intended to crystallize the acquired international treaty rights of Member States to the detriment of the EEC Treaty's objectives or of the Community interest. Finally, even if Article 234 (1) did apply, the Member States concerned would nevertheless be obliged to take all appropriate steps to eliminate incompatibility between their obligations *vis-à-vis* third countries and the EEC rules. This applies in particular where Member States acting collectively have the statutory possibility to modify the international convention in question as required, e.g. in the case of the Eutelsat Convention.

141.　As to the WATTC Regulations, the relevant provisions of the Regulations in force from 9 December 1988 are flexible enough to give the parties the choice whether or not to implement them or how to implement them.

In any event, EEC Member States, by signing the Regulations, have made a joint declaration that they will apply them in accordance with their obligations under the EEC Treaty.

142.　As to the International Telegraph and Telephone Consultative Committee (CCITT) recommendations, competition rules apply to them.

143.　Members of the CCITT are, pursuant to Article 11 (2) of the International Telecommunications Convention, 'administrations' of the Members of the ITU and recognized private operating agencies ('RPOAs') which so request with the approval of the ITU members which have recognized them. Unlike the members of the ITU or the Administrative Conferences which are States, the members of the CCITT are telecommunications administrations and RPOAs. Telecommunications administrations are defined in Annex 2 to the International Telecommunications Conventions as *tout service ou département gouvernemental responsable des mesures à prendre pour exécuter les obligations de la Convention Internationale des télécommunications et des règlements* [any government service or department responsible for the measures to be taken to fulfil the obligations laid down in the International Convention on Telecommunications and Regulations]. The CCITT meetings are in fact attended by TOs. Article 11 (2) of the International Telecommunications Convention clearly provides that telecommunications administrations and RPOAs are members of the CCITT by themselves. The fact that, because of the ongoing process of separation of the regulatory functions from the business activity, some national authorities participate in the CCITT is not in contradiction with the nature of undertakings of other members. Moreover, even if the CCITT membership became governmental as a result of the separation of regulatory and operational activities of the telecommunications administrations, Article 90 in association with Article 85 could still apply either against the State measures implementing the CCITT recommendations and the recommendations themselves on the basis of Article 90 (1), or if there is no such national implementing measure, directly against the telecommunications organizations which followed the recommendation.[30]

144.　In the Commission's view, the CCITT recommendations are adopted, *inter alia*, by undertakings. Such CCITT recommendations, although they are not legally binding, are agreements between undertakings or decisions by an association of undertakings. In any event, according to the case law of the Commission

---

[30] See Commission Decision 87/3/EEC *ENI/ Montedison*, OJ 1987 L5/13.

and the European Court of Justice[31] a statutory body entrusted with certain public functions and including some members appointed by the government of a Member State may be an 'association of undertakings' if it represents the trading interests of other members and takes decisions or makes agreements in pursuance of those interests.

The Commission draws attention to the fact that the application of certain provisions in the context of international conventions could result in infringements of the EEC competition rules:

—As to the WATTC Regulations, this is the case for the respective provisions for mutual agreement between TOs on the supply of international telecommunications services (Article 1 (5)), reserving the choice of telecommunications routes to the TOs (Article 3 (3) (3)), recommending practices equivalent to price agreements (Articles 6 (6) (1) (2)), and limiting the possibility of special arrangements to activities meeting needs within and/or between the territories of the Members concerned (Article 9) and only where existing arrangements cannot satisfactorily meet the relevant telecommunications needs (Opinion PL A).

—CCITT recommendations D1 and D2 as they stand at the date of the adoption of these guidelines could amount to a collective horizontal agreement on prices and other supply conditions of international leased lines to the extent that they lead to a coordination of sales policies between TOs and therefore limit competition between them. This was indicated by the Commission in a CCITT meeting on 23 May 1990. The Commission reserves the right to examine the compatibility of other recommendations with Article 85.

—The agreements between TOs concluded in the context of the Conventions on Satellites are likely to limit competition contrary to Article 85 and/or 86 on the grounds set out in paragraphs 126 to 128 above.

---

[31] See *Pabst & Richarz/BNIA*, OJ No 1976 L231/24, *AROW/BNIC*, OJ 1982 L379/1, and Case 123/83 *BNIC* v *Clair* (1985) ECR 391.

AMENDED PROPOSAL FOR A COUNCIL DIRECTIVE

COM (92) 422 final — SYN 287

on the protection of individuals with regard to the processing of personal data and on the free movement of such data*

submitted by the Commission on 16 October 1992, pursuant to Article 149 (3) of the EEC Treaty

THE COUNCIL OF THE EUROPEAN COMMUNITIES,

A8.1 Having regard to the Treaty establishing the European Economic Community and in particular Articles 100 a and 13 thereof,

Having regard to the proposal from the Commission,

In cooperation with the European Parliament,

Having regard to the opinion of the Economic and Social Committee, (OJ 1991 C159/38)

1. Whereas the objectives of the Community, as laid down in the Treaty, as amended by the single European Act, include establishing an ever closer union among the peoples of Europe, fostering closer relations between the States belonging to the Community, ensuring economic and social progress by common action to eliminate the barriers which divide Europe, encouraging the constant improvement of the living conditions of its peoples, preserving and strengthening peace and liberty and promoting democracy on the basis of the fundamental rights recognized in the constitutions and laws of the Member States and in the European Convention for the Protection of Human Rights and Fundamental Freedoms;

2. Whereas data-processing systems are designed to serve society; whereas they must respect the fundamental freedoms and rights of individuals, notably the right to privacy, and contribute to economic and social progress, trade expansion and the well-being of individuals;

3. Whereas the establishment and the functioning of an internal market in which, in accordance with Article 8 a of the Treaty, the free movement of goods, persons, services and capital is ensured require not only that personal data should be able to flow freely from one Member State to another, but also that the fundamental rights of individuals should be safeguarded;

4. Whereas increasingly frequent recourse is being had in the Community to the processing of personal data in the various spheres of economic and social activity; whereas the progress made in information technology is making the processing and exchange of such data considerably easier;

5. Whereas the economic and social integration resulting from the establishment and functioning of the internal market within the meaning of Article 8 a of the Treaty will necessarily lead to a substantial increase in crossborder flows of personal data between all those involved in a private or public capacity in economic and social activity in the Member States; whereas the exchange of personal data between undertakings in different Member States is set to increase; whereas the national authorities in the various Member States are being called upon, by virtue of Community law, to collaborate and exchange personal data so

---

* OJ 1992 C311/30.

230

as to be able to perform their duties or carry out tasks on behalf of an authority in another Member State within the context of the area without internal frontiers as constituted by the internal market;

6. Whereas, furthermore, the increase in scientific and technical cooperation and the coordinated introduction of new telecommunications networks in the Community necessitate and facilitate cross-border flows of personal data;

7. Whereas the difference in levels of protection of the rights and freedoms of individuals, notably the right to privacy, with regard to the processing of personal data afforded in the Member States may prevent the transmission of such data from the territory of one Member State to that of another Member State; whereas this difference may therefore constitute an obstacle to the pursuit of a number of economic activities at Community level, distort competition and impede authorities in the discharge of their responsibilities under Community law; whereas this difference in levels of protection is due to the existence of a wide variety of national laws, regulations and administrative provisions;

8. Whereas in order to remove the obstacles to flows of personal data, the level of protection of the rights and freedoms of individuals with regard to the processing of such data must be equivalent in all the member States; whereas this objective is vital to the internal market but cannot be achieved by the Member States alone, especially in view of the scale of the divergences which currently exist between the relevant laws in the Member States and the need to coordinate the laws of the Member States so as to ensure that the cross-border flow of personal data is regulated in a consistent manner that is in keeping with the objective of the internal market as provided for in Article 8 a of the Treaty; whereas Community action

to approximate those laws is therefore needed;

9. Whereas the object of the national laws on the processing of personal data is to protect fundamental rights and freedoms, notably the right to privacy which is recognized both in Article 8 of the European Convention for the Protection of Human Rights and Fundamental Freedoms and in the general principles of Community laws; whereas, for that reason, the approximation of those laws must not result in any lessening of the protection they afford but must, on the contrary, seek to ensure a high level of protection in the Community;

10. Whereas the principles of the protection of the rights and freedom of individuals, notably the right to privacy, which are contained in this Directive, give substance to and amplify those contained in the Council of Europe Convention of 28 January 1981 for the Protection of Individuals with regard to Automatic Processing of Personal Data;

11. Whereas the protection principles must apply to all processing of personal data by any person whose activities are governed by Community laws; whereas processing carried out by a Member State's own authorities, organizations or other bodies in the course of activities which are not governed by Community law should, as is provided for in the Resolution of the representatives of the Governments of the Member States of the European Communities meeting within the Council of . . ., be subject to the same protection principles set out in national laws; whereas processing carried out by a natural person for purely private purposes in connection, for example, with correspondence or the maintenance of lists of addresses must be excluded;

12. Whereas, in order to ensure that individuals are not deprived of the protection to which they are entitled under this Directive, any processing of personal data in the Community

must be carried out in accordance with the law of one of the Member States; whereas, in this connection, processing carried out by a person who is established in a Member State should be governed by the law of that State; whereas, the fact that processing is carried out by a person established in a third country must not stand in the way of the protection of individuals provided for in this Directive; whereas, in that case, the processing should be governed by the law of the Member State in which the means used are located, and there should be guarantees to ensure that the rights and obligations provided for in this Directive are respected in practice;

13. Whereas Member States may more precisely define in the laws they enact or when bringing into force the measures taken under this Directive the general circumstances in which processing is lawful; whereas, however, more precise rules of this kind cannot serve as a basis for supervision by a Member State other than the member State of residence of the person responsible for the processing, since the obligation on the part of the latter to ensure, in accordance with this Directive, the protection of rights and freedoms with regard to the processing of personal data is sufficient, under Community law, to permit the free flow of data;

14. Whereas the principles of protection must be reflected, on the one hand, in the obligations imposed on persons, public authorities, enterprises or bodies carrying out processing, in particular regarding quality, technical security, notification to the supervisory, and the circumstances under which processing is admissible, one such possible circumstance being that the data subject has consented, and, on the other hand, in the rights conferred on individuals, the data on whom are the subject of processing, to be informed that processing is taking place, to consult the data, to demand corrections and even to object to processing;

15. Whereas any processing of personal data must be lawful and fair to the person concerned; whereas, in particular the data must be relevant and not excessive in relation to the purposes for which they are processed; whereas such purposes must be explicit and lawful;

16. Whereas, in order to be lawful, the processing of personal data must be carried out with the consent of the data subject or with a view to the conclusion or performance of a contract, binding on the data subject, or be required by Community law, by national law, by the general interest or by the interest of an individual, provided that the data subject has no legitimate grounds for objection; whereas, in particular, in order to maintain a balance between the interests involved, while guaranteeing effective competition, Member States remain free to determine the circumstances in which personal data may be disclosed to a third party for mailing purposes or research being carried out by an organization or other association or foundation, of a political nature for example, subject to the provisions allowing a data subject to object to the disclosure of data regarding him, at no cost and without having to state his reasons;

17. Whereas data which are capable by their nature of infringing fundamental freedoms or privacy should not be processed unless the data subject gives his written consent; whereas, however, processing of these data must be permitted if it is carried out by an association the purpose of which it to help safeguard the exercise of those freedoms; whereas, on grounds of important public interest, notably in relation to the medical profession, exemptions may be granted by law or by decision of the supervisory authority laying down the limits and suitable safeguards for the processing of these types of data;

18. Whereas the processing of personal data for purposes of journalism should qualify for exemption from

the requirements of this Directive wherever this is necessary to reconcile the fundamental rights of individuals with freedom of information and notably the right to receive and impart information, as guaranteed in particular in Article 10 of the European Convention for the protection of Human Rights and Fundamental Freedoms;

19. Whereas, if the processing of data is to be fair, the data subject must be in a position to learn of the existence of a processing operation and must be given accurate and full information where data are collected from him, and not later than the time when the data are first disclosed to a third party if the data subject was not informed at the time the data were collected;

20. Whereas any person must be able to exercise the right of access to data relating to him which are being processed, in order to verify the accuracy of the data and the lawfulness of the processing; whereas, therefore, any person should be entitled to object to the processing of the data on legitimate grounds;

A8.4 21. Whereas the protection of the rights and freedoms of data subjects with regard to the processing of personal data requires that appropriate technical measures be taken, both at the time of the design of the techniques of processing and at the time of the processing itself, particularly in order to maintain security and thereby to prevent any unauthorized processing;

22. Whereas the notification procedures are designed to ensure disclosure of the purposes and main features of any processing operation, for the purpose of verification that the operation is in accordance with the national measures taken under this Directive; whereas, in order to avoid unsuitable administrative formalities, exemption from the obligation to notify and simplification of the notification required must be provided for by Member States in cases where processing does not adversely

affect the rights and freedoms of data subjects provided that it is in accordance with a measure taken by a Member State and specifying its limits;

23. Whereas *ex post facto* verification by the competent authorities must, in general, be considered a sufficient measure; whereas, however, Member States must provide for checking by the supervisory authority prior to any processing which poses a particular threat to the rights and freedoms of data subjects by virtue of its nature, scope or purpose, such as processing which has as its object the exclusion of data subjects from a right, a benefit or a contract; whereas Member States should be entitled to replace such prior checking by means of a legislative measure or a decision of the supervisory authority authorizing the processing operation and specifying suitable safeguards;

24. Whereas, if the person carrying out processing fails to respect the rights of data subjects, national legislation must provide for a judicial remedy; whereas any damage which a person may suffer as a result of unlawful processing must be compensated for by the person responsible for the processing, who may be exempted from liability only if he proves that he has taken suitable security measures; whereas dissuasive penalties must be imposed on any person, whether governed by private or public law, who fails to comply with the national measures taken under this Directive;

25. Whereas cross-border flows of personal data are necessary to the expansion of international trade; whereas the protection of individuals guaranteed in the Community by this Directive does not stand in the way of transfers of personal data to third countries which ensure an adequate level of protection; whereas the adequacy of the level of protection afforded by a third country must be assessed in the light of all the circumstances surrounding the

transfer operation or set of transfer operations;

26. Whereas, on the other hand, the transfer of personal data to a third country which does not ensure an adequate level of protection must be prohibited; whereas provision should be made for exemptions in certain circumstances where the data subject has given his consent or has been informed or where protection of the public interest so requires; whereas particular measures may be taken to rectify the lack of protection in a third country in cases where the person responsible for the processing offers appropriate assurances; whereas, moreover, provision must be made for procedures for negotaitions between the Community and such third countries;

27. Whereas Member States may also provide for the use of codes of conduct drawn up by the business circles concerned and approved by the supervisory authority, with a view to adapting the national measures taken under this Directive to the specific characteristics of processing in certain sectors;

A8.5   28. Whereas Member States must encourage the business circles concerned to draw up Community codes of conduct so as to facilitate the application of this Directive; whereas the Commission will support such initiatives and will take them into account when it considers the appropriateness of additional specific measures in respect of certain sectors;

29. Whereas the establishment in each Member State of an independent supervisory authority is an essential component of the protection of individuals with regard to the processing of personal data; whereas such an authority must have the necessary means to perform its duties, including powers of investigation or intervention and powers in connection with notification procedures; whereas such authority must help to ensure transparency of processing in the Member State within whose juris-

diction it falls; whereas the authorities in the different Member States will need to assist one another in performing their duties;

30. Whereas, at Community level, a Working Party on the Protection of Individuals with regard to the Processing of Personal Data must be set up and be completely indepedent in the performance of its functions; whereas, having regard to its specific nature, it must advise the Commission and, in particular, contribute to the uniform application of the national rules adopted pursuant to this Directive;

31. Whereas the adoption of additional measures for applying the principles set out in this Directive calls for the conferment of rule-making powers on the Commission and the establishment of an advisory committee in accordance with the procedures laid down in Council Decision 87/373/EEC (OJ 1987 L197/33);

32. Whereas the principles set out in this Directive regarding the protection of the rights and freedoms of individuals, notably their right to privacy, with regard to the processing of personal data may be supplemented or clarified, in particular as far as certain sectors are concerned, by specific rules based on those principles;

33. Wheres Member States should be allowed a period of not more than three years from the entry into force of the national measures transposing this Directive in which to apply such new national rules gradually to all processing operations already under way;

34. Whereas this Directive does not stand in the way of a Member State's regulating market research activities aimed at consumers residing in its territory in so far as such regulation does not concern the protection of individuals with regard to the processing of personal data,

HAS ADOPTED THIS REGULATION:

Chapter 1

General provisions

Article 1

Object of the Directive

A8.6 1. In accordance with this Directive, Member States shall protect the rights and freedoms of natural persons with respect to the processing of personal data, and in particular their right of privacy.

2. The Member States shall neither restrict nor prohibit the free flow of personal data between Member States for reasons connected with the protection afforded under paragraph 1.

Article 2

Definitions

For the purpose of this Directive:

A8.7 (a) 'personal data' means any information relating to an identified or identifiable natural person ('data subject'); an identifiable person is one who can be identified, directly or indirectly, in particular by reference to an identification number or to one or more factors specific to his physical, physiological, mental, economic, cultural or social identity;

Data presented in statistical form, which is of such a type that the persons concerned can no longer be reasonably identified, are not considered as personal data;

(b) 'processing of personal data' ('processing') means any operation or set of operations which is performed upon personal data, whether or not by automatic means, such as collection, recording, organization, storage, adaptation or alteration, retrieval, consultation, use, disclosure by transmission, dissemination or otherwise making available, alignment or combination, blocking, erasure or destruction;

(c) 'personal data file' ('file') means any structured set of personal data, whether centralized or geographically dispersed, which is accessible according to specific criteria and whose object or effect is to facilitate the use or alignment of data relating to the data subject or subjects;

(d) 'controller' means any natural or legal person, public authority, agency or other body who processes personal data or causes it to be processed and who decides what is the purpose and objective of the processing, which personal data are to be processed, which operations are to be performed upon them and which third parties are to have access to them;

(e) 'processor' means any natural or legal person who processes personal data on behalf of the controller;

(f) 'third party' means any natural or legal person other than the data subject, the controller and any person authorized to process the data under the controller's direct authority or on his behalf;

(g) 'the data subject's consent' means any express indication of his wishes by which the data subject signifies his agreement to personal data relating to him being processed, on condition he has available information about the purposes of the processing, the data or categories of data concerned, the recipient of the personal data, and the name and address of the controller and of his representative if any.

The data subject's consent must be freely given and specific, and may be withdrawn by the data subject at any time, but without retrospective effect.

Article 3

Scope

1. This Directive shall apply to the processing of personal data wholly or partly by automatic means, and to the processing otherwise than by automatic means of personal data which forms part of a file or is intended to form part of a file. **A8.8**

2. This Directive shall not apply:

—to the processing of data in the course of an activity which falls outside the scope of Community law,

—to the processing of personal data by a natural person in the course of a purely private and personal activity.

235

Article 4

National law applicable

A8.9 1. Each Member State shall apply the national provisions adopted under this Directive to all processing of personal data:

(a) of which the controller is established in its territory or is within its jurisdiction;

(b) of which the controller is not established in the territory of the Community, where for the purpose of processing personal data he makes use of means, whether or not automatic, which are located in the territory of that Member State.

2. In the circumstances referred to in paragraph 1 (b) the controller must designate a representative established in the territory of that Member State, who shall be subrogated to the controller's rights and obligations.

Chapter II

General rules on the lawfulness of the processing of personal data

Article 5

A8.10 Member States shall provide that the processing of personal data is lawful only if carried out in accordance with this Chapter.

Subject to this Chapter, Member States may more precisely determine the circumstances in which the processing of personal data is lawful.

Section I

Principles relating to data quality

Article 6

A8.11 1. Member States shall provide that personal data must be:

(a) processed fairly and lawfully;

(b) collected for specified, explicit and legitimate purposes and used in a way compatible with those purposes;

(c) adequate, relevant and not excessive in relation to the purposes for which they are processed;

(d) accurate and, where necessary, kept up to date; every step must be taken to ensure that data which are inaccurate or incomplete having regard to the purposes for which they were collected are erased or rectified;

(e) kept in a form which permits identification of data subjects for no longer than is necessary for the purposes in view; Member States may lay down appropriate safeguards for personal data stored for historical, statistical or scientific use.

2. It shall be for the controller to ensure that paragraph 1 is complied with.

Section II

Principles relating to the grounds for processing data

Article 7

Member States shall provide that personal   **A8.12** data may be processed only if:

(a) the data subject has consented;

(b) processing is necessary for the performance of a contract with the data subject, or in order to take steps at the request of the data subject preliminary to entering into a contract;

(c) processing is necessary in order to comply with an obligation imposed by national law or by Community law;

(d) processing is necessary in order to protect the vital interests of the data subject;

(e) processing is necessary for the performance of a task in the public interest or carried out in the exercise of public authority vested in the controller or in a third party to whom the data are disclosed; or

(f) processing is necessary in pursuit of the general interest or of the legitimate interests of the controller or of a third party to whom the data are disclosed, except where such interests are overridden by the interests of the data subject.

Section III

Special categories of processing

Article 8

The processing of special categories of data

A8.13 1.   Member States shall prohibit the processing of data revealing racial or ethnic origin, political opinions, religious beliefs, philosophical or ethical persuasion or trade-union membership, and of data concerning health or sexual life.

2.   Member States shall provide that data referred to in paragraph 1 may be processed where:

(a) the data subject has given his written consent to the processing of that data, except where the laws of the Member State provide that the prohibition referred to in paragraph 1 may not be waived by the data subject giving his consent;

(b) processing is carried out by a foundation or non-profit-making association of a political, philosophical, religious or trade union character in the course of its legitimate activities and on condition that the processing relates solely to members of the foundation or association and to persons who have regular contact with it in connection with its purposes and that the data are not disclosed to third parties without the data subjects's consent; or

(c) the processing is performed in circumstances where there is manifestly no infringement of privacy or fundamental freedoms.

The processing of data referred to at point (b) shall not be subject to the obligation to notify imposed in Section VIII of this Chapter.

3.   Member States may, on grounds of important public interest, lay down exemptions from paragraph 1 by national legislative provision or by decision of the supervisory authority, stating the types of data which may be processed, the persons to whom such data may be disclosed and the persons who may be controllers, and specifying suitable safeguards.

4.   Data concerning criminal convictions may be held only by judicial and law-enforcement authorities and by the persons directly concerned with those convictions or by their representatives; Member States may, however, lay down exemptions by means of a legislative provision which shall specify suitable safeguards.

5.   Member States shall determine the conditions under which a national identification number or other identifier of general application may be used.

Article 9

Processing of personal data and freedom of expression

With a view to reconciling the right to   **A8.14**
privacy with the rules governing freedom of expression, Member States shall prescribe exemptions from this Directive in respect of the processing of personal data solely for journalistic purposes by the press, the audio-visual media and journalists.

Section IV

Information to be given to the data subject

Article 10

The existence of a processing operation

1.   Member States shall ensure that any   **A8.15**
person is entitled, on request, to know of the existence of a processing operation, its purposes, the categories of data concerned, any third parties or categories of third party to whom the data are to be disclosed, and the name and address of the controller and of his representative, if any.

2.   Member States may lay down exemptions from paragraph 1 in the circumstances referred to in Article 14 (1).

Article 11

Collection of data from the data subject

1.   Member States shall provide that the   **A8.16**
controller must ensure that a data subject from whom data are collected be informed at least of the following:

(a) the purposes of the processing for which the data are intended;

(b) the obligatory or voluntary nature of any reply to the questions to which

237

answers are sought;

(c) the consequences for him if he fails to reply;

(d) the recipients or categories of recipients of the data;

(e) the existence of a right of access to and rectification of the data relating to him; and

(f) the name and address of the controller and of his representative if any.

2. Paragraph 1 shall not apply to the collection of data where to inform the data subject would hinder or prevent the exercise of or the cooperation with the supervision and verification functions of a public authority or the maintenance of public order.

Article 12

Disclosure to a third party

A8.17 1. Member States shall provide that in the cases referred to in Article 7 (b), (c), (e) and (f) the controller must satisfy himself that at the appropriate time, and no later than the time when the data are first disclosed to a third party, the data subject is informed of this disclosure and of the following information at least:

(a) the name and address of the controller and of his representative, if any;

(b) the purposes of the processing;

(c) the categories of data concerned;

(d) the recipients or categories of recipients; and

(e) the existence of rights of access, rectification and objection

2. Paragraph 1 shall not apply where:

—the data subject has already been informed that the data are to be or may be disclosed to a third party,

—disclosure to a third party is required by a legal provision which lays down an exemption from the obligation to inform,

or

—the data are disclosed to a third party for one of the reasons listed in Article 14 (1).

3. Where the provision of information to the data subject proves impossible or involves a disproportionate effort, or runs counter to the overriding legitimate interests of the controller or similar interests of a third party, Member States may em-

power the supervisory authority to authorize an exemption, laying down any suitable safeguards.

Section V

The data subject's right of access to data

Article 13

Right of access

Member States shall grant all data subjects the following rights: A8.18

1. to obtain, on request, at resonable intervals and without excessive delay or expense, confirmation of the existence of personal data relating to him, communication to him of such data in an intelligible form, an indication of their source, and general information on their use.

Member States may provide that the right of access to medical data may be exercised only through a medical practitioner;

2. To refuse any demand by a third party that he should exercise his right of access in order to communicate the data in question to that third party or to another party, unless the third party's request is founded on national or Community law;

3. to obtain, as the case may be, the rectification of inaccurate or incomplete data or the erasure or blocking of such data if they have been processed in breach of this Directive;

4. where point 3 applies, to be notified of the rectification, erasure or blocking to any third party to whom the data have been disclosed;

5. to be informed of the reasoning applied in any automatic processing operations the outcome of which is invoked against him.

Article 14

Exceptions to the right of access

1. Unless obliged to do so by a provision   A8.19 of Community law, Member States may restrict the exercise of the rights provided for in Article 10 (1) and in point 1 of Article 13 where such restriction is necess-

ary to safeguard:

(a) national security;

(b) defence;

(c) criminal proceedings;

(d) public safety;

(e) a duly established paramount economic and financial interest of a Member State or of the Community;

(f) a monitoring or inspection function performed by a public authority or an activity undertaken to assist the performance of such a function;

(g) an equivalent right of another person and the rights and freedoms of others.

2. In the circumstances described in paragraph 1, the supervisory authority shall be empowered to carry out the necessary checks, at the data subject's request, so as to verify the lawfulness of the processing within the meaning of this Directive, respecting the interests to be protected in accordance with paragraph 1.

3. Member States may limit the right of access of the person concerned to data temporarily kept in personal form and which is intended to serve statistical ends of such a type that the persons concerned can no longer be reasonably identified.

Section VI

The data subject's right to object

Article 15

Objection on legitimate grounds

A8.20 1. Member States shall grant the data subject the right to object at any time on legitimate grounds to the processing of data relating to him.

2. Where there is a justified objection, the controller shall cease the processing.

3. The controller must ensure that the opportunity to have data erased without cost has been expressly offered to a data subject before personal data are disclosed to third parties or used on their behalf for the purposes of marketing by mail.

Article 16

Automated individual decisions

1. Member States shall grant the right to **A8.21** every person not to be subjected to an administrative or private decision adversely affecting him which is based solely on automatic processing defining a personality profile.

2. Subject to the other Articles of this Directive, Member States shall provide that a person may be subjected to a decision of the kind referred to in paragraph 1 if that decision:

(a) is taken in the course of the entering into or performance of a contract, provided any request by the data subject has been satisfied, or that there are suitable measures to safeguard his legitimate interests, which must include arrangements allowing him to defend his point of view; or

(b) is authorized by law which also lays down measures to safeguard the data subject's legitimate interests.

Section VII

Security of processing

Article 17

1. Member States shall provide that the **A8.22** controller must take appropriate technical and organizational measures to protect personal data against accidental or unlawful destruction or accidental loss and against unauthorized alteration or disclosure or any other unauthorized form of processing.

Such measures shall ensure, in respect of the automatic processing of data, a suitable level of security having regard to the state of the art and the nature of the data to be protected, and an evaluation of the potential risks involved. To that end, the controller shall take into consideration any recommendations on data security and network interoperability made by the Commission in accordance with the procedure referred to in Article 33.

2. Methods ensuring an appropriate level of security shall be chosen for the

239

transmission of personal data within a network.

3. Where an opportunity is provided for remote access, the controller shall utilize the hardware and software in such a way that the access takes place within the limits of the lawfulness of the processing.

4. The obligations referred to in paragraphs 1, 2 and 3 shall also be incumbent on persons who share responsibility for carrying out the processing, and, in particular, the processor.

5. Any person who, in the course of his work, has access to personal data shall not disclose it to third parties without the controller's agreement, unless he is required to do so under national or Community law.

Section VIII

Notification

Article 18

Obligation to notify the supervisory authority

A8.23

1. Member States shall provide that the controller or his representative, if any, must notify the supervisory authority referred to in Article 30 before carrying out any wholly or partly automatic processing or a set of processing operations of the same type intended to serve a single purpose or several related purposes.

2. Member States shall specify the information to be given in the notification. It shall include at least:
(a) the name and address of the controller and of his representative, if any;
(b) the purpose or purposes of the processing;
(c) the category or categories of data subject;
(d) a description of the data or of the categories of data to which the processing relates;
(e) the third parties or categories of third party to whom the data might be disclosed;
(f) proposed transfers of data to third countries;
(g) a description of the measures taken pursuant to Article 17 to ensure security of processing.

3. Any change affecting the information referred to in paragraph 2 must be notified to the supervisory authority.

4. Before processing which poses specific risks to the rights and freedoms of individuals commences, the supervisory authority shall examine such processing within a period of 15 days commencing with the date of the notification at the end of which period the authority shall give its conclusions.

5. Member States may provide that some of the processing operations referred to in paragraph 4 shall be authorized beforehand either by law or by decision of the supervisory authority.

Article 19

Simplication of and exemption from the obligation to notify

1. Member States shall provide for the   **A8.24**
taking of measures to simplify or exempt from the obligation to notify in the case of certain categories of processing operation which do not adversely affect the rights and freedoms of data subjects. Such categories of processing include the production of correspondence or papers, the satisfaction of legal, accounting, tax or social security duties or the consultation of documentation services accessible to the public.

2. Simplication or exemption measures shall be adopted either by or after consulting the supervisory authority. Such measures shall particularly specify, for each category of processing operation:
—the purposes of the processing,
—a description of the data or categories of data undergoing processing,
—the category or categories of data subject,
—the third parties or categories of third party to whom the data are to be disclosed,
—the length of time the data are to be stored,
—where appropriate, the conditions under which the processing is to be carried out.

3. Simplication or exemption from the obligation to notify shall not release the controller from any of the other obligations resulting from this Directive.

Article 20

Manual processing operations

A8.25 Member States may lay down the conditions under which Articles 18 and 19 are to apply to non-automatic processing operations involving personal data contained in files.

Article 21

Register of notified processing operations

A8.26 Member States shall provide that a register of notified processing operations must be maintained by the supervisory authority. The register shall, as a minimum, in the cases provided for in Articles 18 and 19, contain the information listed in Article 18 (2) (a) to (f). It may be inspected by any person subject to such restrictions as may be imposed by Member States on the same grounds as are set in Article 14 (1).

Chapter III

Judicial remedies, liability and penalties

Article 22

Judicial remedies

A8.27 Member States shall provide for the right of every person to a judicial remedy for any breach of the rights guaranteed by this Directive.

Article 23

Liability

A8.28 1. Member States shall provide that any person whose personal data are undergoing processing and who suffers damage as a result of an unlawful processing operation or of any act incompatible with the national provisions adopted pursuant to this directive is entitled to receive compensation from the controller for the damage suffered.

2. Member States may provide that the controller may be exempted, in whole or in part, from his liability for damage resulting from the loss or destruction of data or from unauthorized access if he proves that he has taken suitable steps to satisfy the requirements of Articles 17 and 24.

Article 24

Processing on behalf of the controller

A8.29 1. Member States shall provide that the controller must, where processing is carried out on his behalf, ensure that the necessary security and organizational measures are taken and choose a processor who provides sufficient guarantees in that respect.

2. The processor shall carry out only such processing of personal data as is stipulated in his contract with the controller and shall take instructions only from the latter. He shall comply with the national provisions adopted pursuant to this Directive.

3. The contract shall be in writing and shall state, in particular, that personal data processed there under may be disclosed to a third party by the processor or his employees only with the controller's agreement.

Article 25

Penalties

A8.30 Each Member State shall provide for the imposition of dissuasive penalties on any person who does not comply with the national provisions adopted pursuant to this Directive.

Chapter IV

Transfer of personal data to third countries

Article 26

Principles

A8.31 1. Member States shall provide that the transfer, whether temporary or permanent, to a third country of personal data which are undergoing processing or which have been collected with a view to processing may take place only if the third country in question ensures an adequate level of protection.

Notwithstanding the first subparagraph, Member States shall provide that a transfer to a third country which does not

241

ensure an adequate level of protection may take place on condition that:

—subject, where appropriate, to Article 8 (2) (a), the data subject has consented to the proposed transfer in order to take steps preliminary to entering into a contract,

—the transfer is necessary for the performance of a contract between the data subject and the controller, on condition that the data subject has been informed of the fact that it is or might be proposed to transfer the data to a third country which does not ensure an adequate level of protection,

—the transfer is necessary on important public interest grounds,

or

—the transfer is necessary in order to protect the vital interests of the data subject.

2.   The adequacy of the level of protection afforded by a third country shall be assessed in the light of all the circumstances surrounding a data transfer operation or set of data transfer operations; particular account shall be taken of the nature of the data, the purpose or purposes and duration of the proposed processing operation or operations, the legislative provisions, both general and sectoral, in force in the third country in question and the professional rules which are complied with in that country.

3.   Member States shall inform the Commission of cases where they consider that a third country does not ensure an adequate level of protection.

4.   Where the Commission finds, either on the basis of information supplied by Member States or on the basis of other information, that a third country does not ensure an adequate level of protection and that the resulting situation is likely to harm the interests of the Community or of a Member States, it may enter into negotiations with a view to remedying the situation.

5.   The Commission may decide, in accordance with the procedure laid down in Article 34 (2) that a third country ensures an adequate level of protection by reason of the international commitments it has entered into or of its domestic law.

6.   Measures taken pursuant to this Ar-

ticle shall be in keeping with the obligations incumbent on the Community by virtue of international agreements, both bilateral and multilateral, governing the protection of persons with regard to the automatic processing of personal data.

Article 27

Particular measures

1.   Subject to the second subparagraph   **A8.32**
of Article 26 (1), a Member State may authorize a transfer or category of transfers of personal data to a third country which does not ensure an adequate level of protection where the controller adduces sufficient justification in particular in the form of appropriate contractual provisions guaranteeing, especially, the effective exercise of data subjects' rights.

2.   The Member State shall inform the Commission and the other Member States in good time of its proposal to grant authorization.

3.   If a Member State or the Commission objects before the authorization takes effect, the Commission shall take appropriate measures in accordance with the procedure laid down in Article 34 (2).

Chapter V

Codes of conduct

Article 28

National codes

1.   Member States may provide that   **A8.33**
codes of conduct drawn up by trade associations may make additional provision for the specific features of particular sectors, subject to the national measures taken under this Directive.

2.   The draft codes shall be reviewed by the national supervisory authority, which shall ascertain whether or not they are justified and the representativeness of the organizations which prepared them. The authority shall seek the views of data subjects or their representatives.

3.   Member States shall ensure the official publication of codes which have been the subject of a favourable opinion on the part of the supervisory authority.

4.   Any extension or amendment of the

codes shall be subject to identical procedures.

Article 29
Community codes

A8.34   1. Member States and the Commission shall encourage the trade associations concerned to participate in drawing up Community codes of conduct intended to contribute to the proper application of this Directive in the light of the specific characteristics of each sector.

2. The Commission may, for the purposes of information, publish codes of conduct in the *Official Journal of the European Communities*, together with the opinion of the working party provided for in Article 31 on the content of the codes and the representativeness at Community level of the organizations which prepared them. The working party shall seek the views of data subjects or their representatives.

Chapter VI

Supervisory authority and working party on the protection of individuals with regard to the processing of personal data

Article 30
Supervisory authority

A8.35   1. Each Member State shall designate an independent public authority to supervise the protection of personal data. The authority shall be responsible for monitoring the application of the national provisions adopted pursuant to this Directive and for performing all the functions entrusted to it by this Directive. Each Member State may designate more than one supervisory authority.

2. Each supervisory authority shall have:

—investigative powers including the right of access to data forming the subject-matter of processing operations covered by this Directive and the right to collect all the information necessary for the performance of its supervisory duties;

—effective powers of intervention such as ordering the blocking or erasure of data, a temporary or definitive ban on processing or the destruction of data matereial, or warning the controller,

—the power to bring an action before the courts where it finds that the national provisions implementing this Directive have been infringed.

3. Each supervisory authority shall hear complaints lodged by any person concerning the protection of persons with regard to the processing of personal data. The person concerned shall be informed of the outcome of the complaint.

4. Each supervisory authority shall produce an annual report. The report shall be made public.

5. Member States' authorities shall cooperate with one another to the extent necessary for the performance of their supervisory duties, *inter alia* by exchanging useful information or exercising their powers of investigation or intervention.

6. Member States shall provide tht the supervisory authority, its members and its staff are to be subject to a duty of confidence.

Article 31
Working party on the protection of individuals with regard to the processing of personal data

1. A working part on the protection of   **A8.36** individuals with regard to the processing of personal data, hereinafter referred to as 'the working party', is hereby set up. The working party, which shall have advisory status, shall act independently. It shall be composed of representatives of the supervisory authorities provided for in Article 30 and of a representative of the Commission. Where a Member State designates more than one supervisory authority, those authorities shall appoint joint representatives who, within the working party, shall have the same rights and obligations as the other representatives of the other authorities.

2. The working party shall elect its chairman. The chairman's term of office shall be two years. His appointment shall be renewable.

3. The working party's secretariat shall

be provided by the Commission.

4. The working party shall adopt its own rules of procedure.

5. The working party shall consider items placed on its agenda by its chairman, either on his own initiative or at the reasoned request of a representative of the supervisory authorities, or at the Commission's request.

Article 32

Tasks of the working party

A8.37 1. The working party shall:
(a) contribute to the uniform application of the national measures taken under this Directive;
(b) give an opinion on the level of protection in the Community and in third countries;
(c) advise the Commission on any proposed amendment of this Directive, on any additional or specific measures to safeguard the rights and freedoms of natural persons and on any other proposed measures affecting such rights and freedoms;
(d) give an opinion on codes of conduct drawn up at Community level.

2. If the working party finds that serious divergences are arising between the laws or practices of Member States concerning the protection of persons with regard to the processing of personal data and that those divergences might affect the equivalence of protection in the Community, it shall inform the Commission accordingly.

3. The working party may, on its own initiative, make recommendations on all matters relating to the protection of persons with regard to the processing of personal data in the Community.

4. The working party's opinions and recommendations shall be recorded in its minutes and shall be transmitted to the Commission; they may also be transmitted to the advisory committee referred to in Article 34.

5. The Commission shall inform the working party of the action it has taken in response to its opinions and recommendations. It shall do so in a report which shall also be transmitted to the European Parliament and to the Council. The report shall be made public.

6. The working party shall draw up an annual report on the situation regarding the protection of natural persons with regard to the processing of personal data in the Community and in third countries, which it shall transmit to the Commission, the European Parliament and the Council. The report shall be made public.

Chapter VII

Rule-making powers of the Commission

Article 33

Exercise of rule-making powers

The Commission shall, in accordance with the procedure laid down in Article 34 (2), adopt such technical measures as are necessary to apply this Directive to the specific characteristics of particular sectors or classes of processing, and the measures necessary to ensure the consistent application of this Directive. **A8.39**

Article 34

Advisory Committee

1. The Commission shall be assisted by a committee of an advisory nature composed of the representatives of the Member States and chaired by a representative of the Commission. **A8.39**

2. The representative of the Commission shall submit to the committee a draft of the measures to be taken. The committee shall deliver its opinion on the draft within a time limit which the chairman may lay down according to the urgency of the matter, if necessary by taking a vote. The opinion shall be recorded in the minutes; in addition each Member State shall have the right to ask to have its position recorded in the minutes. The Commission shall take the utmost account of the opinion delivered by the committee. It shall inform the committee of the manner in which its opinion has been taken into account.

244

Final provisions

Article 35

A8.40   1. The Member States shall bring into force the laws, regulations and administrative provisions necessary to comply with this Directive by 1 July 1994.

When Member States adopt these provisions, these shall contain a reference to this Directive or shall be accompanied by such reference at the time of their official publication. The procedure for such reference shall be adopted by Member States.

2. Member States shall set a date after which processing operations which began before 1 July 1994 must be compatible with the national provisions adopted pursuant to this Directive; the date set may be no later than 30 June 1997.

3. Member States shall communicate to the Commission the texts of the provisions of national law which they adopt in the field covered by this Directive.

Article 36

The Commission shall report to the Council and the European Parliament at regular intervals on the implementation of this Directive, attaching to its report, if necessary, suitable proposals for amendments. The report shall be made public.   **A8.41**

Article 37

This Directive is addressed to the Member States.   **A8.42**

AMENDED PROPOSAL FOR A EUROPEAN PARLIAMENT AND COUNCIL DIRECTIVE

COM(94) 128 final — COD 288

concerning the protection of personal data and privacy in the context of digital telecommunications networks, in particular the integrated services digital network (ISDN) and digital mobile networks*

(Submitted by the Commission pursuant to Article 189a (2) of the EC Treaty on 14 June 1994)

THE EUROPEAN PARLIAMENT AND THE COUNCIL OF THE EUROPEAN UNION,

A9.1 Having regard to the Treaty establishing the European Community, and in particular Article 100a thereof,

Having regard to the proposal from the Commission (OJ 1990 C277/12),

Having regard to the opinion of the Economic and Social Committee (OJ 1991 C159/38),

1. Whereas Council Directive .../.../ EEC, concerning the protection of individuals with regard to the processing of personal data and the free movement of such data, exhorts Member States to ensure the rights and freedom of natural persons with regard to the processing of personal data, and in particular their right to privacy, in order to ensure the free flow of personal data in the Community.

2. Whereas currently in the European Community new advanced digital public telecommunications networks are emerging which give rise to specific requirements concerning the protection of personal data and privacy of the user;

3. Whereas this is the case, in particular, with the introduction of the integrated services digital network (ISDN) and digital mobile networks;

4. Whereas the Council, in its resolution of 30 June 1988 on the devel-

opment of the common market for telecommunications services and equipment up to 1992 (OJ 1988 C257/1) has called for steps to be taken to protect personal data, in order to create an appropriate environment for the future development of telecommunications in the Community; whereas the Council has re-emphasized the importance of the protection of personal data and privacy in its resolution of 18 July 1989 on the strengthening of the coordination for the introduction of the integrated services digital network (ISDN) in the European Community (OJ 1989 C196/4);

5. Whereas the European Parliament has underlined the importance of the protection of personal data and privacy in telecommunications networks, in particular with regard to the introduction of the integrated services digital network (ISDN) (OJ 1987 C7/334) (OJ 1989 C12/69) (OJ 1989 C12/66);

6. Whereas in the case of telecommunications networks, specific legal, regulatory, and technical provisions must be made in order to protect personal data and the privacy of users with regard to the increasing risks connected with computerized storage and processing of personal data in such networks;

7. Whereas several Member States **A9.2** have already adopted diverging provisions in this area; whereas a number of Member States are currently developing legislation which bears

---

* OJ 1994 C200/4.

246

the risk to increase the existing differences;

8. Whereas these divergent legal, regulatory, and technical provisions concerning the protection of personal data and privacy in the context of the implementation of telecommunications networks in the Community, in particular the integrated services digital network (ISDN) and digital mobile networks, create obstacles to the creation of an internal market for telecommunications in conformity with the objective set out in Article 8 A of the Treaty; whereas the importance of these differences and the necessity to ensure the freedom of transborder telecommunications within the Community require specific harmonization at Community level; whereas the harmonization envisaged is strictly limited, pursuant to the principle of subsidiarity, to the specific requirements which have arisen as a result of the introduction of new functionalities in telecommunications networks;

9. Whereas for all matters concerning protection of personal data and privacy in the context of telecommunications networks, which are not covered by the provisions of this Directive, including the rights of individuals, the Council Directive .../.../EEC, shall apply;

10. Whereas the personal data processed to establish calls are highly sensitive, in particular in the case of digital mobile networks; whereas the storage of these data should be limited to the period strictly necessary for the provision of the service;

11. Whereas currently diverging rules exist in the Member States with regard to the provision of itemized bills; whereas this Directive must provide for harmonization of the Member States' rules concerning the privacy in the field of itemized billing in order to avoid obstacles to the development of trans-European services;

12. Whereas, it is necessary, as regards the calling line identification, to protect both the right of the calling party to remain anonymous and the privacy of the called party with regard to unidentified calls; whereas, however, it is justified to override the elimination in specific exceptional cases;

13. Whereas directories are widely distributed and publicly available; whereas the right to privacy requires that the subscriber himself is able to determine to which extent his personal data are published in a directory;

14. Whereas measures must be taken to　**A9.3** prevent the unauthorized access to communications in order to protect the confidentiality of communications;

15. Whereas safeguards must be provided for the users against intrusion into their privacy by means of forwarded calls as well as unsolicited calls and telefaxes;

16. Whereas it is necessary to ensure that the introduction of technical features of telecommunications equipment for data protection purposes is harmonized in order to be compatible with the implementation of the internal market of 1992;

17. Whereas where the rights of the users and subscribers are not respected, national legislation must provide for judicial remedy; whereas sanctions must be imposed on any person, whether governed by private or public law, who fails to comply with the national measures taken under this Directive;

18. Whereas Member States, industries concerned and the European Community will have to cooperate in developing and manufacturing the technologies necessary for the implementation of this Directive; this cooperation will have to respect in particular the competition rules of the Treaty;

19. Whereas this Directive does not address issues of protection of personal data and privacy related to activities, such as national security, which are not governed by Community law; whereas processing carried out by a Member State's own authorities, organizations or other bodies in

the course of activities which are not governed by Community law should be governed by the protection principles provided for in the resolution of the representatives of the Governments of the Member States of the European Communities meeting within the Council of . . .;

20. Whereas the processing of personal data may not be used to give telecommunications organizations any undue competitive advantage over other service providers;

A9.4 21. Whereas it is useful in the field of application of this Directive to draw on the experience of the Working Party on the protection of individuals with regard to the processing of personal data composed of representatives of the supervisory authorities of the Member States, set up in Article 31 of Council Directive . . .;

22. Whereas such measures must be prepared with the assistance of the Committee composed of representatives of the Member States set up by Council Directive . . .;

HAVE ADOPTED THIS DIRECTIVE:

Article 1

Objective

A9.5 1. This Directive provides for the harmonization of the provisions required to ensure an equivalent level of protection of personal data and privacy in the Member States and to provide for the free movement of telecommunications equipment and services in the Community.

2. The Member States shall adopt the necessary specific provisions in order to guarantee the protection of personal data and privacy in the telecommunications sector in accordance with this Directive.

Article 2

Definitions

A9.6 In addition to the definitions given in Directive . . ./. . ./EEC., for the purposes of this Directive:

1. 'telecommunications organization' means a public or private body to which a Member State grants special or exclusive rights for the provision of a public telecommunications network

and, where applicable, public telecommunications services;

2. 'service provider' means a natural or legal person providing services whose provision consists wholly or partly in the transmission and routing of signals on a public telecommunications network, with the exception of radio broadcasting and television;

3. 'subscriber' means any natural or legal person having subscribed to a telecommunications service of a telecommunications organization or another service provider;

4. 'user' means any person using a telecommunications service for private or business purposes without necessarily having subscribed to this service;

5. 'public telecommunications network' means the public telecommunications infrastructure which permits the conveyance of signals between defined network termination points by wire, by microwave, by optical means or by other electromagnetic means;

6. 'public telecommunications service' means a telecommunications service whose supply Member States have specifically entrusted *inter alia* to one or more telecommunications organizations.

Article 3

Services concerned

1. Without prejudice to the provisions of **A9.7** Council Directive . . ./. . ., this Directive applies to the processing of personal data by telecommunications organizations in connection with the provision of public telecommunications services in public digital telecommunications networks in the Community, in particular via the integrated services digital network (ISDN) and public digital mobile networks.

2. The principles concerning network security, billing data, subscriber directories, technical features and standardization as well as judicial remedies and sanctions as set out in Articles 4, 5, 6, 11, 14 and 16 of this Directive shall apply *mutatis mutandis* to public digital telecommunications services of service providers other than telecommunications organiz-

ations and to other telecommunications services provided to the public over the public telecommunications network.

The measures necessary for the application of other provisions of this Directive to service providers other than telecommunications organizations or measures that may prove necessary to give better effect to the application of the above paragraph shall be adopted by the Commission after consultation of the Working Party referred to in Article 17 and in accordance with the procedure laid down in Article 18.

3. Member States shall ensure that the provisions of this Directive will, where technically possible, be also applied to the processing of personal data in connection with services provided via analogue networks.

Article 4

Security

A9.8 In case of particular risk of a breach of the security of the network, for example in the field mobile radio telephony, the telecommunications organization must inform the subscribers concerning such risk and offer them encryption facilities.

Article 5

Billing data

A9.9 1. For the purpose of billing, data containing the number or identification of the subscriber station, the address of the subscriber and the type of station, the total number of units to be charged for the accounting period, the called, subscriber number, the type and duration of the calls made and/or the data volume transmitted as well as other information needed for billing such as advance payment by instalments, disconnection and reminders, may be processed. Access to the storage of such data has to be restricted to the persons in charge of billing.

2. Such a storage of billing data is permissible only up to the end of the statutory period during which the bill may be challenged.

Article 6

Traffic data

A9.10 Traffic data containing the personal data processed to establish calls and stored in

the switching centres of the telecommunications organizations must be erased as soon as it is no longer necessary to provide the service required.

Article 7

Itemized billing

Where, upon application of the sub- **A9.11**
scriber, an itemized bill is produced, Member States shall ensure the privacy of calling users and called subscribers is preserved.

Article 8

Calling-line identification

1. Where calling-line identification is **A9.12**
offered, the calling subscriber must have the possibility to eliminate via a simple means the transmission of his/her subscriber number for the purpose of calling-line-identification on a per-call basis.

2. Member States shall ensure that, upon application, the subscriber obtains from the telecommunications organization a per-line elimination of the transmission of the subscriber number for the purpose of calling-line identification.

3. Member States shall ensure that, upon application, the subscriber obtains from the telecommunications organization a per-line elimination of the identification of all incoming calls; Member States shall ensure that in other cases the subscribers are able to prevent the access to the identification of incoming calls by unauthorized persons.

The called subscriber must be able to limit the acceptance of incoming calls to those where the identification of the calling subscriber's number has not been eliminated.

4. The provisions set out in paragraphs (1) and (2) shall also apply with regard to calls to third countries originating in the Community; the provisions set out in paragraph (3) shall also apply to incoming calls originating in third countries.

5. The options set out in this Article must be offered free of charge.

Article 9

Exceptions

1. Member States shall ensure that, for a **A9.13**
limited period of time, the telecommuni-

cations organization may override the elimination of the calling line identification in exceptional cases:

(a) upon application of a subscriber requesting the tracing of malicious calls; in this case, the data containing the identification of the calling subscriber will be stored by the telecommunications organization and be made available upon request to the public authority charged with the prevention or pursuit of criminal offences of the Member State concerned;

(b) upon specific court order, in order to prevent or pursue serious criminal offences.

2. Member States shall ensure that a permanent override function is made available upon request:

(a) to organizations recognized by a Member State which answer and deal with emergency calls; and

(b) to fire brigades operated or recognized by a Member State.

3. The telecommunications organizations shall take the necessary steps to ensure that the overide function is operational on a national and Community-wide basis.

Article 10

Call forwarding

A9.14 Calls may be forwarded from the called subscriber to a third party only if this party has agreed; for this purpose ways and means of agreement by a third party will have to be developed and provided for as well as the possibility to stop automatic forwarding.

Article 11

Directories

A9.15 Personal data contained in a directory should be limited to what is strictly necessary to identify a particular subscriber, unless the subscriber has given his consent to the publication of additional personal data. The subscriber shall be entitled, free of charge, not to have his or her sex indicated and to be omitted from the directory at his or her request.

Article 12

Surveillance of communications

1. Member States shall take appropriate   **A9.16** measures to ensure that listening or tapping devices or other means of interception or surveillance of communications by third parties are applied only subject to authorization by the competent judiciary or administrative national authorities in conformity with national legislation.

2. Member States shall ensure that the content of telephone calls must not be made accessible to third parties via technical devices, such as loudspeakers or other on-hook equipment, or be stored on tape for own use or use by third parties without the consent of the users concerned.

3. Paragraph (2) does not apply in cases covered by Article 9 (1).

Article 13

Unsolicited calls

1. Notwithstanding the provisions of Di-   **A9.17** rective .../../EC, on the protection of consumers in respect of contracts negotiated at a distance (distance selling), Member States shall take appropriate measures to ensure that unsolicited calls for promotional or advertising/research purposes are not allowed in respect of subscribers who do not wish to receive these calls.

2. The use of automatic cell devices for transmitting pre-recorded messages may only be used in respect of subscribers who have given their consent.

3. Paragraphs (1) and (2) apply accordingly to telefax messages.

Article 14

Technical features and standardization

1. In implementing the provisions of this   **A9.18** Directive, Member States shall ensure, subject to paragraphs (2) and (3) of this Article, that no mandatory requirements for specific technical features are imposed on terminal or other telecommunications equipment which could impede the placing of equipment on the market and the free circulation of such equipment in and between Member States.

2.   Where provisions can only be implemented by requiring specific technical features, Member States shall inform the Commission according to the procedures provided for by Council Directive 83/189/ EEC (OJ 1983 L109/8) which lays down a procedure for the provision of information in the field of technical standards and regulations.

3.   Where required, the Commission will ensure the drawing up of common European standards for the implementation of specific technical features, in accordance with Council Directive 91/263/EEC on the approximation of the laws of the Member States concerning telecommunications terminal equipment, including the mutual recognition of their conformity (OJ 1991 L128/1), and Council Decision 87/95/EEC of 27 December 1986 on standardization in the field of information technology and telecommunications (OJ 1987 L36/31).

Article 15

Technical application and modification

A9.19   The details of the application of this Directive and the modifications necessary to adapt this Directive to new technical developments shall be determined by the Commission in accordance with the procedure laid down in Article 18.

Article 16

Judicial remedy and sanctions

A9.20   1.   Member States shall ensure that any individual has a judicial remedy if the rights guaranteed in this Directive are violated.

2.   Each Member State shall make provision in its law for the application of dissuasive sanctions applicable to any person not complying with the national provisions taken pursuant to this Directive.

Article 17

Working Party on the protection of individuals with regard to the processing of personal data

A9.21   1.   The Working Party on the protection of individuals with regard to the process-

ing of personal data established according to Article 31 of Directive .../.../EEC shall carry, out the tasks laid down in Article 32 of the abovementioned Directive also with regard to the data protection measures which are the subject of this Directive.

2.   The Working Party will be specifically constituted for the purpose of his Directive.

Article 18

Procedure

1.   The Commission shall be assisted by   **A9.22** the Committee established by Article 34 of Directive .../.../EEC which for the purposes of this Directive will act according to the following procedure:

The representative of the Commission shall submit to the committee a draft of the measures to be taken, the Committee shall deliver its opinion on the draft within a time limit which the chairman may law down according to the urgency of the matter, if necessary by taking a vote.

The opinion shall be recorded in the minutes; in addition each Member State shall have the right to ask to have its position recorded in the minutes.

The Commission shall take the utmost account of the opinion delivered by the committee. It shall inform the committee of the manner in which its opinion has been taken into account.

2.   The Committee established in the framework of that procedure will be constituted specifically for the purposes of this Directive.

Article 19

Implementation of the Directive

1.   The Member States shall bring into   **A9.23** force the laws, regulations, and administrative provisions necessary for them to comply with this Directive one year after the adoption of this Directive at the latest.

When Member States adopt these provisions, these shall contain a reference to this Directive or shall be accompanied by such a reference at the time of their official publication. The procedure for such reference shall be adopted by Member States.

251

2.   The Member States shall communicate to the Commission the texts of the provisions of national law which they adopt in the field governed by this Directive.

Article 20

Addressees

This Directive is addressed to the Member States.   **A9.24**

UNDERTAKING MADE BY MICROSOFT TO THE EC COMMISSION

1. Introduction

A10.1 Microsoft undertakes in good faith to carry out the obligations set out in this Undertaking. The purpose of this Undertaking is to assist the Commission of the European Communities ("the Commission") in satisfying itself that Articles 85 and 86 of the EC Treaty and Articles 53 and 54 of the EEA Agreement are not infringed.

2. Definitions

A10.2 A. "Covered Product(s)" means binary code of (i) MS-DOS 6.22, (ii) Microsoft Windows 3.11, (iii) Windows for Workgroups 3.11, (iv) predecessor versions of the aforementioned products, (v) the product currently codenamed "Chicago", and (v) successor versions of or products marketed as replacements for the aforementioned products, whether or not such successor versions or replacement products could also be characterized as successor versions or replacement products of other Microsoft Operating System Software products, that are made available (a) as stand-alone products to OEMs pursuant to License Agreements, or (b) as unbundled products that perform Operating System Software functions now embodied in the products listed in subsections (i) through (v). The term "Covered Products" shall not include "Customized" versions of the aforementioned products developed by Microsoft; nor shall it apply to Windows NT Workstation and its successor versions, or Windows NT Advanced Server.

B. "Customised" means the substantial modification of a product by Microsoft to meet the particular and specialized requirements of a final customer of a computer system. It does not include the adaptation of such a product in order to optimize its performance in connection with a Personal Computer System manufac-tured by an OEM.

C. "Duration" means, with respect to a License Agreement, the period of time during which an OEM is authorized to license, sell or distribute any of the Covered Products.

D. A "License Agreement" means any licence, contract, agreement or understanding, or any amendment thereto, written or oral, express or implied, pursuant to which Microsoft authorizes an OEM to license, sell or distribute any Covered Product with its Personal Computer System(s).

E. A "Minimum Commitment" means an obligation of an OEM to pay Microsoft a minimum amount under a License Agreement, regardless of actual sales.

F. "Lump Sum Pricing" means any royalty payment for a Covered Product that does not vary with the number of copies of the Covered Product that are licensed, sold or distributed by the OEM or of Personal Computer Systems distributed by the OEM.

G. "New System" means a system not included or designated in a Per System License.

H. "NDA" means any non-disclosure agreement for any pre-commercial release of a Covered Product that imposes any restriction on the disclosure or use of any such pre-commercial release of any Covered Product or any information relating thereto.

I. "OEM" means an original equipment manufacturer or assembler of Personal Computer Systems or Personal Computer System components (such as motherboards or sound cards) or peripherals (e.g., printers or mice) that is a party to a License Agreement.

J. "Per Copy License" means any License Agreement pursuant to which the OEM's royalty payments are calculated by multiplying (i) the number of copies of each Covered Product licensed, sold or distributed during the term of the License Agreement, by (ii) a per copy royalty rate agreed upon by the OEM and Microsoft, which rate may be determined as povided in Section IV.H.

K. "Per Processor License" means a License Agreement under which Microsoft requires the OEM to pay Microsoft a royalty for all Personal Computer Systems that contain the particular microprocessor type(s) specified in the License Agreement.

L. "Per System License" means a License Agreement under which Microsoft requires the OEM to pay Microsoft a royalty for all Personal Computer Systems which bear the particular model name(s) or number(s) which are included or designated in the License Agreement by the OEM to Microsoft, at the OEM's sole option and under the terms and conditions as set for herein.

M. "Personal Computer System" means a computer designed to use a video display and keyboard (whether or not the video display and keyboard are actually included) which contains an Intel x86, or Intel x86 compatible microprocessor.

N. "Operating System Software" means any set of instructions, codes, and ancillary information that controls the operating of a Personal Computer System and manages the interaction between the computer's memory and attached devices such as keyboards, display screens, disk drives, and printers.

3. Applicability

This Undertaking applies to Microsoft and to each of its officers, directors, agents, employees, subsidiaries, successors and assigns.

4. Prohibited conduct

A10.3 A. Microsoft shall not enter into any License Agreement for any Covered Product that has a total Duration that exceeds one year (measured from the end of the calendar quarter in which the agreement is executed). Microsoft may include as a term in any such License Agreement that the OEM may, at its sole discretion, at any time between 90 and 120 days prior to the expiration of the original License Agreement, renew it for up to one additional year on the same terms and conditions as those applicable in the original license period.

The License Agreement shall not impose a penalty or charge of any kind on an OEM for its election not to renew all or any portion of a License Agreement. In the event that an OEM does not exercise the option to renew a License Agreement as provided above, and a new License Agreement is entered between Microsoft and the OEM, the arm's length negotiation of different terms and conditions, specifically including a higher royalty rate(s), will not by itself constitute a penalty or other charge within the meaning of the foregoing sentence.

The Duration of any License Agreement with any OEM not domiciled in the United States or the European Economic Area that will not be effective prior to regulatory approval in the country of its domicile may be extended at the option of Microsoft or the OEM during the time required for any such regulatory approval.

License Agreement provisions that do not bear on the licensing or distribution of the Covered Products may survive expiration or termination of the License Agreement.

B. Microsoft shall not enter into any License Agreement that by its terms prohibits or restricts the OEM's licensing, sale or distribution of any non-Microsoft Operating System Software product.

C. Microsoft shall not enter into any Per Processor License.

D. Except to the extent permitted by Section IV.G. below, Microsoft shall not enter into any License Agreement other than a Per Copy License.

E. Microsoft shall not enter into any License Agreement in which the terms of that agreement are expressly

254

or impliedly conditioned upon:

1. the licensing of any other Covered Product, Operating System Software product or other product (provided, however, that this provision in and of itself shall not be construed or prohibit Microsoft from developing integrated products); or

2. the OEM not licensing, purchasing, using or distributing any non-Microsoft product.

F. Microsoft shall not enter into any License Agreement containing a Minimum Commitment. However, nothing contained herein shall prohibit Microsoft and any OEM from developing non-binding estimates of projected sales of Microsoft's Covered Products for use in calculating royalty payments.

A10.4 G. Microsoft's revenue from a License Agreement for any Covered Product shall not be derived from other than Per Copy or Per System Licenses, as defined herein. In any Per System License:

(i) Microsoft shall not explicitly or implicitly require as a condition of entering into any License Agreement, or for purposes of applying any volume discount, or otherwise, that any OEM include under its Per System License more than one of its Personal Computer Systems;

(ii) Microsoft shall not charge or collect royalties for any Covered Product on any Personal Computer System unless the Personal Computer System is designated by the OEM in the License Agreement or in a written amendment. Microsoft shall not require an OEM which creates a New System to notify Microsoft of the existence of such a New System, or to take any particular actions regarding marketing or advertising of that New System, other than creation of a unique model name or model number that the OEM shall use for internal and external identification purposes. The requirement of external identification may be satisfied by placement of the

unique model name or model number on the machine and its container (if any), without more. The OEM and Microsoft may agree to amend the License Agreement to include any new model of Personal Computer System in a Per System License. Nothing in this clause shall be deemed to preclude Microsoft from seeking compensation from an OEM that makes or distributes copies of a Covered Product in breach of its License Agreement or in violation of copyright law;

(iii) The License Agreement shall not impose a penalty or charge on account of an OEM's choosing at any time to create a New System. Addition of a New System to the OEM's License Agreement so that Covered Products are licensed for distribution with such New System and royalties are payable with respect thereto shall not be deemed to constitute a penalty or other charge of any kind within the meaning of the foregoing sentence;

(iv) All OEMs with existing Per System Licenses, or Per Processor Licenses treated by Microsoft under Section IV.J as Per System Licenses, will be sent within 30 days following entry of this Undertaking in a separately mailed notice printed in bold, boxed type which shall begin with the sentence "You are operating under a Microsoft Per System License" and shall continue with the language contained in the first four quoted paragraphs below. All new or amended Per System Licenses executed after September 1, 1994 shall contain a provision that appears on the top half of the signature page in bold, boxed type shall begin with the sentence "This is a Microsoft Per System License," and which shall continue with the language contained in the first four quoted paragraphs below.

"As a Customer, you may create a "New System" at any time that does not require the pay-

255

ment of a royalty to Microsoft unless the Customer and Microsoft agree to add it to the License Agreement."

"Any New System created may be identical in every respect to a system as to which the Customer pays a Per System royalty to Microsoft provided that the New System has a unique model number or model name for internal or external identification purposes which distinguishes it from any system the Customer sells that is included in a Per System License. The requirement of external identification may be satisfied by placement of the unique model name or model number on the machine and its container (if any), without more."

"If the customer does not intend to include a Microsoft operating system product with a New System, the customer does not need to notify Microsoft at any time of the creation, use or sale of any such New System, nor does it need to take any particular steps to market or advertise the New System."

"Under Microsoft's License Agreement, there is no charge or penalty if a Customer chooses at any time to create a New System incorporating a non-Microsoft operating system. If the Customer intends to include a Microsoft operating system product with the New System, the Customer must so notify Microsoft, after which the parties may enter into arm's lenth negotiation with respect to a license to apply to the New System."

In the case of OEMs with Per Processor Licenses treated as Per System Licenses pursuant to Section IV.J., the notice shall include the following paragraph at the beginning of the notice:

"All models covered by your Per Processor License are now treated as subject to a Per System License. You may exclude any such model from being treated as subject to a Per System License by notifying Microsoft in writing. Such notice to Microsoft must include the model designation to be excluded from the Per System License. Such exclusion shall take effect on the first day of the calendar quarter next following Microsoft's receipt of such notice."

H. Microsoft may not use any form of **A10.5** Lump Sum Pricing in any License Agreement for Covered Product(s) executed after the date of this Undertaking. It is not a violation of this Undertaking for Microsoft to use a form of royalty rates, including rates embodying volume discounts agreed upon in advance with respect to each individual OEM, each specific version or language of a Covered Product, and each designated Personal Computer System model subject to the License Agreement, provided, however, that this Undertaking does not sanction any particular implementation of such form.

I. OEMs that currently have a License Agreement that is inconsistent with any provision of this Undertaking may, without penalty, terminate the License Agreement or negotiate with Microsoft to amend the License Agreement to eliminate such inconsisten provisions. An OEM desiring to terminate or amend such a License Agreement shall give Microsoft ninety (90) days written notice at any time prior to January 1, 1995.

J. If an OEM has a License Agreement that is inconsistent with any provision of this Undertaking, Microsoft may enforce that License Agreement subject to the following:

(i) if the License Agreement is a Per Processor License, Microsoft shall treat it as a Per System License for all existing OEM models that contain the microprocessor type(s) specified in the License Agreement, except those models that the OEM opts in writing to exclude, and such exclusion shall take effect on the first day of the calendar quarter next following Microsoft's receipt of such notice; and

(ii) Microsoft may not enforce prospectively any Minimum Commitment.

K. Microsoft shall not enter into any NDA:

(i) whose duration extends beyond (a) commercial release of the product covered by the NDA, (b) an earlier public disclosure authorized by Microsoft of information covered by the NDA, or (c) one year from the date of disclosure of information covered by the NDA to a person subject to the NDA, whichever comes first; or

(ii) that would restrict in any manner any person subject to the NDA from developing software products that will run on competing Operating System Software products, provided that such development efforts do not entail the disclosure or use of any Microsoft proprietary information during the term of the NDA; or

(iii) that would restrict any activities of any person subject to the NDA to whom no information covered by the NDA has been disclosed.

L. The form of standard NDAs will be approved by a Microsoft corporate officer and all non-standard language in NDAs that pertains to matters covered in Section (K) above will be approved by a Microsoft senior corporate attorney.

M. Within thirty (30) days of the entry of this Undertaking, Microsoft will provide a copy of this Undertaking to all OEMs with whom it has License Agreements at that time except for those with licenses solely under the Small Volume Easy Distribution (SVED) program or the Delivery Service Partner (DSP) program.

5. Administrative provisions

A. Microsoft acknowledges that it may be necessary for the Commission to determine the extent to which this Undertaking is implemented. For this purpose, Microsoft will supply such information as the Commission may from time to time request.

B. All License Agreements shall be made in writing. Copies of such agreements shall be retained by Microsoft and submitted to the Commission at the Commission's request.

C. Microsoft shall produce to the Commission, within forty-five (45) days, any documents provided to the Antitrust Division of the US Department of Justice ("DOJ"), in connection with its monitoring or securing of compliance with any Final Judgment against Microsoft that realtes to Microsoft's licensing of any Covered Product. In addition, Microsoft shall not object to disclosure to the Commission by the DOJ of any other information provided by Microsoft to the DOJ, or to cooperation between the Commission and the DOJ in the enforcement of this Undertaking, provided that Microsoft shall receive in advance a detailed description of the information to be provided. The Commission will accord Microsoft information received from the DOJ and all Microsoft License Agreements provided pursuant to Section V.A.2 above the maximum confidentiality protection available under applicable law. Thus, the Commission will abide by its obligation of professional confidentiality set out in Article 20(2) of Regulation 17, even though the Microsoft information will not have been obtained pursuant to that Regulation and even though the information may not have been designated specifically as containing business secrets. The Commission shall take precautions to ensure the security and confidentiality of Microsoft information provided in electronic form.

D. This Undertaking shall remain in force for six and one-half ($6\frac{1}{2}$) years or until the entry into effect of a Commission Decision with respect to the subject matter of this Undertaking, whichever is the earlier.

E. This Undertaking (and all correspondence, memoranda or discussions with respect thereto) is made without prejudice and may not be used in any way by Microsoft in this or any other proceeding and does not constitute in any way an admission by Microsoft, and shall not be enforceable by any other natural or legal person or any national authority or agency.

F. This Undertaking shall take immediate effect.

Index